Representing Workers

Employment relations are at a crossroad. Worker representation has historically been dominated by trade union channels in the advanced economies, but with the decline in union membership other forms of representation are increasingly significant.

Representing Workers is the result of significant research addressing key issues underlying these developments. A group of internationally renowned employment relations specialists, under the Leverhulme Foundation Future of Trade Unionism Programme, consider issues such as

- trends in trade union membership;
- factors behind the decline of union membership;
- young workers and trade unionism;
- the law and union recognition;
- European influences on worker representation;
- non-union representation;
- trade unionism in the context of new forms of representation;
- enhancing the appeal of unions.

This timely study of worker representation presents powerful analysis of such issues. *Representing Workers* is one of the most broad-ranging studies of representation, and is essential reading for anyone studying or working in employment relations.

Howard Gospel is Professor of Management at King's College, London, Research Associate at the Centre for Economic Performance, London School of Economics, and Fellow at Said Business School, University of Oxford.

Stephen Wood is Research Professor and Deputy Director of the Institute of Work Psychology at the University of Sheffield, and Research Associate at the Centre for Economic Performance, London School of Economics. He is also co-director for the ESRC Centre for Organization and Innovation, and Chief Editor of the *British Journal of Industrial Relations*.

The future of trade unions in Britain
The Centre for Economic Performance

This groundbreaking new series on trade unions and employment relations is the result of the largest research grant ever awarded by the Leverhulme Trust, and the three series titles both analyse and evaluate the nature of unionization in Britain. With a multidisciplinary approach, the series brings together experts in the field of employment relations to offer three of the most informed, broad-ranging and up-to-date studies available. Essential reading for anyone studying or working professionally within employment relations in Britain.

Representing Workers
Trade union recognition and membership in Britain
Edited by Howard Gospel and Stephen Wood

Representing Workers

Trade union recognition and
membership in Britain

Edited by Howard Gospel
and Stephen Wood

Routledge
Taylor & Francis Group

LONDON AND NEW YORK

First published 2003 by Routledge
11 New Fetter Lane, London EC4P 4EE

Simultaneously published in the USA and Canada
by Routledge
29 West 35th Street, New York, NY 10001

Routledge is an imprint of the Taylor & Francis Group

Typeset in Sabon by Wearset Ltd, Boldon, Tyne and Wear
Printed and bound in Great Britain by TJ International Ltd,
Padstow, Cornwall

British Library Cataloguing in Publication Data
A catalogue record for this book is available from the British
Library

Library of Congress Cataloging in Publication Data
Representing workers: trade union recognition and membership
in Britain / edited by Howard Gospel and Stephen Wood.
   p. cm. – (The future of trade unions in Britain; 1)
Simultaneously published in the USA and Canada.
Includes bibliographical references and index.
1. Labor unions–Great Britain. 2. Industrial relations–Great
Britain. I. Gospel, Howard F. II. Wood, Stephen, 1948–
III. Series.
 HD6664 .R46 2003
 331.88′0941–dc21
                                        2002152698

ISBN 0–415–28727–8 (hbk)
ISBN 0–415–28728–6 (pbk)

Contents

Illustrations

Figures

Boxes

Tables

Contributors

Helen Bewley Research Assistant, Centre for Economic Performance, London School of Economics.

Alex Bryson Principal Research Fellow, Policy Studies Institute.

Andy Charlwood Lecturer in Industrial Relations and Human Resource Management at Leeds University Business School, Leeds; Research Associate, Centre for Economic Performance, London School of Economics.

Wayne Diamond Senior Research Officer, Employment Relations Directorate, Department of Trade and Industry.

Keith Ewing Professor of Law, King's College, London.

Sue Fernie Lecturer in Industrial Relations; Research Associate, Centre for Economic Performance, London School of Economics.

Richard Freeman Professor of Economics at Harvard and Co-Director of the Centre for Economic Performance, London School of Economics; Director of Labor Studies at National Bureau of Economic Research, Cambridge, Massachusetts.

Rafael Gomez Lecturer in Management, Interdisciplinary Institute of Management, London School of Economics.

Howard Gospel Professor of Management, King's College, London; Research Associate, Centre for Economic Performance, London School of Economics; Fellow, Said Business School, University of Oxford.

Thomas A. Kochan George M. Bunker Professor of Work and Employment Research, Sloan School of Management, Cambridge, Massachusetts, Massachusetts Institute of Technology.

Stephen Machin Professor of Economics, University College London; Director of the DfES Centre for the Economics of Education and Programme Director (Skill and Education), Centre for Economic Performance, London School of Economics.

Sian Moore Research Officer, Centre for Economic Performance, London School of Economics.

Paul Willman Ernest Button Professor of Management Studies, University of Oxford; Fellow, Balliol College, Oxford.

Stephen Wood Research Professor, Deputy Director, Institute of Work Psychology, and Co-Director, ESRC Centre for Organization and Innovation, University of Sheffield; Research Associate, Centre for Economic Performance, London School of Economics.

Foreword

Profound changes have taken place during the last quarter of a century in both employee representation and voice. Union membership has declined by over five million, the closed shop is almost extinct, half the present workforce has never belonged to a union and now, in the private sector, only one worker in five is a member. Simultaneously there has been a big move away from representative voice to direct voice. Representative voice occurs via a recognized trade union or works council. Direct voice bypasses these intermediate institutions. Instead, management and employees communicate directly with one another through, for example, team briefings, regular meetings between senior management and the workforce, and problem solving groups such as quality circles.

The Leverhulme Trust realised that these alterations in industrial relations required more attention and initiated a research programme on the Future of Trade Unions in Modern Britain. This research is being carried out in the Centre for Economic Performance and the Industrial Relations Department at the London School of Economics, and includes colleagues from other institutions like King's College London, Oxford and Sheffield Universities and the Policy Studies Institute. The team are very grateful to the Leverhulme Trust for this financial support. In particular the successive Directors, Barry Supple and Sir Richard Brook, have greatly helped us with their wisdom and flexibility.

Programme research is organized around a number of themes: membership; interaction with employers and the state; adapting to change; performance outcomes; and public sector and public policy (see http://cep.lse.ac.uk/future_of_unions. The various outputs will be distilled into a trilogy to be published by Routledge over the next two years. This volume, edited by Howard Gospel and Stephen Wood, focuses on trade union recognition and membership. It analyses the reasons for the decline in membership, what unions do for younger workers and women, the willingness to unionize among non-union workers and the impact of new laws governing trade union recognition and information and consultation. The team much appreciates the cooperation and input from Francesca Poynter and Rachel Crookes of Routledge in bringing this volume to fruition.

Volume 2, to be edited by John Kelly and Paul Willman, will be about union organization and activity. It will cover organizing campaigns, unions and the Internet, union structures, representing workers in the new economy, and interactions with employers including social partnership. Volume 3, to be edited by Sue Fernie and myself, will present different approaches to the future of unions and examine performance outcomes. The approaches include organization theory, social movements and standard economic analysis. The performance outcomes cover economic and industrial relations performance in both the public and private sector.

David Metcalf
Director
Leverhulme Trust Programme on Future of Trade Unions in Modern Britain

Acknowledgements

This book is based on research that is part of the Leverhulme Future of Trade Unions in Modern Britain programme. We would like to thank the Leverhulme Foundation for their financial support for the programme, the Centre for Economic Performance at the London School of Economics for providing the programme's home, and David Metcalf for his overall co-ordination of the programme. We are also grateful to the authors for their contributions to this book, and to Linda Cleavely and Janet Taylor for their help in its preparation.

Howard Gospel and Stephen Wood

Chapter 1

Representing workers in modern Britain

Howard Gospel and Stephen Wood

What is happening to trade unions is a key question at the beginning of the twenty-first century. In the majority of advanced market economies, their membership has shrunk, their ability to achieve strong bargaining relations with employers has declined, and their influence with national governments is less than in the past. In the UK, union density in the private sector has fallen to the lowest levels since the interwar years and the proportion of the workforce covered by collective bargaining has similarly contracted. Nevertheless, trade unions still have strength in some areas of the private sector and especially in the public sector; they have strongly influenced developments at the national level, most notably in campaigning for a minimum wage and statutory union recognition procedures; and there are new opportunities for them to exploit, such as those provided by European Union-inspired legislation and the heightened concerns of workers regarding issues such as job security, family-friendly practices, equality of opportunity, and training and career development.

This book is the first of a series of three concerned with examining the current state and future prospects of trade unions, derived from the Centre for Economic Performance–Leverhulme Foundation research programme on the Future of Trade Unions in Modern Britain. This book focuses on the interconnected areas of union membership, employer recognition and employee representation; the second will concentrate on questions of recruitment, organization and the structure of unions; and the third will examine the effects of unions on outcomes, such as economic performance and social justice. The series reports major research studies that together present a wide-ranging analysis of contemporary developments in industrial relations.

The waxing and waning of trade unions

Historically, trade unions were a vital concomitant of the process of industrialization and political liberalization in most countries. As their influence grew to unprecedented heights after the Second World War, social theorists saw them as a key ingredient of the capitalist economy and social democracy. Unions were seen to offer workers a channel to voice their grievances and to ensure due process in the workplace; they provided a means by which the benefits of productivity growth could be distributed in a fairer way than might otherwise have been the case; and they were seen as critical intermediaries in the model of the pluralist society that was the base of liberal democracy.

Yet through the 1960s and 1970s their activities increasingly became a source of concern to employers, governments and the public, not least in the UK. The purported role of unions in fuelling cost-plus inflation as well as their perceived adverse effect on unit costs, technological innovation and productivity growth was given particular prominence. Wages and conditions in unionized firms were certainly more favourable than those in non-union firms in economies such as the UK and USA, where decentralized bargaining made such comparisons possible. The effect of union activity on innovation and productivity was less clearly established. Moreover, some commentators argued that they could have positive effects on performance by providing workers with a collective voice and helping management to legitimize change. This view was subsequently confirmed by some academic research (Freeman and Medoff, 1984; Kochan *et al.*, 1986a; Metcalf, 1990). Nonetheless, from the mid-1970s onwards employers and governments increasingly downplayed any positive effects of union representation or argued that these came at the expense of innovation and performance.

In the UK, the short, often unofficial, strike posed a question about the representativeness of union lay officials at workplace level and the authority and control of full-time officials at national level. The question was often posed as to whether the officials' politics were more radical than those of their members. Within the labour movement itself there were also questions asked about the limits of collective bargaining. Issues surrounding redundancies, closures and investment policies were seen as requiring strategies and tactics that extend beyond traditional negotiations; there was also debate about how far the law should be used to further worker rights and extend industrial democracy; while the ability of collective bargaining to deal with rapidly rising concerns about gender and racial inequality in the workplace was questioned, with some even implicating a union movement founded on male manual workers in the generation of inequality.

Collective bargaining had certainly been the trade unions' main mode of relating to employers, and indeed their *raison d'être*. In many countries, through the years of union growth, there was usually some kind of state support (direct or indirect) for collective bargaining. However, from the late 1960s this support began to be constrained. Thus, for example, wage policies were developed to control the alleged inflationary effects of unionism. In countries where relations between the trade unions and the social democratic political parties were strong enough to facilitate the development of what were known as corporatist relations between central government, employers and trade unions, these policies had some success. In the UK, however, the weakness of the central employer and trade union bodies, coupled with the increasing trend away from industry-level bargaining, militated against such arrangements. As a result, more direct and stronger measures were conceived by government. Under the Thatcher administrations, laws designed to outlaw the closed shop, curtail the ability of unions to strike and remove the support for collective bargaining were introduced. More fundamental economic policies of eliminating exchange rate controls, abandoning full employment as a primary economic objective, refusing to subsidize ailing enterprises, and the privatization and marketization of public sector activities fundamentally altered the context in which trade unions had previously flourished.

The Conservative years from 1979 onwards consequently marked a watershed in industrial relations. The main indices – union density, union recognition, collective bargaining coverage, strike levels – all declined (Millward *et al.*, 2000). Such developments were especially stark when viewed in comparison with countries that entered the 1980s with more corporatist and cooperative arrangements, such as Germany and the Scandinavian countries (Boyer, 1995).

The effects of these changes were such that by the time the Conservatives lost the 1997 election, the landscape of industrial relations had been transformed. The 1998 Workplace Employee Relations Survey, covering workplaces with 25 or more employees, revealed the depth of change in both union and non-union workplaces. Union density fell in such workplaces from 65 per cent in 1980 to 36 per cent in 1998, and if workplaces of between 10 and 25 employees are included the density was 30 per cent. The proportion of workplaces with a union presence fell from 73 per cent in the early 1980s to 54 per cent in the late 1990s. Unions were recognized in around 64 per cent of workplaces in the early 1980s, in 53 per cent in 1990, and in only 42 per cent by the late 1990s (Cully *et al.*, 1999:

234–8). The failure of trade unions to organize new workplaces was a particularly important factor in this downward trend. In addition, the proportion of employees whose terms and conditions of employment were determined in some way by collective agreements fell from well over 80 per cent before 1979 to 70 per cent in 1984 and to 41 per cent in 1998, a decline especially pronounced in the private sector. Analysis at the individual level, based on the 1999 Labour Force Survey, shows that by the end of the twentieth century only 23 per cent of employees were both in a union and covered by a collective agreement, with as many as 7 per cent of union members not having their terms and conditions subject to collective agreement (Metcalf, 2001: 26). The majority of employees (57 per cent in 1999) are now neither in a union nor have their terms and conditions determined by collective agreement.

Even where collective bargaining has been maintained, the institutional arrangements have changed so that multi-employer bargaining is rare and bargaining is increasingly insulated within the company and/or the individual workplace. The content of bargaining has also changed, reflecting changes in the approach of employers, and perhaps trade unions, to employment relations. The main reduction in the scope of bargaining over non-pay issues occurred in the 1980s (Millward *et al.*, 2000: 167–9), and by the late 1990s there were significant cases where unions were recognized but little or no bargaining occurred, even over pay (Brown *et al.*, 1999). The break-up of the public utilities following privatization and the contracting-out of public services has further contributed to the decentralization of bargaining and a decline in its scope. The introduction of performance-related pay has in some cases curtailed collective bargaining, although, particularly in the public sector, this has not necessarily been at the expense of bargained salary scales. In addition the number of firms with multi-union bargaining has decreased so that by 1998 43 per cent of unionized workplaces had only one union and of these 72 per cent had a single-union agreement, while in 88 per cent of those with more than one union negotiations were on a joint (single-table) basis.

The precise role these changes have played in the economy is uncertain. Since the mid-1980s, inflation has fallen, unemployment has fluctuated downwards, and the British economy has grown over the business cycle at reasonably comparable rates to other economies. Performance within the unionized sector compared with the non-unionized sector has improved considerably, and on some indicators there is now no differential between the two. At the same time, however, there are persistent uncertainties about job security, the growth of precarious part-time and temporary jobs, fears that working hours and labour intensity are increasing, and attempts to increase wage flexibility and levels of pay inequality unmatched at any time in the twentieth century.

What is certain is that collective bargaining is no longer the dominant method of conducting employment relations. Whether this has been replaced by what some call the 'authoritarian workplace' or 'take-it-or-leave-it management' (Fernie and Metcalf, 1995: 381; Metcalf, 1999: 14), or by more sophisticated management practices and alternative consultative voice mechanisms, is unclear, not least because the precise nature and extent of so-called high involvement human resource management (HRM) – typically associated with some form of high involvement model – and its relation to unionism is uncertain. There has been some growth in non-union forms of joint consultation in the private sector, and a very significant growth of direct forms of employee involvement. However, it is clear that in large areas of the economy management has come to be unilaterally in control of employment relations. In parallel with this, any decline in union membership and industrial action does not necessarily signal a significant reduction in dissatisfactions and grievances in workplaces, as is evidenced by the increasing number of enquiries to the Advisory Conciliation and Arbitration Service and to Citizens' Advice Bureaux, and cases to Employment Tribunals.

What lies behind these changes is a set of processes involving the interplay between macro-economic factors, government economic and employment policies, and the policies and practices of both employers and unions. Attempts to explain the decline in union density in terms of a single cause – business cycle (Carruth and Disney, 1988), compositional changes in the economy (Booth, 1989), or increased labour legislation (Freeman and Pellitier, 1990) – are likely to be in vain, and tend to lead to over-deterministic conclusions. Strong cyclical downturns and compositional changes have occurred in other countries without the same effects on unionism. The downward trend in union density continued during cyclical upturns in the economy, suggesting that there is nothing inevitable about union revival on the back of a buoyant economy. Nor is it inevitable that service-sector workers remain largely unorganized, as is revealed by the relative success of the UK compared with the USA in recruiting white-collar workers in the 1960s and 1970s or levels of unionization among such employees in some Scandinavian countries. As for the law, it is difficult to sustain an argument that it has had such an overall effect as some have suggested.

The Thatcher legislative programme had direct effects on industrial relations – for example, the demise of the closed shop, sympathy strikes and secondary action may be largely accounted for by the law. However, changes in the membership and role of unions and in employment relations have been significantly affected by broader economic factors (Brown and Wadhwani, 1990; Dunn and Metcalf, 1996: 3). Since the late 1970s two deep recessions, with high unemployment, intensified product and financial market competition, and changes in the composition of the labour force, have compounded any impact of the law on membership. Market pressures were often the initial stimulus for employers to search for new ways of managing their labour forces, but high unemployment and labour legislation undoubtedly gave management more freedom to do this.

The agency of the actors is also crucial in explaining trends in trade unionism. This includes employers who have discretion in how they respond to the intensification of competition; it includes the broader government policy that lay behind the legal interventions; and it also includes unions whose greatest problem has been deciding on how best to overcome their past emphasis on servicing existing members and how to recruit and represent new members.

An important legacy of the Thatcher policies is its impact on the attitudes of employers, employees and union officials. Collective bargaining is no longer the taken-for-granted norm for employment relations. It is seen by employers as at best an instrument by which the employees' voice may be obtained but which is unable to solve the key motivational problems of employment relations and may have undesirable side effects, and at worst as being disruptive of working relations and an inhibition on the kind of employee involvement and commitment that employers say they desire. Moreover, the perceived relevance of trade unions to employees is in question, particularly in the case of young workers, who are increasingly unlikely to be in unions (Disney *et al.*, 1998). For trade union officials, however, collective bargaining remains the prime means of improving the conditions of workers and, along with representation of individual members, the prime purpose of trade unionism. At the same time they are increasingly aware of the need to develop new policies to attract new members, as well as new types of relationships with employers, as they face increased pressure to justify themselves in the eyes of employers.

The Labour government, elected in 1997, has maintained key elements of Conservative policy, especially its labour laws, emphasis on low inflation and preference for market relations over state intervention. Other initiatives have been in line with the previous Conservative governments' policy, such as the further encouragement of private finance and performance-related pay in the public sector and of share ownership in private companies. Nonetheless, changes have been made, most notably the new statutory recognition procedures introduced under the Employment Relations Act (1999); the introduction of a national minimum wage for the first time in the UK; and the signing of the EU Social Chapter, with its implication for working time regulations and transnational consultative arrangements. The government has also (albeit with some reluctance) now accepted the EU Directive on Information and Consultation rights in national level undertakings. This will eventually cover over three-quarters of the labour force and will establish for the first time in the UK general consultative councils, which may be union-based or not, with statutory rights to be informed and consulted.

From the mid-1990s, in the face of the decline in their fortunes, British trade unions became more proactive. Achieving a Labour government was always paramount. First, they sought the restoration of a statutory union recognition procedure. Second, they began to orientate themselves towards organizing and recruiting new members so that they no longer concentrated on servicing existing members. Third, they became more positive towards EU-inspired labour policies and increasingly accepted the idea that there might be dual channels of representation through both voluntary collective bargaining and legally-inspired joint consultation.

Employers, for their part, have continued to seek as much freedom as possible to decide how they conduct their employment relations. The emphasis in their representations to the Labour government has been on the need for flexibility, and they have argued that the balance and scope of legislation was right when the Conservative government left office and that any rebuilding of trade unionism may herald a return to the conflictual industrial relations and the economic and political problems of the 1960s and 1970s. Thus, employers' organizations opposed the principle of a statutory union recognition procedure and the EU proposals on information and consultation. Alongside this, the growth of management-initiated direct involvement is continuing and is the favoured method, especially for work-related issues (Millward *et al.*, 2000: 127).

With these developments, it is timely to take stock of a number of key aspects of industrial relations. First, what lies behind the decline in trade unionism and collective bargaining and to what extent is a revival in membership and activity possible, perhaps taking advantage of the statutory recognition procedures and other EU-inspired changes? Second, what are union strategies in terms of recruitment and organization, and how have these affected the structure and governance of unions? Does revival require further changes in union strategies, perhaps involving so-called partnership agreements and accommodation to new forms of employee involvement and management methods? Or, again, does revival require more radical policies that reject such arrangements and pursue a more militant approach? Third, what are the main effects of trade unions on outcomes such as benefits for members, organizational performance and social justice? The series of books, of which this is the first, has been designed to deal with these three sets of issues; this book focuses on the first issue.

The focus of the book

The main issues addressed by this book are: the respective role of new workplaces and young workers in the decline of union recognition and membership; the latent demand for trade unionism amongst non-union members, particularly the young, women, and those who have never been in a union; the effect of enhanced state support for trade unionism provided by the Labour government; employer support for and opposition to trade unionism; and the growth of forms of representation other than collective bargaining and their link to trade unionism.

In Chapter 2, Stephen Machin examines the relative importance of new workplaces and young workers in the economy and their effect on union decline. First, he demonstrates that rates of union recognition and union membership are substantially lower in workplaces established after 1980. Unions have clearly been less successful in gaining recognition in new workplaces than in the past. Second, young workers are shown to be considerably less likely to be union members than they were in the past – a fact that applies even more to male than to female workers. Finally, addressing the question of whether the age of the workplace or the age of the worker matters most, Machin concludes that the workplace is more significant. Those industries with more new establishments experienced the greatest decline, even when differences in worker age remain constant.

In Chapter 3, Richard Freeman and Wayne Diamond then examine in more detail young workers, their attitudes to trade unions, and their likelihood of becoming members. Their research confirms that the proportion of young persons who are unionized in the UK has fallen sharply in the past two decades. However, young workers have no less favourable views of unions than older workers, and Freeman and Diamond reject this explanation for the low and declining level of membership among the young. Young workers, they suggest, do not see unions as vestiges of the past that are more appropriate for their parents than for modern-day employees. The young people studying in Colleges of Further Education and whose knowledge of trade unions they tested were found to be not unfavourable to trade unions in principle, but rather largely ignorant of them. As such, any latent demand for trade unionism is largely dormant and, by implication, requires a trade union to activate it. Consistent with Machin's findings, Freeman and Diamond find that young workers are more concentrated in the non-union sectors of the economy than older workers; however, their low and declining rate of unionization is also affected by the fact that they are less likely to be union members than older workers even in unionized plants. Assessing several union initiatives designed to appeal to young workers, Freeman and Diamond conclude that special youth programmes have not worked well, whereas programmes that seek to help young workers as employees have greater potential for success. They also surmise that because young workers, like others, are favourable to consultative committees and works councils, a strong union initiative in this direction may increase the attractiveness of unions.

In Chapter 4, Andrew Charlwood analyses the willingness of non-union members to join or not join trade unions. He hypothesizes that individuals join unions for one or more of three main reasons: dissatisfaction with the working environment, a belief in the ability of unions to do something about this, and sympathy with the union movement that stems from broader political beliefs or normative values acquired through socialization in the family and local community. Charlwood shows that in the UK the relationship between job dissatisfaction and willingness to join a union is weak. Some workers are predisposed towards unions because of their ideological disposition, but perceived union instrumentality is by far the most important predictor of willingness to join a union. Judgements about instrumentality are made in the context of the workplace. Consequently, union organizing campaigns have an important role to play in shaping the individual workers' perception of union instrumentality and effectiveness.

Since union instrumentality is important to the decision to join unions, Chapter 5, by Alex Bryson and Raphael Gomez, focuses on how employees, including the rising numbers of employees who have never been in a union, can discover the benefits of membership. The relative benefits of unions may be less obvious than in the past, since the union wage premium has fallen and there are increasingly other forms of employee voice available to prospective members. Moreover, the non-wage benefits of unionism are normally not readily apparent without being experienced either directly or indirectly through contact with relatives and friends who have knowledge of them. If fewer people are joining unions, then less people are coming into indirect contact with unions and are less likely to perceive their benefits. In this way, the worker ignorant of unions, highlighted by Freeman and Diamond, will become the norm. Faced with this vicious circle, Bryson and Gomez analyse the ways in which unions might increase their appeal: by lowering the costs of employees gaining a first experience of the union (e.g. through discounting membership fees for new recruits), or by increasing the benefits (e.g. through offering new forms of protection and stimulating organizations to provide certain types of benefits). Both these tactics will depend on unions overcoming the lack of awareness of their activities, and hence require unions to make the existence and benefits more visible.

In Chapter 6, Helen Bewley and Sue Fernie focus on what unions do for women workers. In the past unions concentrated mostly on male, full-time workers, in part due to the difficulty of organizing the sectors in which women are concentrated. However, women now account for 47 per cent of union membership. The authors examine a major potential source of appeal to women workers, namely the role unions can play in developing equal opportunity and family-friendly practices in workplaces. They show that employees are more likely to have access to gender-based equal opportunities policies and to certain family-friendly employment policies where a union is recognized. Moreover, employers offering family-friendly policies have better performance than those without. Thus family-friendly and equal opportunity practices provide a potential new union mark-up, for both women and men, that may not be associated with an adverse cost to employers. Bewley and Fernie, having considered a number of recent campaigns for workplace equal opportunities, conclude that unions need to develop these further by building on the evidence that unions do make a difference.

In Chapter 7, Stephen Wood, Sian Moore and Keith Ewing focus on the role of government legislation and concentrate on the achievement of employer recognition, which other chapters suggest is vital for the future of trade unionism. The authors outline how the UK's statutory recognition procedure, introduced in 2000, is intended to encourage the voluntary settlement of recognition disputes and in so doing may stimulate recognition agreements outside of the statutory procedure. To have this effect, the legislation must be perceived to be working. Their research shows that, in its own terms, the procedure is largely working, and that it has stimulated recognitions. However, so far the numbers of workers affected through either the use of the statutory procedure or voluntary recognition agreements is small, and aspects of the operation of the statutory procedure may be limiting the exercise of workers' right to recognition.

In Chapter 8, Howard Gospel and Paul Willman examine union representation in the context of forms of representation other than collective bargaining, and particularly joint consultation, which may or may not involve union representatives. They show that as collective bargaining has decreased in importance direct involvement methods have increased, and the use of consultation mechanisms, though far from ubiquitous, has remained constant. The British system of industrial relations is now multi-channel rather than union-based. Reflecting this, the preference amongst employees for collective rather than individual voice mechanisms does not necessarily translate into a desire for union representation, and certainly not for a union monopoly of representation. The EU Directive on Information and Consultation will reinforce the move towards multiple forms of representation within organizations and add to the increased variety of arrangements across the economy. The authors suggest that the advent of the Directive offers British trade unions an important opportunity to reinforce their effectiveness and attractiveness to employees.

In the final chapter, Tom Kochan takes a transatlantic perspective on developments in the UK. He points to a number of similarities between the USA and the UK: the long-term decline in union membership, an increasing failure of young people to join unions, and a desire for voice arrangements that resemble works councils more than unions. In both countries he suggests that there are some similar factors driving these developments: the failure of unions to organize new workplaces; market pressures on management searching for new forms of flexibility; the development over the last two decades of the kind of human resource practices associated with the high involvement model; and the growing decentralization of industrial relations, which makes it hard to recruit and service members. However, Kochan also notes a number of differences between the USA and the UK that are rather more encouraging for the latter country: the membership mass in the UK is still significantly higher than in the USA, British employers are on average less aggressively hostile to trade unions, and the EU offers some opportunities for British unions that are not available in the USA. Kochan then suggests a number of ways forward for unions, similar to those put forward by other authors, such as the provision of new services, the use of information technology, and the engagement of young people in activities that interest them and addressing issues critical to women, thereby demonstrating the value of trade unions. He warns that the traditional organizing model, based on organizing workplaces around dissatisfaction and instrumentality, has limitations. Rather he proposes an organizing approach based not on organizing workplaces but on organizing individuals, who retain their membership as they move between jobs.

The future of trade unions

Collectively, the chapters have important implications for the debate about the future of trade unions in the UK. First, a number of chapters suggest that workers do want collective representation at work. However, trade unions must now be viewed within the context of multiple forms of representation more than they have in the past. Workers may be represented by bodies other than trade unions, such as joint consultative committees or works councils. In addition, many managements claim employees are given voice through direct participation via mechanisms such as direct workforce meetings, briefing groups and problem-solving circles. Moreover, these alternative forms of representation and involvement may indeed be perceived as valuable by employees. In addition, union representation itself no longer means high levels of union membership, given the demise of the closed shop. Even when a union is recognized, the topics of representation may be severely limited and workers may turn elsewhere for representation – such as to a Citizens' Advice Bureau or an Employment Tribunal without the aid of a union. Yet some of these alternative forms of representation may be additives and not substitutes for one another. There is indeed no strong evidence to suggest that new direct methods of involvement associated with human resource management are generally substitutes for unionism. Nonetheless, workers in some situations may be content with such methods and thus perceive unions as irrelevant to them. How well alternative forms of involvement and representation perform in the eyes of employees seems increasingly likely to affect whether they will join a trade union and remain in one throughout their working lives. For unions, they have to find ways of turning such arrangements to their advantage.

A second implication is that the difficulty unions have had in obtaining recognition in new workplaces and among young workers must be the starting point of any diagnosis of the unions' problems. In the case of new workplaces, it is important to realize that these problems extend across the whole private sector and not just services. The new workplace effect is more important than the decline of union membership within recognized workplaces or any effect that non-union-based employee involvement methods may have on the desire for union voice. However, in the case of young workers the declining probability of their joining trade unions does not appear to signify any weaker desire on their part, relative to older workers, for a voice at work, or hostility towards unions. It appears simply to be the case that there is a lower awareness amongst young workers of the nature and relevance of trade unionism. Consistent with this, a large part of the reducing rate of union membership amongst young workers reflects the fact that they are disproportionately likely to be employed in young workplaces.

Third, the government's emphasis on choice in employment relations, particularly for employers, means that support for collective bargaining remains limited. While the trend towards an increasing juridification of industrial relations and the conferment of individual employment rights, in part fostered by EU membership, has continued, the effect of government policy is likely to mean the increasing coexistence of a range of forms of employee involvement and representation. It would seem that the recognition procedures and now the information and consultation procedures are as far as the current Labour government or any government in the immediate future is likely to go in terms of promoting trade unions.

Fourth, there is currently little likelihood of any revival of the managerial support that may have underpinned some of the extension of trade unionism in the 1970s. While recognition agreements are being signed, they are in the shadow of the law, and the initiation of such discussions by management is rare and likely to be a means of averting a claim from an alternative union. Employers' policies continue to extend across the whole spectrum from 'active support' to 'peaceful competition' and 'forcible opposition', to use Bain's terms (1970: 131–5), but there is still forcible opposition in the UK to trade unions. However, as Kochan points out, this is in no way as aggressive or widespread as in the USA, and derecognition has not been a major factor in the decline of trade unionism. Chapters 5 and 8 suggest that peaceful competition via direct employee involvement and indirect forms of joint representation, such as joint consultative committees and councils, are a major challenge to trade unions at the present time. However, these forms of representation may also complement trade unionism and offer unions an opportunity to extend their membership. Chapter 6 also suggests that the increasing need of employers to address equal opportunity and family-friendly working issues may provide fertile grounds for trade unions to influence corporate policies and demonstrate their value to employees.

Finally, the implications for union strategy are various. It would be wrong to read any simple lessons from these research studies, but they clearly show that neither government legislation nor managerial support will act as substitutes for trade union organizing and campaigning. The book also points to the need for unions to target new workplaces as a way of accessing young workers if they are to replenish the stock of union members, let alone return to the kind of growth they enjoyed in the 1970s. It also suggests that there is a need to demonstrate their benefits to women workers, as well as to workers from ethnic minorities. If the reality is that workers who will never join a union are becoming typical, it is vital that unions recruit young workers within the early years of their working lives unless they are to lose them forever. This implies that making young people aware of unions at as early an age as possible and a two-pronged approach to union recognition (aimed at workplaces and at individuals) is necessary. Nonetheless, there are estimated to be around three million workers who are covered by a recognition agreement at their workplace but who are not union members, and a cost–benefit analysis of recruitment activity might suggest that unions (or at least specific ones) could be better off concentrating on such free riders (Metcalf, 2001: 29).

Conclusions

The overall conclusion is that unions are not outmoded institutions of little relevance to modern employees. A majority of workers want voice, albeit not always exclusively via a union, and workers have dissatisfactions that may be increasing, particularly regarding job security, training, career opportunities and the intensity of work. Knowledge of the benefits of unions is limited, and is a major factor behind relatively low membership amongst young workers. While assessments of unionism must be coloured by their failure to avert job losses and enhanced workloads in major industries, including the public sector, the benefits that unions offer remain highly salient – including new areas such as family-friendly working arrangements and equal opportunities practices. Nonetheless, it is unlikely that the decline of unions in the UK will be reversed in any significant way in the near future, short of unions organizing beyond their existing territories and new groups of workers. Moreover, in the future representation will be different from in the past, with more mixed forms of representation via unions, joint consultation and other arrangements. The unions of the future will thus not be mirror images of those of the past. As a contribution to understanding the current challenges and opportunities that trade unions face, this book provides an assessment of the key issues involved in union membership, recognition and representation.

Chapter 2

Trade union decline, new workplaces and new workers

Stephen Machin

Union activity in Britain is at its lowest level since the Second World War, with less than 30 per cent of employees being trade union members. In the private sector, less than one in five people in employment are members of a union. This compares to the heyday years of unionism in the late 1970s, when just over 13 million people – or 58 per cent of employees – were trade union members, and over 70 per cent of employees' wages were set by collective bargaining. Since reaching its peak in 1979, unionization (however measured) has fallen relentlessly year on year to the very low levels seen today.

The reasons for this decline are becoming better understood. While Pencavel (2002) refers to union retreat in Britain as 'surprising', he emphasizes that a combination of several factors has marginalized union presence in the labour market (see also Metcalf, 1991, 2001). This said, it appears that a key factor underpinning the rapid and sizeable deunionization of the British labour market has been a failure of trade unions to organize workers in new establishments (see Disney *et al.*, 1995, 1996; Machin, 2000). It also seems that unions are rarely derecognized in existing workplaces (Smith and Morton, 1993; Gall and McKay, 1994, 1999, 2002), and the evidence from the 1980s (Machin, 1995) shows no role of unions in closing down establishments. Putting these together emphasizes that new workplace entry and the unions' inability to get a foot in the door of these new workplaces are key to understanding union decline.

This chapter focuses on the links between unionization and new workplaces. It begins by reporting evidence, drawn from and extending earlier work on union recognition and age of establishment, from the Workplace Industrial/Employee Relations Surveys (WIRS/WERS). However, establishment age is not the only important age-related feature of trade union decline. The union membership rate amongst young workers is currently very low, and much lower than in the past. Box 2.1 shows changes in the

---

Box 2.1 *Individual case study of union decline*

What has happened to unionization rates for archetypical union members and union workplaces?

The probability of being a union member has fallen sharply, but at a much faster rate for younger people.

Archetypical union member:
1975 probability of union membership for male aged 45, working in manufacturing industry in the north: 0.80.
1975 probability of union membership for male aged 25, working in manufacturing industry in the north: 0.74.
2001 probability of union membership for male aged 45, working in manufacturing industry in the north: 0.42.
2001 probability of union membership for male aged 25, working in manufacturing industry in the north: 0.19.

The probability of a workplace having a union recognized for collective bargaining purposes has fallen sharply, but at a much faster rate for younger workplaces.

Archetypical union workplace:
1980 probability of union recognition for workplace over 25 years old in manufacturing industry in the north: 0.84.
1980 probability of union recognition for workplace less than 25 years old in manufacturing industry in the north: 0.69.
1998 probability of union recognition for workplace over 25 years old in manufacturing industry in the north: 0.67.
1998 probability of union recognition for workplace less than 25 years old in manufacturing industry in the north: 0.17.

---

unionization rates of what many would view as an archetypical union member and workplace (a male manufacturing worker in the north, and a northern manufacturing workplace). It clearly confirms very important workplace-age and age-of-worker declines in union membership rates between 1975 and 2001. In fact, in 2001 union membership and recognition rates amongst the younger people and workplaces are seen to be extremely low. This chapter therefore also presents an analysis of how the relationship between individual union membership and worker age has altered through time. Finally, further analysis, whilst not conclusive, suggests that workplace age may be the more important age-based factor in the recent era of union decline.

Union decline in Britain: the role of age of workplace

Table 2.1 uses data from the Workplace Industrial/Employee Relations Surveys of 1980, 1984, 1990 and 1998 to demonstrate the scale of union decline in Britain since 1980. Panel A reports information on the proportion of establishments that recognized trade unions for collective bargaining purposes between 1980 and 1998. By 1998 only 42 per cent of all workplaces recognized any union(s), as compared to 64 per cent eighteen years earlier. Other measures of union presence at the workplace (e.g. union density, union coverage) also show large falls (see Machin, 2000: 634; Millward *et al.*, 2000: 83–137). By any standards this corresponds to a large and rapid deunionization of the British labour market, and in international terms the scale and pace of union decline is both larger and faster than that experienced by other countries over as long a time period. Indeed, in some other countries (e.g. Germany and the Scandinavian countries) union collective bargaining coverage has not fallen. In those where it has (such as Australia, Japan and the USA), the percentage decrease is nowhere near as marked as in Britain.

The question is, why has this happened? It is clear that there has been a very marked shift linked to age. This chapter studies the dimensions of this age-based shift, looking at both age-of-worker and age-of-workplace effects on union decline. The remainder of this section begins by considering the pattern of union change across different-aged workplaces.

Union recognition and age of workplace

The lower panels of Table 2.1 show how patterns of union recognition are linked to the age of the workplace. Panel B clearly shows that the relationship with workplace age has altered through time. Rates of union recognition are substantially lower in newer establishments (defined as less than ten years old at the survey date) in the later surveys. According to the 1990 and 1998 data, union recognition rates were a very large 0.25 (1990) and 0.23 (1998) points lower in establishments less than ten years old. In the 1980 and 1984 surveys the gaps related to workplace age were much smaller, at 0.06 and 0.10 respectively.

The age differences can be re-formulated in terms of changes through time, and this has been done in Panel C, which shows markedly lower rates of union recognition in the workplaces set up after 1980. For the 1990 and 1998 surveys (the two with reasonably large samples of workplaces set up post-1980), recognition is over 0.25 points lower than in workplaces set up in 1980 or before.

Table 2.1 Trade union recognition in Britain: 1980–98

	1980	1984	1990	1998
A. Aggregate				
Proportion of establishments with any union recognized for collective bargaining purposes	0.64	0.66	0.53	0.42
B. Patterns by age of establishment				
Proportion of establishments with any union recognized for collective bargaining purposes, age of workplace < 10 years	0.59	0.58	0.34	0.27
Proportion of establishments with any union recognized for collective bargaining purposes, age of workplace ⩾ 10 years	0.65	0.68	0.59	0.50
Difference across age groups (standard error)	−0.06 (0.03)	−0.10 (0.03)	−0.25 (0.02)	−0.23 (0.02)
C. Patterns by decade of set-up date				
Proportion of establishments with any union recognized for collective bargaining purposes, workplace set up after 1980	–	0.54	0.35	0.30
Proportion of establishments with any union recognized for collective bargaining purposes, workplace set-up 1980 or before	0.64	0.66	0.61	0.56
Difference across set-up date groups (standard error)	–	−0.12 (0.07)	−0.25 (0.02)	−0.26 (0.02)

D. Set-up date differences from statistical models controlling for compositional changes

	1980–1998 pooled	1998
Set up after 1980	−0.117 (0.017)	−0.109 (0.026)
Sample size	7862	1883

Aggregate (i.e. all establishments with 25 or more workers) proportions taken from the sourcebooks for the 1980, 1984 and 1990 WIRS and the 1998 WERS (Daniel and Millward, 1983; Millward and Stevens, 1986; Millward et al., 1992; Cully et al., 1999). 1998 recognition data recodes recognition to zero for fifteen workplaces that recognized teacher unions but who in fact had pay set by the Pay Review Bodies (this follows the same procedure as in Chapter 10 of Cully et al., 1999). John Forth and Neil Millward kindly provided the serial codes for these fifteen workplaces. In Panels B and C standard errors are reported in parentheses for the differences across age and set-up date. The Panel D differences are marginal effects (associated standard errors in parentheses) from statistical probit models that control for establishment size (five dummy variables compared to a base of 25–49 workers), whether the establishment was single-site or foreign owned, the proportion of part-time workers, dummies for broad sector (private manufacturing and public sector as compared to the base of private services) and, in the pooled models, dummies for the relevant survey.

These descriptive statistics point to an important workplace age-related decline in union recognition. They clearly reveal a pattern showing a failure of unions to organize in new workplaces. Coupled with the evidence for the 1980s that unions did not seem to close workplaces (Machin, 1995), this emphasizes the role that the dynamics of workplace entry and exit in the product market has played in recent years. This is exacerbated by the fact that it is now the level of workplace that matters most for union bargaining in Britain (unlike some other countries, where unions retain an important role at industry or even national levels).

However, these statistics should be treated with caution as over the time period under consideration there have also been some important compositional changes, such as the increased incidence of smaller workplaces and the move away from manufacturing to services. So the next step is to present empirical estimates of the age-based recognition decline derived from statistical models that control for such shifts in composition.

Empirical models of establishment union recognition

Panel D of Table 2.1 reports recognition differences between workplaces set up after 1980 as compared to those established earlier, derived from statistical models that control for compositional changes. The specific variables measuring changes in workplace composition are entered into the statistical models for two reasons: first, they reflect a need to define variables consistently through time; second, they are chosen on the basis of judgement of what are likely to have been the most important compositional changes in the economy over the time period under study. The variables entered measure establishment size, whether the establishment is single-site or foreign owned, the proportion of part-time workers, broad sector (private manufacturing and public sector as compared to private services), and, in the pooled models, controls for the survey year.

Estimates of recognition differences related to workplace age derived from two specifications are reported – the first from all four surveys pooled together, and the second from the most recent 1998 survey only. The reason for reporting two specifications is that the establishment age variables are not identical across surveys (Machin, 2000: 644; Millward *et al.*, 2000: 103). Table 2.1 reports marginal effects that show the proportionate difference in recognition between workplaces established post-1980 as compared to those set up before, holding constant the control variables. They show a very similar pattern in both specifications. It is clear that the composition variables entered matter, as the marginal effects associated with being established after 1980 variables are halved relative to a model that does not control for them. Nonetheless, in the specification using pooled data, workplaces set up post-1980 have recognition of 0.12 lower than those set up before. Much the same picture emerges when focusing on the 1998 data alone, where the marginal effect is estimated to be of similar magnitude (-0.11).

Overall, these results highlight the importance of the workplaces set up since the start of the 1980s in accounting for union decline. Unions have clearly been less successful in gaining recognition in newer workplaces in the last couple of decades than they were before.

Union decline in Britain: the role of age of worker

When considering data on unionization, the other significant age-based factor is age of worker. It matters in that its relationship with union status has also changed over time. Young workers are today considerably less likely to be union members than they were in the past. This section considers connections between worker age and union status, and how they have shifted through time. The analysis utilizes a data source from the mid-1970s, a period when union membership was high and growing, and compares patterns of unionization to those seen in current (2001) data, when membership is low and has been falling for over twenty years.

Union membership and age of worker

Panels A and B of Table 2.2 report some descriptive statistics on individual union membership in 1975 and in 2001. The 1975 figures come from the National Training Survey (NTS), a survey carried out by the Manpower Services Commission of around 54,000 people (Manpower Services Commission, 1978; Stewart, 1983). The 2001 data are drawn from the Autumn 2001 Labour Force Survey (LFS).

Table 2.2 clearly demonstrates the sharp fall in union membership density that took place in the last quarter century. In 1975, 55 per cent of people were members of a union (or staff association); in 2001, this had plummeted to just 29 per cent. The fall is strongly significant in statistical terms; the downtrend in union membership has been a rapid one. One interesting observation is that the fall is much more marked for males than for females, with 66 per cent of men being union members in 1975 and only 30 per cent in 2001. The corresponding fall for women is from 40 to 29 per cent, revealing a clear gender convergence in union status (see Machin, 2002, for a fuller analysis of factors of convergence and divergence in union membership).

Table 2.2 Individual union membership and worker age: 1975–2001

	1975	2001	Change (standard error)
A. Aggregate			
All	0.55	0.29	−0.26 (0.003)
Men	0.66	0.30	−0.36 (0.004)
Women	0.40	0.29	−0.12 (0.005)
B. Patterns by age of worker			
All age <30	0.48	0.15	−0.33 (0.006)
All age ≥ 30	0.59	0.34	−0.25 (0.004)
All, difference across age groups (standard error)	−0.11 (0.01)	−0.18 (0.01)	−0.07 (0.007)
Men age <30	0.54	0.15	−0.39 (0.008)
Men age ≥ 30	0.72	0.36	−0.36 (0.005)
Men, difference across age groups (standard error)	−0.17 (0.01)	−0.20 (0.01)	−0.03 (0.010)
Women age <30	0.39	0.16	−0.23 (0.008)
Women age ≥ 30	0.41	0.33	−0.08 (0.006)
Women, difference across age groups (standard error)	−0.01 (0.01)	−0.16 (0.01)	−0.15 (0.010)
C. Age differences from statistical models controlling for compositional changes			
All: age (× 100)	0.474 (0.024)	0.628 (0.018)	0.154 (0.018)
All: age <30	−0.130 (0.007)	−0.160 (0.004)	−0.030 (0.003)
Men: age (× 100)	0.469 (0.029)	0.656 (0.026)	0.187 (0.030)
Men: age <30	−0.142 (0.008)	−0.162 (0.006)	−0.020 (0.004)
Women: age (× 100)	0.373 (0.038)	0.582 (0.026)	0.209 (0.032)
Women: age <30	−0.085 (0.010)	−0.152 (0.006)	−0.067 (0.008)

Sample covers all people aged 18–64 inclusive in each year. Sample sizes for descriptive statistics are: 1975 National Training Survey, 35,371, 2001 Labour Force Survey, 49,600. In Panel B standard errors are reported in parentheses for the differences across age groups. Each row in Panel C corresponds to a marginal effect on age (or an age <30 dummy variable), with associated standard errors in parentheses, from probit models estimated separately for 1975 and 2001. These control for gender (in the all models), full-time status, no qualifications, non-white, regional dummies (5), industry dummies (8) and size of workplace dummy variables (2). Sample sizes are: All 1975 – 30,848; All 2001 – 48,862; Men 1975 – 17,965; Men 2001 – 24,200; Women 1975 – 12,883; Women 2001 – 24,662.

Panel B of Table 2.2 considers the union membership–worker age relation by breaking down the temporal change in union membership by age of worker. A number of observations are relevant. First, whilst membership rates were lower in both years for people aged below 30, the gap widens over time. In 1975 union membership density was 11 percentage points lower for younger people (at 48 per cent compared to 59 per cent), but by 2001 the age gap was 19 percentage points. Expressed differently, the rate of union membership fell more rapidly amongst the under 30s between 1975 and 2001 as the union gap opened out by (a statistically significant) 7 percentage points.

Second, the fall in union membership was more neutral with respect to age for men. Within both age groups male union membership fell a long way, by 39 percentage points (from 54 to 15 per cent) for young men and by 36 percentage points (from 72 to 36 per cent) for men aged 30 and over. There is still a widening of the age-of-worker gap in union status, but only of 3 percentage points. On the other hand, whilst female membership fell by less, it fell much more sharply amongst the younger group of women. For those aged below 30 the percentage of union members fell from 39 to 16 per cent, as compared to a fall from 41 to 33 per cent for the older group of women, implying a large (15 percentage points) opening up of the age-based union status gap over time.

This analysis confirms that whilst union membership fell for all age–gender comparisons, an important dimension is the opening up of the age-of-worker gap in union status. However, as in the case of the establishment models considered above, it may also be the case that other relevant factors (correlated with both age and unionization) changed at the same time. Panel C of Table 2.2 therefore considers temporal shifts in the relation between union membership and worker age derived from statistical models that control for other factors.

Empirical models of individual union membership

Panel C of Table 2.2 presents the age effects derived from statistical models controlling for the determinants of individual-level union membership in 1975 and 2001. The variables controlled for include gender and industry (see Table notes for the full list). Six different estimates are presented for each year; two each for all individuals and separately for men and women. The two models per group basically differ in the way that age was entered into the statistical model, being a continuous age variable in the first and a dichotomous variable comparing people aged less than 30 to older people in the second.

First, the age effect for all individuals is considered. In both years the age variable attracts a strongly significant coefficient showing that older workers are substantially more likely to be union members (or alternatively that those aged less than 30 are substantially less likely to be members). However, this relationship has strengthened through time. The estimated age coefficient (which is multiplied by 100 for ease of presentation) rises by 0.154 between 1975 and 2001 and the coefficient on the age less than 30 variable falls by 0.030. Both of these changes are strongly significant. This is despite the inclusion of the control variables.

The separate gender specifications also show the rising importance of worker age. The linear age coefficient rises by 0.187 for men and by 0.209 for women. Perhaps more striking is the age less than 30 effect, which falls by a statistically significant 0.020 for men and by a much more sizeable 0.067 for women. This confirms the opening up of the age-based union gap, and that this widening has been particularly marked amongst female workers. It also reveals how the simple observation of gender convergence in unionization noted above obscures an important age-related difference in patterns of change by gender through time. It seems then that age of worker, as well as age of workplace, has a potentially important role in explaining union decline in Britain in the last 25 years or so.

Patterns of union membership across industries

If age of worker matters for union membership, it is interesting to observe and isolate situations where membership rates are higher or lower. Table 2.3 considers one possibility by looking at which industries have higher or lower unionization rates amongst all workers, and specifically amongst younger workers (again defined as aged less than 30). The industries with the ten highest and ten lowest membership densities are reported for each group, using 2001 LFS data.

Even in 2001, when the average is low, there is substantial variation in union status across industries. The high end of the list is, not surprisingly, dominated by public sector industries. However, even within these sectors, at the high end the young worker rate is markedly lower than the overall membership density.

There seem to be two sorts of industries clustered into the low membership zone. First, there are the traditionally low-wage industries that have in the past never really offered much in the way of prospects to join trade unions (e.g. agriculture, personal services, wholesale trade). Second, some of the more high-tech and new sectors of the economy, like the computer industries towards the bottom of the list, have very low overall union

Table 2.3 Industry rankings of individual union membership for all workers and workers aged less than 30 in 2001, calculated from 58 industry classifications in the Labour Force Survey of Autumn 2001

All workers		Workers aged < 30	
Highest 10 industries		*Highest 10 industries*	
Public administration	0.56	Education	0.45
Electricity, gas and water	0.56	Public administration	0.42
Air transport	0.56	Manufacture of transport equipment (other)	0.37
Education			
Post and telecommunications	0.50	Manufacture of leather products	0.36
Water	0.49	Electricity, gas and water	0.32
Manufacture of transport equipment (other)	0.45	Health and social work	0.31
		Air transport	0.29
Manufacture of basic metals	0.45	Land transport	0.27
Health and social work	0.45	Manufacture of motor vehicles	0.27
Manufacture of motor vehicles	0.44	Manufacture of basic metals	0.27
Lowest 10 industries		*Lowest 10 industries*	
Manufacture of office machinery and computers	0.13	Other business activities (legal, advertising, cleaning)	0.06
Wholesale trade	0.09	Oil and gas	0.05
Other business activities (legal, advertising, cleaning)	0.09	Renting of machinery and equipment and personal household goods	0.05
Personal services	0.07	Manufacture of wood products	0.05
Agriculture	0.07	Sale, maintenance and repair of motor vehicles	0.04
Renting of machinery and equipment and personal household goods	0.06		
		Agriculture	0.03
Sale, maintenance and repair of motor vehicles	0.06	Hotels and restaurants	0.02
		Computer and related activities	0.02
Hotels and restaurants	0.06	Personal services	0.02
Computer and related activities	0.05	Private households	0.00
Private households	0.01		

membership rates – extremely low amongst the young. These industries are sizeable employers of British workers and, of course, many are characterized by having large numbers of newly established workplaces.

Union decline in Britain: age of workplace or age of worker?

This last observation raises the question as to whether age of worker or age of establishment matters more for union decline, or whether they operate in conjunction with one another (i.e. if young workers and young workplaces are more likely to be matched to one another). At the outset, it should be acknowledged that to conduct a strong test of this hypothesis longitudinal data on workers and workplaces are required, coupled with union data for each. Such data do not currently exist. Nevertheless, this section presents two pieces of suggestive evidence. While based on two different approaches – one using matched worker–firm data at one point in time and the other using industry data through time – both point to age of workplace being more important for union decline.

Union recognition and workplace set-up date by age of worker

As noted, ideally matched worker–firm data over time are required to look at this question. Unfortunately, the only currently available data along these lines are for one point in time, namely the cross-sectional employee-level data matched to workplaces in the 1998 WERS. This data source contains information on worker age (grouped into age bands), so one possibility is to see if the estimated coefficient on the post-1980 variable differs by age of worker.

This is considered in Machin (2000), where estimates of individual membership equations including age of workplace effects were presented separately for workers of different ages. In that analysis, the pattern of estimated coefficients on workplace age always revealed a significant negative 'set-up post-1980' association with recognition, but shows the post-1980 effect to be of very similar magnitude across different worker ages. An updated set of estimates shows that for workers aged less than 30 the coefficient and associated standard error on the post-1980 variable is −0.061 (0.018). This compares with −0.058 (0.014) for those aged 30 or more. As such, the results suggest that establishment age matters to much the same extent for both ages of worker.

Industry level union recognition and age of workplace and worker

The other evidence that can be brought to bear on the age of worker versus age of workplace question is derived from creating a data set following the same industries over time. This can be used to estimate separate age-of-worker and age-of-workplace effects on rates of industry unionization. Aggregating the WIRS/WERS data for 1980 and 1998 to industry level for 44 consistently defined industries in both years makes this analysis possible. To this, data on worker age can be added from the LFS (in the nearest available years of 1981 and 1998).

Table 2.4 reports estimates of the relation between industry recognition

Table 2.4 Industry-level regressions of union recognition on age of worker and age of workplace

	Proportion of workplaces in industry with recognized unions			
Average age of workers	−0.003 (0.015)		−0.003 (0.015)	
Proportion of workers aged < 30		−0.204 (0.387)		−0.194 (0.378)
Proportion of workplaces aged < 10 years		−0.253 (0.140)	−0.253 (0.145)	−0.252 (0.144)
Industry dummies	yes	yes	yes	yes
Year dummy	yes	yes	yes	yes
R-squared	0.90	0.90	0.91	0.91
Sample size	88	88	88	88

All regressions include dummy variables for industry and year so as to study within-industry changes over time; regressions weighted by WIRS/WERS relative cell sizes; standard errors in parentheses.

and the two age variables. All specifications are configured in an appropriate statistical way so as to ensure that the analysis asks the right question: if age of worker or age of workplace shifts within industries through time, what does that do to union recognition? The specifications differ as to which age variables are considered, with age of worker being entered in the two forms already considered and age of workplace being entered in a consistent way for the two years. The two age-of-worker variables are therefore aggregated versions of those considered earlier: the average age of workers in the industry and the proportion aged less than 30. The age-of-workplace variables are constrained by the 1980 WIRS data (which has age banded into five intervals), and therefore reconfigures the 1998 data to be consistent and looks at the proportion of workplaces in the industry aged less than ten years.

The pattern of results is clear. Only the workplace-age variable matters statistically, as it is only the proportion of workplaces less than ten years old variable that attracts a significant negative coefficient. This indicates that those industries with greater influxes of newer establishments between 1980 and 1998 experienced greater union decline. This is true even in statistical specifications that hold constant the industry differences in worker age, as reported in the final two columns of Table 2.4. As such it is in line with the 1998 WERS evidence that, if anything, it seems that workplace age is what matters more in explaining union decline.

Conclusions

This chapter has focused on the way in which union decline in Britain has been characterized by age-of-workplace and age-of-worker effects. The relationship between union presence and both age variables has clearly altered over time, as the union status gap between newer and older workplaces and between younger and older workers has widened. The analysis presented here uses several data sources from the last 25 years to document this, and to ascertain the scale of the shifts. It reports strong evidence of sizeable age-based shifts in union status linked to age of workplace and age of worker. Whilst clearly not the only factors behind the rapid de-unionization of the British labour market, both are central to understanding the patterns of union decline seen in the last quarter century. Finally, some suggestive evidence shows that age of workplace is perhaps more important than age of worker in accounting for union decline.

These findings may be related to recent work in this area. Other commentators have noted the importance of the dynamics of workplace entry and exit for labour market outcomes, and in particular for trade union presence. Pencavel (2002) argues that the more competitive nature of product and labour markets in Britain means that 'unions in the future will need to run much faster to stay in the same place', and that 'to extend their reach, unions have to run even faster' (Pencavel, 2002: 44). It is very clear from the results reported in this chapter, showing an increased failure of unions to organize newer workplaces and younger workers, that the recent past has not seen this happen. As such this has resulted in unions falling behind, perhaps reflecting an inability to adapt to the demands of the so-called New Economy. All this is further reinforced by the fact that recent union organizing campaigns are heavily skewed towards sectors with traditionally strong union activity – manufacturing and the public sector (Gall and McKay, 2002). That employment is declining here and growing in the sectors characterized by new (principally non-union) work-places and workers only acts to make the swimming upstream pheno-menon more marked.

Acknowledgements

I am very grateful to Tanvi Desai and Joanne Roberts for all the hard work they put in to get the National Training Survey data into a usable format, and to Jo Blanden for comments and research assistance. Some of the work on this chapter was done during the author's leave during the 2001/2 academic year in the Economics Department at MIT, whose hospitality and support are gratefully acknowledged.

Chapter 3

Young workers and trade unions

Richard Freeman and Wayne Diamond

Young workers are much less likely to be unionized than older workers in Great Britain. In 2001, the Labour Force Survey (for the UK) reported that 16 per cent of employees aged up to 29 years were union members compared to 34 per cent of workers aged 30 years and older (see Table 3.1). From the 1980s and through the 1990s the proportion of workers who were in unions fell more rapidly among younger workers than among older workers. As a result the young worker share of union membership dropped to extraordinarily low levels. Data from the MORI Social Research Institute's aggregate Omnibus survey (which involves about 65,000 interviews per year and, like all the data in this chapter except the Labour Force survey is for Great Britain) shows that in 1998 just 7 per cent of union members were aged 18–24 whereas a decade earlier 14 per

Table 3.1 Union membership of employees by age in 2001

Members	BWRPS 2001	BSAS 2001	Labour Force Survey 2001
	%	%	%
All employees	35	31	29
Up to 29 years	17	20	16
30 and over	41	33	34
Difference	−24	−13	−18

(Source: British Workers Representation and Participation Survey (BWRPS, 2001); British Social Attitudes (BSAS, 2001). Weighted base of 1,546, 1,351 un-weighted observations.)

1. Questions: BWRPS, 'Are you currently a member of a union, or similar body, at your workplace?'; BSAS, 'Are you now a member of a trade union or staff association?' Weighted base of 1,652, 1,536 un-weighted observations.

2. The BWRPS was conducted in summer 2001 to find out how British workers saw their workplace and employer, the problems they had at work, the services they wanted from workplace organizations, and their assessment of the ability of unions to deliver those services. The survey was carried out by face-to-face interviews of some 1,300 workers by BMRB, based on a random location sampling design to assure a representative non-biased sample.

cent of all union members were in this age group (Mori, 2000). While the number of workers that join unions typically rises with age, membership among British young persons dropped to sufficiently low levels to constitute a serious problem for the future of unions.

One interpretation of the low and declining rate of union membership among young workers is that young persons, many of whom were brought up during the Thatcher and Major years, have developed an individualistic orientation that conflicts with the collectivism that leads people to join unions. According to this analysis, young Britons see unions as dinosaur institutions that suited their parents but that are not helpful to them in the workplace. The analysis in this chapter shows that this is an incorrect reading of the low and falling rate of union membership among young workers. Differences in attitudes towards unions by age are modest. Rather than being biased against unions, young persons have a slight positive orientation towards unions. However, they have little knowledge of unions before they take jobs and so their response to unions depends critically on their actual workplace experiences.

Another explanation for the low and declining rate of union membership among young workers is that it reflects the disproportionate representation of young workers in the non-union sectors of the economy – particularly in service industries, where the union presence has always been less than in manufacturing. Analysis shows that the type of jobs held by young persons contributes to their low membership in unions, but this is far from the dominant cause. Young workers are less likely to be union members than older workers even in organized workplaces. We attributed this difference in part to the failure of union representatives to interact with or even to try to sign up young employees.

British unions have responded to the low rate of membership among young workers by developing special programmes to improve their attractiveness to this group. These programmes appear at best to have had only a marginal impact, in part because unions are bureaucratic organizations that cannot easily modify their operations to fit specific groups and in part because the programmes ghettoize young members. There may be greater opportunities for unions to attract youths through programmes that help young persons as workers rather than as youths per se. Because young workers are as favourably inclined to European Union (EU)-style works councils at their workplaces as older workers, strong union initiatives to develop works councils as the voice of labour within firms, consistent with the UK's acceptance of the EU Directive on Information and Consultation in national level undertakings, offers a more promising way to attract young workers than special youth programmes.

Low unionism among young workers

The starting point for this chapter is the fact that young workers are less likely to be members of trade unions than are older workers. This is documented in Table 3.1, which records the percentage of workers who are union members by age in 2001 in three surveys: the British Workplace Representation and Participation Survey (BWRPS), conducted in summer 2001; the British Social Attitudes Survey (BSA), which has been conducted annually since 1981 (Jowell *et al.*, 1999); and the Labour Force Survey (LFS), which has asked about unionization regularly since the early 1990s (Office of National Statistics, 2001). All three surveys show that young workers – defined here as those aged less than 30 years old – have a much lower rate of unionism than older workers. The gap is largest in the BWRPS (24 percentage points) and least in the BSAS (13 percentage points), with the LFS gap almost halfway in between (18 percentage points). The differences reflect the design of the surveys as well as sampling variability in the BWRPS and BSAS, which have relatively small samples of young workers. Sampling variability can be important because both the BWRPS and BSAS cover approximately 1,300 workers. By contrast, the LFS covers 60,000 or so workers. Since only about 10 per cent of the working population is in the young age group, the sample sizes for young persons in the BWRPS and BSAS are relatively small.

By itself, the low unionization of young workers in 2001 tells us little about whether unions should worry more about their inability to attract young members than about their inability to organize other workers. Perhaps the same pattern of relatively low union membership among the young also held 20 or 30 years ago, when union density was higher. If young workers are disproportionately non-union because they have not had sufficient time or opportunity to join unions and naturally age into unionism as they grow older, differential rates of unionism by age would be a life-cycle phenomenon of little consequence to the long-term status of unions.

To examine this possibility, the proportion of workers less than 30 years old and the proportion aged 30 and over in unions over time were calculated, using time series data from the BSA and LFS surveys. Figure 3.1 displays the results for the BSA from 1983 to 2001. The gap in unionization between the younger and older workers trends upward, albeit with considerable year-to-year fluctuations. In 1983–7 the gap averaged 8.3 percentage points; in 1998–2001 it averaged 14.5 percentage points. Measured in percentage terms, the trend in the gap is even more dramatic. Whereas in 1983–7 young workers were just 16 per cent less likely to be

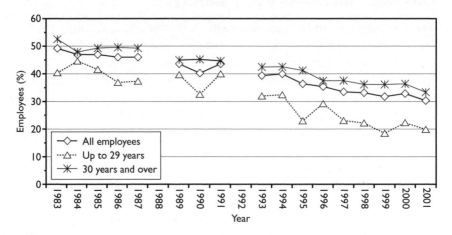

Figure 3.1 Union membership of employees by age, 1983–2001 (BSAS)

From 1985 onwards, respondents were asked if they belonged to a union or staff association at their workplace. The above chart counts staff association members as union members. Responses weighted using standard BSAS weighting variables. Respondents were employees working 10 or more hours per week. No survey was conducted in 1988 or 1992.

union members than older workers, in 1998–2001 young workers were nearly 60 per cent less likely to be union members than older workers.

Figure 3.2 displays the 1990s trend in unionization by age in the LFS. The gap in the rates between younger and older workers widens over the ten-year period covered. In 1992–3, young workers were 14 percentage points less likely to be unionized than older workers – a 35 per cent differential in the probability of unionization. In 2000–1, young workers were 18 percentage points less likely to be union members than older workers, which translates into a 53 per cent differential in the probability of union members given the low rate of unionization in this year.

Since unionization fell among older workers as well as among younger workers, the drop in union membership among the young cannot simply be a matter of postponing the age at which they join unions. If that were the case, the rate of unionization would fall only among young workers and the rate would jump for cohorts as they aged over the period. The data show no such pattern.

Another way to see the problem that the falling unionization among younger workers poses for unions is to consider unionism as a social phenomenon that one generation of workers passes on to the next generation. To examine this, we used a Markov chain transition rate model that links the union status of a parent with that of a younger working person. Formally, let α be the probability that a young person from a union home

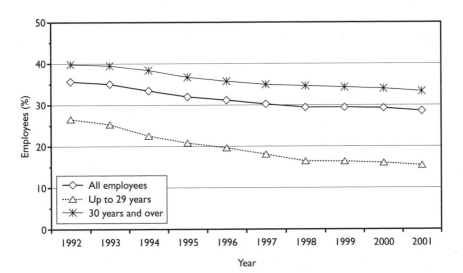

Figure 3.2 Union membership of employees by age, 1992–2001 (LFS)

Membership levels are for all in employment, but exclude members of the armed forces, unpaid family workers, and those on college-based schemes. Since 1992, union membership has been assessed in the autumn quarter. Those who did not report their union status or were not contactable in the autumn quarter have been allocated on a *pro-rata* basis.

becomes a union member, and β be the probability that a young person from a non-union home becomes a union member. Then if U is the proportion of the population of parental homes that are unionized, the proportion of young persons who will be unionized will be $U\alpha + (1 - U)\beta$ – a weighted average of the parental union status transmission rates. With a given set of transmission rates, the long-term or steady-state equilibrium rate of unionization (U*) that would result if the given transmission rates were constant over time can then be calculated as $U^* = \beta/(1 - \alpha + \beta)$.

The hard part of estimating this model is finding data on the transmission probabilities. Here, Labour Force Survey questions about the union status of all respondents in a given family unit were used to estimate the probabilities α and β. The estimates are imperfect since they are limited to young people who are working and still residing in their parents' home and exclude young persons who are not living with their parents, who may have a different unionization rate to those living with their parents. To minimize the danger that these estimates would be non-representative, we focused on a relatively young age group, 16–25-year-olds, where over half of the employed persons live at home. In the sample of 16–25-year-old employees living at home in 2001, 9.3 per cent were union members compared to 13.3 per cent of workers aged 16–25 not living at home. For the age group as a whole, the proportion unionized was 11.2 per cent. This suggests that the unionized proportion was understated by just 1.9 percentage points, or 17 per cent. In 1990, the LFS data show that 21.0 per cent of employed 16–25-year-olds living at home were in unions compared to 23.6 per cent of all 16–25-year-old employees – or a modest 2.6 percentage point (11 per cent) understatement. Thus, while imperfect, our sample of 16–25-year-olds living at home provides a reasonable picture of unionization in this age group.

Table 3.2 records the estimated transmission probabilities of union status from parent to offspring in 1990 and 2001. The family was categorized as union when at least one parent was a union member. The transition probabilities show that young workers from union families have much higher probabilities of being in a union than young workers from non-union families. The sizeable difference in the probabilities indicates that treating unionization as something that parents pass on to children has some empirical bite. In multivariate regressions that control for diverse characteristics of individuals, parental status remains a key determinant of whether or not a young person becomes a union member (Diamond and Freeman, 2002a). This is consistent with the Gomez *et al.* (2002) and Bryson and Gomez (Chapter 5 of this book) analysis of unionism as an experience good: if parents are members their children are more

Table 3.2 The proportion of employed 16–25-year-olds living at home in unions, by parental union status, and the implicit equilibrium rate of unionization: 1990 and 2001

| | Proportion of 16–25-year-olds in union | | |
	1990	*2001*	*% Change*
Parental union status			
Either parent member	0.261	0.128	−51
Neither parent member	0.145	0.065	−55
Implied equilibrium rate of unionization	0.182	0.081	−55

(Source: tabulated from Household Labour Force Survey, 1990 and 2001)

The 1990 survey had 1,964 persons aged 16–25 employed and thus potential union members. The 2001 survey had 509 persons aged 16–25. Union is defined by member in union or staff association. The LFS family unit comprises either a single person or a married or co-habiting couple or lone parents with never-married children who have no children of their own.

We have adjusted the equilibrium rates of unionization calculated from the Markov transition probabilities for the downward bias in the unionization rate of 16–25-year-olds living at home compared to 16–25-year-olds living on their own. We raised the 1990 implied equilibrium rate based on the transition probabilities by 11 per cent (from 16.4 per cent to the 18.2 per cent in the Table). We raised the 2001 implied equilibrium rate by 17 per cent (from 6.9 per cent to 8.1 per cent). In both cases we used the figures reported in the text for the union rates of 16–25-year-olds in total and for 16–25-year-olds living at home for our adjustment.

favourable towards this institution, since they experience it indirectly (assuming of course that the typical experience is a positive one).

The critical finding in Table 3.2 for the future of unions is that the probabilities of transmission of status fell sharply from 1990 to 2001 for both union and non-union families. At the 1990 rates of transmission of union status from parent to offspring, the equilibrium rate of unionization is 18.2 per cent. At the 2001 rates of transmission of union status from parent to offspring the equilibrium rate of unionization is just 8.1 per cent. Since these rates are below unionization rates in those years, the implication is that if all else remained the same, union density would fall for the foreseeable future, towards the equilibrium rates. With fewer persons coming from union families, it will be more difficult to engage young workers in trade unions.

In sum, we conclude that the drop in union membership among young workers poses a major challenge to British unions. Unions cannot readily rejuvenate themselves as a dynamic force in the labour market unless they are able to attract young workers.

Have young workers given up on unionism?

There is a widespread view that young workers do not join unions because they regard them as dinosaur institutions irrelevant to their needs, whereas older workers view them as an important force in their working lives. Existing research on young persons' attitudes towards unions, which is largely Canadian-based, shows that young persons do not have exceptionally negative views of trade unions, but these studies do not contain comparable data on the attitudes of older workers (Brammel and Cortiz, 1987; Cregan and Johnston, 1990; Barling et al., 1991; Cregan, 1991; Kelloway and Watts, 1994; Kelloway and Newton, 1996; Kelloway et al., 1996; Wagar and Rahman, 1997; Dekker et al., 1998), an exception being Gomez et al. (2002). Our research, based on interviews with young workers, confirms the finding that the young are not noticeably averse to unions. In addition, however, we compare the attitudes of younger persons with those of older persons in the BWRPS and other surveys and find that age per se is not to be a major determinant of attitudes towards unions in Great Britain. Thus we reject the notion that the low rate of unionization of young British workers is due to their having drastically different attitudes towards unions than those of older workers.

To find out how young people view unions, in spring 2000 we interviewed some 50 students who were about to enter the job market from Croydon College of Further Education and Kingsway College of Further

Education, both in London. We quantified what students told us about trade unions and how they felt about unions by asking them to fill out a short questionnaire. The principal finding from this analysis is that young persons have very little knowledge about trade unions – that they are largely 'blank slates' with regard to unions when they enter the job market. This is again consistent with the Gomez and Bryson model of unionism as an experience good (see Chapter 5) – that is, a good about which people form solid preferences only if and when they experience them. Until young people experience unions at their workplace, they have diffuse expectations about what unions do.

Table 3.3 summarizes the results from the Croydon interview/survey that led to the blank-slate interpretation of young workers' view of unions. We asked students twenty factual questions about unions – for instance, whether the letters TUC stand for The Union Council or something else; whether a worker has to be 25 years old or older to join a union; whether many unions provide credit cards and other services for members. By random chance, the students should have answered 50 per cent of the

Table 3.3 Attitudes of young persons towards unions

Source	Question	Response
Croydon college of FE survey		
Group interviews/survey 2000	20 basic true/false questions on trade unions in Britain	48% correct
n = 50 students	Attitude towards union, scaled −1 to 1	
	Instrumentality, 4 questions	0.28
	Big labour, 6 questions	0.00
	Attitude towards collectivism, scaled −1 to 1	
	Average 6 questions	0.23
TUC–Mori survey of 16–24-year-olds		
1996	Now thinking about trade unions, how much, if anything, do you know about them?	
n = 1,000	A great deal	1%
	A fair amount	12%
	Not very much	44%
	Nothing at all	42%
	From what you know or have heard, how favourable or unfavourable would you say you feel towards trade unions?	
	Very/mainly favourable	37%
	Mixed/don't know	54%
	Very/mainly unfavourable	9%

questions correctly. In fact, they answered, on average, 48 per cent correctly. We also asked students about the ability of unions to help workers (the instrumentality of unionism) and about union influence and power in the society (designed around the images associated with the UK union movement in the 1970s). The sum of responses to these questions were scaled from −1 to 1, with negative scores reflecting badly on unions and positive scores reflecting positively. As Table 3.3 shows, the students' replies were modestly favourable to unions being able to help workers and evenly divided around the more negative Big Labour image. We also asked whether they thought collective action was fruitful or not, and obtained responses slightly favourable towards collective activity.

It is impossible to generalize from a small group of young people to the attitudes of interviews with young British workers. However, the blank-slate hypothesis finds support in other surveys. Table 3.3 also summarizes a 1996 TUC–Mori survey of 16–24-year-olds that we discovered after undertaking our interviews. This survey asked young persons how much they knew about trade unions. Forty-two per cent said that they knew nothing at all, while 44 per cent said that they knew 'not very much'. The survey also asked whether young persons had favourable or unfavourable impressions of unions. Consistent with the blank-slate assessment, over half of respondents reported that they had either mixed impressions or no impressions about unions. Thirty-seven per cent had favourable views compared to 9 per cent that had unfavourable views, further rejecting the notion that the young look upon unions negatively.

Comparison of attitudes of younger and older workers

As our interviews and the TUC–MORI survey both deal only with young people, they do not provide comparative data on older workers. It could be that the mildly favourable views that young workers have towards unions are markedly less favourable than the views that older workers have towards unions. This would support the notion that there is a substantial age difference in attitudes that might help to explain the age difference in rates of union membership. To see if this is the case, we examined the responses to questions about unions by younger and older workers on three surveys: the BWRPS, the BSAS and the British Household Panel Survey (BHPS).

Panel A of Table 3.4 contains the results for questions regarding unions in general. In the BWRPS a split sample design was used, asking half of the sample one question and half of the sample another question on the same

Table 3.4 Attitudes of employees towards trade unions by age

	Up to 29 years (%)	30 and over (%)
Panel A: Views of unions in general		
BWRPS 2001		
Trade unions are old-fashioned	28	27
Trade unions have no future in modern Britain	18	17
Strong trade unions are needed to protect the working conditions and wages of employees	70	70
BHPS W7 1997		
Strong trade unions are needed to protect the working conditions and wages of employees	63	47
Panel B: Views of unions at own workplace		
BWRPS 2001		
Workplace better with a union:		
All employees	31	39
Employees with union at workplace only	44	57
Employees with no union at workplace only	24	19
BSAS 1998		
Workplace better with a union:		
All employees	30	36
Employees with union at workplace only	48	52
Employees with no union at workplace only	17	17

(Source: BWRPS, 2001)

Q34 'Please tell us how much you agree or disagree with the following statements . . .'
Q34 item 3 'Strong trade unions are needed to protect the working conditions and wages of employees'
Q34 item 4 A variant 'Trade unions are old-fashioned'
Q34 item 4 B variant 'Trade unions have no future in modern Britain'
Q37 (Union at workplace) 'Do you think your workplace would be a better or worse place to work if there was NO union?'
Q39 (No union at workplace) 'Do you think your workplace would be better or worse off with a union?'

BHPS Wave 7 (1997)
GOPSOCF 'Strong trade unions are needed to protect the working conditions and wages of employees' (5-point scale)

BSAS 1998
Q640 'Do you think that your workplace would be a better or worse place to work if there were no union or would it make no difference?'
Q638 'Do you think that your workplace would be a better or worse place to work if there were a trade union, or would it make no difference?'

All questions were originally recorded on 5-point scales, and have been recoded to 3-point scales for ease of use.

phenomenon. Providing two different statements reduces the danger that answers will depend on the particular way that a question is posed. Specifically, respondents were asked to assess two different statements: 'trade unions are old-fashioned' and 'trade unions have no future in Britain'. Few workers of any age agreed that unions are old-fashioned or have no future.

The BWRPS and BHPS asked workers to assess the statement 'strong trade unions are needed to protect the working conditions and wages of employees'. In both surveys the vast majority of younger workers agreed with this statement. In the BWRPS the response for younger workers was similar to that for older workers, while in the BHPS the proportion of younger workers supporting this proposition exceeded the proportion of older workers supporting the proposition, suggesting that the young have, if anything, more favourable views of unions than older workers.

Panel B of Table 3.4 turns from views of unions in general to views of what unions can do for workers at the workers' own workplace. Both the BWRPS and the BSAS asked how unions might affect a worker's current workplace. Both surveys asked non-union workers if their workplace would be better with a union, and asked union workers if their workplace would be better without a union. Taking the union and non-union samples together, we find that a smaller proportion of young workers than of older workers believe that unionization would make their workplace better (or that de-unionization would make their workplace worse). This would seem to show that young persons have less positive views about the efficacy of unions at their workplace than do older persons. However, dividing the sample by union status tells a more complicated story. The big difference in workers' views about whether or not unions make a workplace better occurs not between workers of different ages, but between workers with different union status. The low rate of unionization among young workers explains much of their lower belief in the efficacy of unions.

Consider first the pattern of responses by age by union status. According to the non-union sample in the BWRPS, young workers are more likely than older workers to believe that a union would make their workplace better, contrary to the result for all workers. In the BSAS, young non-union workers are as likely to believe that a union would make their workplace better as older non-union workers. By contrast, in the union samples in both surveys, younger union members are less likely to believe that unions make the workplace better than are older union members. The implication is that unions are failing to service their younger members as well as they service their older members.

Consider next the differences in attitudes by union status. These differences dwarf the differences in attitudes by age. Workers in a union workplace are far more likely to believe a union makes a workplace better than are workers in a non-union workplace. According to the BWRPS, 44 per cent of young workers at a union workplace believe that unions make workplaces better compared to 24 per cent of young workers at a non-union workplace – a massive 20-point gap. Similarly, 57 per cent of older workers at a union workplace believe that unions make workplaces better compared to 24 per cent of older workers at a non-union workplace – an even larger 33-point gap. The BSAS data show a similar pattern. The difference in the view of what unions do between workers in union workplaces and workers in non-union work-places is sufficiently ubiquitous in data sets in the USA and UK that we have labelled it the 'incumbency effect' (Diamond and Freeman, 2000) – the tendency for people in a union workplace to believe that unionism is necessary for the workplace to operate effectively for workers. Experience with unions, not the age of the worker, determines attitudes towards unions.

In sum, we reject the claim that young British workers are less likely to be union members because they have less favourable attitudes towards unions than other workers. Young workers enter the job market as blank slates with respect to unions, and develop attitudes similar to those of other workers as they experience unionism on the job. Proportionately fewer young workers than older workers believe that their workplace would be better with a union, largely because the young work in non-union workplaces where such views are more prevalent. The one piece of evidence indicating that young persons have more adverse views of unions is that at union workplaces they are less likely to believe that unions make the workplace better.

Are young workers less unionized because they work in non-union sectors?

If differential attitudes towards unionism do not explain the low union membership of young workers, could the low rate be due to the fact that young workers are concentrated in less organized occupations and sectors?

Young workers are more likely than older workers to be employed in industries and occupations with low union presence. However, this explains only a modest part of the youth/adult difference in union membership. We base this conclusion on a logistic probability model of the effect of the type of work that a person does on the differential probability that younger and older workers are unionized in the BWRPS. Analysis is simple: first we estimate the impact of a 0/1 dummy variable for being a young worker (less than 30 years of age) on unionization; then add measures for the characteristics of the job the person holds (industry, occupation and level of pay) and contrast the coefficient regarding the young-worker variable under these two specifications. Including the pay variable in this calculation biases upwards the analysis of the structural effect. This is because part of the relation between earnings and unionization is due to unions raising pay. However, as recent estimates of the impact of British unions on pay suggest only very slight impacts, much of the link found is probably due to the type of jobs that are unionized rather than to the union wage effect. In any case, the decline in the absolute value of the coefficient regarding young workers reflects the degree to which characteristics of the person's job, including wage, can explain their low rate of unionization.

Table 3.5 gives the results. Column 1 shows that, absent any covariates, young workers have a substantially lower chance of being union members than do older workers. Addition of the gender, age and schooling measures in column 2 barely affects this result. However, addition of dummy variables for public or private sector of work, managerial/non-managerial occupation and level of pay reduces the coefficient by approximately 30 per cent from -1.228 to -0.877. This implies that less than a third of the lower unionization of young workers can be attributed to the types of jobs they hold.

Going beyond industry and occupation, young workers are more likely to be in less unionized enterprises than older workers within the same sector. After all, young workers work more in new enterprises, which are less organized than older enterprises. In addition, employment has grown more slowly in union enterprises than in non-union enterprises (Bryson, 2001). If the only reason young workers are less unionized than older workers is that they are more likely to be in non-union workplaces, addition of this variable to the regression would reduce the coefficient on the young-age dummy variable to null. If, by contrast, young workers are less unionized even in organized workplaces, the negative coefficient on the young worker dummy variable would still remain. The statistics in column 4 show that, even controlling for union status of the workplace, the young are less likely to be union members than other workers. The coefficient on the young-person dummy falls to -0.797, still sizeable and statistically significant. Finally, we added the years a worker has been with the firm (job tenure) to the calculation on the notion that the youth effect might be largely the result of young workers being with a firm for a short period of time. Column 5 of the table shows that even the addition of tenure, which

Table 3.5 Logistic regression estimates of the effect of youth on union membership among British employees

	1 coeff	SE	2 coeff	SE	3 coeff	SE	4 coeff	SE	5 coeff	SE
Age group of employee (Under 30=1)	−1.202	0.157	−1.228	0.161	−0.877	0.191	−0.797	0.224	−0.626	0.233
Gender (male = 1)			✓		✓		✓		✓	
Race (white = 1)			✓		✓		✓		✓	
Highest qualification (5 levels)[1]			✓		✓		✓		✓	
Public/private sector (public = 1)[2]					✓		✓		✓	
Manager/non-managerr (Manager = 1)[3]					✓		✓		✓	
Pay (gross)[4]					✓		✓		✓	
Union at workplace							✓		✓	
Tenure									✓	
Constant	−0.383	0.064	−0.878	0.279	−1.733	0.376	−3.395	0.485	−3.539	0.489
Observations	1,351		1,351		1,089		1,072		1,072	
Pseudo R-squared	0.040		0.060		0.152		0.384		0.388	

(Source: BWRPS, 2001)

1 Highest qualification achieved: none; GCSE; A-level; degree; postgraduate or equivalent
2 Coded from SIC (A to I and O coded as 'Private')
3 Coded from SOC (major group I and 2 coded as management)
4 Mid-point of gross pay category.

Table 3.6 Workers with union at their workplace, by age

	Respondent age group		
	Up to 29 years (%)	30 and over (%)	Difference (% age points)
1 Percentage who are union members	42	71	29
2 Percentage who are non-members who say they were not asked to join	37	15	7
3 Percentage who are non-members who say they were asked to join	21	14	22
4 Percentage of non-members who say they would join if asked now	42	33	11
5 Additional percentage of members if all non-members were asked (4) × [(2) + (3)]	24	10	14
6 Percentage likely to be union members if all non-members are asked to join (1) + (5)	68	81	13

(Source: BWRPS, 2001)

Q41 'Has anyone ever asked you to join a union at your current workplace?'
Q43 'If someone from the union at your workplace asked you to join, how likely is it that you would do so?'

is highly correlated with age and union membership, does not eliminate the effect of being young per se.

Why are the young less unionized in union workplaces?

Table 3.6 examines the lower unionization rate of young workers than of older workers in unionized workplaces, using the BWRPS. Line 1 shows that in that survey 42 per cent of workers aged less than 30 years old were union members in workplaces where workers reported that 'a union or similar body such as a staff association represents employees and that people doing your sort of job can join', compared to 71 per cent of workers aged 30 and over who were members. What accounts for this huge percentage point difference in the rate of unionization at organized workplaces?

One reason why young workers in union workplaces may be less likely to join unions than older workers is because union representatives give them less time and attention than the older workers. The BWRPS asked workers, 'how much contact do you have with union or other worker representatives about workplace matters?' Among workers aged 30 and over, 22 per cent said that they had frequent contact with the representative and 48 per cent said that they had occasional contact, giving a total of 70 per cent having some contact with a union representative. Among workers aged less than 30, 16 per cent said that they had frequent contact and 39 per cent said that they had occasional contact, giving a total of 55 per cent with some contact. Union representatives may pay little attention to young workers on the notion that they are more likely to leave the workplace than older workers, because the representatives are busy with existing problems, or because middle-aged representatives have trouble interacting with the young. Whatever the reason, proportionately more younger than older workers have no contact with the union at their workplace and thus may find it hard to see how the union makes working lives better.

To relate contact with the union to actual membership, non-members at union workplaces were asked if anyone at the workplace had asked them to join the union. Lines 2 and 3 of Table 3.6 show that 21 per cent of young workers were non-members who had been asked to join the union (and thus must have refused to join), whereas 37 per cent of the young were non-members who had not been asked to join. These figures imply that unions did not ask 64 per cent $(37/(37 + 21))$ of young non-union members to join, which goes a substantial way towards explaining why so many young workers are not members. This result is consistent with the findings of a 1995 UNISON survey of young workers, where the young reported that one of the top reasons they did not join a union is that they had never been asked (Kerr and Waddington, 1997). By contrast, 14 per cent of older workers were non-members who reported that they had been asked to join the union, while 15 per cent of older workers were non-members who reported that they had not been asked to join. These figures imply that unions did not ask 52 per cent $(15/(15 + 14))$ of older non-union members to join.

To get some indication of how many non-members might join unions if they were asked to, all non-members (those who said they had been asked to join the union in the past as well as those who said that they had never been asked to join) were asked if they would join the union if someone were to ask them to join now. Line 4 of Table 3.6 shows that 42 per cent of the younger non-members compared to 33 per cent of the older non-members said that it was likely they would join the union if someone from the union asked them to do so. Multiplying the proportion of non-members by the proportion who say that they would join if asked suggests that unions would increase membership among young workers by 24 percentage points at union workplaces by asking young non-members to join, and would increase older worker membership by 10 percentage points by asking older non-members to join (line 5). The implication is that 14 percentage points of the 29 percentage point gap in unionization between younger and older workers at union workplaces – nearly half of the gap in union membership by age – would disappear if unions recruited all workers at an organized workplace.

There is also some indication in the survey that this may underestimate the effect of asking persons to join on the rate at which young workers join. Nineteen per cent of younger union members said a reason for their joining was that friends and colleagues were members (compared to 12 per cent of older members who gave this reason), suggesting that signing up one young person may increase the chance that the next young person asked will also join. Even if allowing for this spillover added 2–3 points to the unionization of young workers, there would still remain a sizeable gap, given the 13 percentage point difference shown in line 6 of Table 3.6. To reduce this gap, unions need to do more than simply ask young workers in organized workplaces to join their organization.

Union policies to attract young workers

Recognizing the problem of attracting young workers, many British trade unions have developed special initiatives to recruit and involve young members. Among these initiatives are:

- courses open to members aged 26 or less (the AEEU and GPMU);
- young members' magazines or newsletters (AEEU's *Your Shout*, BECTU – Rooney, 1998);
- reduced or promotional membership fees (GMB London Region, UNISON, nursing, BECTU);
- regional youth officers (GMB, UNISON) and young members' organizations (GMB);
- annual youth conferences (GPMU, UNIFI);
- a network for recent graduates (Connect);
- national and divisional youth committees (USDAW);
- youth weekends (USDAW, 1996);
- a youth network, sponsoring special events for youths (UNIFI).

Boxes 3.1 and 3.2 illustrate two different innovative efforts by unions to appeal to young workers: the UNISON–NUS web site, which offers information and advice to student workers and lets them know that unions are available to help them; and the UNIFI effort to make its internal operations more helpful and friendly to young persons.

For its part, the TUC has developed the TUC Youth Forum and sponsored

Box 3.1 *The UNISON–National Union of Students* **www.troubleatwork.org.uk** *website to provide information and advice to student workers having problems at work*

Healthy Working	trouble spots	
Aches, pains and miserable workmates? Your health and safety problem might find an answer here	At last there's somewhere to go on the web for up-to-date info and advice on work problems. Trouble at Work aims to help people who don't know where to turn when things go pear-shaped . . . more	
Rights at Work		
12-hour shifts and no holidays? Problems on your nursing placement? We've got jargon-free help on your rights here	A company has been fined £50,000 for health and safety breaches following a four year campaign by relatives and friends of a student killed at work...more.	
Respect at Work		
Bullied by customers and the boss is trying it on? If you need help or just the right way to tell them where to shove it, try here	Find out more about UNISON. We will send you an information pack about Britain's biggest union.	

special youth events, including a Union Festival Summer campaign that targeted major rock festivals. It has also developed a student employment service to raise awareness of unions on campus and recruit new members.

There has been no scientific project evaluation of these diverse efforts – for example, by comparing recruitment at a locality where the union devoted special efforts to recruiting youths with recruitment at some otherwise comparable control area, or by seeking to attract some randomly chosen set of young workers rather than some others. Absent such evaluations, the best we can tell from discussion with union officials is that the efforts have not been particularly successful in spurring young workers to become members. They certainly have not produced any observable turnaround in the rate of unionization of youths.

Pursuing a different strategy, the TUC has developed programmes to aid young workers regardless of union status. It has spearheaded efforts to improve safety at work for young workers and pressed the government to raise the minimum wage and eliminate the youth differential in the minimum wage. In a similar vein, UNISON and the National Union of Students have resorted to the Internet to aid student workers, developing a

---

Box 3.2 *UNIFI's improved participation project: developing a young workers' rep.*

1 Of the 400,000 workers under the age of 30 in the finance sector, only a tenth are in membership.

2 UNIFI embarked on an improved participation project in an attempt to address this problem in 2001, its aim being to integrate the union's work in this area ... by developing a strategic committee and providing education to increase the number of youth networks that exist.

3 Initiatives included the establishment of a steering group, the aim being to encourage 'rising stars' into membership and then onto the steering group; UNIFI's annual youth conference was revamped, e.g. the introduction of theatre groups to provide interactive sessions for delegates; a special edition of UNIFI's magazine for members, *FUSION*, devoted to young workers.

4 The union is also developing a higher profile externally, for example through the British Youth Council.

5 The next plan is to pilot a new role: the young workers' rep. To aid the design of this, the union will survey potential members. The rep.'s specific role will be to represent and support workers in their first job, to raise awareness of health and safety and rights, and to organize tailored events. The role of the young workers' rep. could be an accredited position, whether by an education institution or an employer, and the position could be based regionally, in large sites, on the union's executive, or in every branch.

(Source: Richard Blakely, www.unions21.org.uk/newgen/UNIFI.htm)

---

website www.troubleatwork.org.uk that provides advice to students about workplace problems, regardless of union status (see Box 3.1). It offers information about legal rights, and guidance about how to avoid problems at work and how to deal with such problems when they arise. Since the Internet will be a major medium for communication, information and interactivity in the twenty-first century, and since many young people already rely on it for information about almost any subject, unions must have a successful Internet strategy to resuscitate their influence on society (Diamond and Freeman, 2002b; Freeman and Rogers, 2002). Even if unions attract only a few members through sites like www.troubleat-work.org.uk, by expanding the union presence and reaching over the

Internet unions can aid young workers at relatively low cost and thus make the labour market better informed and presumably more efficient for members and non-members alike.

Young workers, works councils and unions

In 2000 the UK government accepted the EU Directive on Information and Consultation rights in national level undertakings, albeit reluctantly and on a slow timetable. At first the UK will restrict application of the directive to businesses with 150 or more employees, all of whom will be covered by 2005. By 2007 the directive will also apply to businesses with 100 or more employees, and by 2008 to ones with 50 or more employees. Since businesses with 50 or more employees account for 75 per cent of UK employees, the Directive will eventually cover the vast bulk of the work force (www.dti.gov.uk/er/consultation/proposal.htm). How do workers view the new form of information and consultation, and the works councils that are likely to form in many non-union as well as union workplaces as a result of the legislation? Do the attitudes of young workers to this forthcoming institutional innovation differ from those of older workers?

To answer this question, workers on the BWRPS were asked about their attitudes towards formal modes of consulting with management. Since many workers may have little knowledge of European works councils or of the specifics of the UK government's acceptance of the EU Directive, we asked what they thought about 'legislation that required management to meet with employees or their representatives', and the nature of any such legislated meetings. In the WRPS (US version) the term 'works council' was not used, but in the BWRPS this term was used after making it clear that a council was an organization that met to discuss issues with management.

Table 3.7 records the results for workers up to age 29, for workers aged 30 and over, and for the two groups taken together. What is striking in Table 3.7 are the modest differences in attitudes between workers by age. The vast majority of younger as well as older workers favour legislation that requires management to meet with employees or their representatives to discuss workplace issues. In addition, there is widespread agreement on the nature of this activity. Young workers as well as older workers want meetings to take place regularly and to choose their own representatives (though more of the young are willing to have management choose representatives or to rely on volunteers); the councils to obtain public domain information; and employee representatives to be protected by law. Asked which of three forms of workplace representation and participation they

Table 3.7 Employee views of alternative forms of workplace representation

	Respondent age group		
	Up to 29 years (%)	30 and over (%)	All employees (%)
All employees In favour of legislation that required management to meet with employees or their representatives	83	81	81
How often should meetings between employee representatives and management take place?			
Regular basis	86	89	88
When management thinks useful	11	7	8
How should employee representatives on works councils be chosen?			
Chosen by management	9	4	5
Elected by employees	66	74	71
Volunteers	22	19	19
Should employee representatives on works councils have access to confidential information?			
Confidential information	38	35	36
Public domain information only	56	57	57
Employee representatives on works councils need legal protection	72	75	74
Do you think your workplace would be better with . . .?			
Works council on its own	24	20	21
Trade union on its own	10	6	7
Works council and trade union	32	48	44
Neither	28	22	24
No union at workplace If a group of workers at your workplace formed a union and asked you to join, how likely is it that you would join?	54	44	47

(Source: BWRPS, 2001)

Q40 'If a group of workers at your workplace formed a union and asked you to join, how likely is it that you would join?'

Q59 'Would you be in favour of legislation that required management to meet with employees or their representatives?'

Q60 'How often should meetings between employee representatives and management take place?'

Q61 'How should employee representatives on works councils be chosen?'

Q62 'Should employee representatives on works councils have access to confidential information?'.

Q63 'Do employee representatives on works councils need legal protection from possible discrimination from employers?'

Q64 'Do you think your workplace would be better with . . .?'

preferred, young workers favoured works councils and a union, as did other workers, though by a smaller amount. More of the younger workers wanted a trade union on its own, and fewer wanted a works council on its own, than did other workers. Consistent with this, among workers in non-union workplaces, substantially more young workers than older workers said that if workers formed a union and asked them to join they would join the union.

The implication is that works councils provide a possible way to engage young workers in union activity along with older workers. By affecting institutions of the workplace directly, the UK's implementation of the EU Directive on Information and Consultation Rights could have a greater impact on youth involvement in trade unions than special programmes for youth.

Conclusion

This chapter has examined the causes of the low and falling unionization of young workers in Great Britain, and has rejected the view that young workers do not join unions because they view unions as dinosaur institutions suitable for their parents but not for them. Rather, we find that differences in attitudes towards unions by age are modest. Far from having a non-union non-collectivist orientation, young persons are largely blank slates when they enter the job market. At union workplaces young workers are less likely to be members than older workers, in part because unions do not recruit the young and have little contact with them. Union efforts to develop special youth programmes have not increased youth membership noticeably, and there is greater promise in programmes that help young workers as workers rather than as youths. Because young workers, like others, are favourable to having workers or their representatives meet with employers on a regular basis, a strong union initiative based on the UK's acceptance of the EU Works Councils Directive could help unions to resuscitate their impact in the job market and attract more young workers.

Chapter 4

Willingness to unionize amongst non-union workers

Andy Charlwood

In Chapter 2, Stephen Machin explained how union membership in Britain has declined dramatically since the late 1970s. Surveying the evidence of union decline from the Workplace Employee Relations Survey series, Millward *et al.* (2000: 92) argued that there has been a 'withering of support' for trade unionism among British workers. Towers (1997: 206–7) took a different view. He argued that union decline resulted in a representation gap, and thus an unfulfilled desire for representation on the part of the non-union workforce offers the union movement the opportunity for renewed growth. Pencavel (2001: 40) surveyed these arguments and concluded that the balance of evidence supported the position of Millward *et al.* over that of Towers. Of course these two views are not mutually exclusive; they can both apply to separate groups of workers. Support for trade unionism may have fallen among previously unionized workers, while demand for trade unionism may have risen among non-union workers. Nonetheless, the debate raises the question of whether or not there is a union representation gap among non-union workers.

This chapter begins by answering this question, and then investigates the factors associated with desire for union representation. The data to investigate these questions come from the 1998 British Social Attitudes Survey (BSAS) and the 2001 British Workers Representation and Participation Survey (BWRPS). These surveys both investigate willingness to unionize, but do not contain identical questions. This is both a weakness and a strength. It is a weakness because it means that identical models of the determinants of willingness to unionize cannot be estimated for both surveys, and it is a strength because it allows the predictive accuracy of two contrasting models of the factors associated with a willingness to unionize to be tested against one another. The BWRPS allows a theoretical model similar to the 'psychological determinants of propensity to unionize' model to be operationalized (Kochan, 1980: 144). This model is contrasted with one using the BSAS data, which incorporates variables that follow from the theoretical insights that (1) union membership is an experience good (see Chapter 5), i.e. the experience of union membership conditions individuals to value the experience, and (2) the way in which individuals attribute causes to events and grievances at work is likely to influence the unionization decision (Kelly, 1998). Investigating this question from the perspectives provided by two different theoretical models should yield richer insights about the relative importance of the probable influences on an individual's willingness to unionize. In the conclusion, the implications of the results for unions and management are investigated through four workers, representative of the type of employee that unions will need to organize if membership is to grow.

Is there a union representation gap?

Table 4.1 summarizes the responses of workers to similar questions about willingness to join a union in 1998 and 2001. According to the 1998 data, 41 per cent of workers described themselves as either very or fairly likely to join a union if one were available at their workplace. The equivalent figure for 2001 data was 50 per cent. However, caution is needed when interpreting these results. They do not mean that willingness to unionize has increased by nine percentage points. First, the question asked by the two surveys is subtly different. BSAS98 asks, 'How likely would you be to join a union if one were available at your workplace?', while BWRPS01 asks, 'How likely would you be to join a union if a group of workers at your workplace formed a union and asked you to join?'. The second question concerns a group of co-workers actively organizing a union, while the first question does not. Workers may be more inclined to combine with a group of familiar co-workers than with an unknown third party, so the

Table 4.1 Willingness to join a union in 1998 and 2001

	Very likely to join (%)	Fairly likely to join (%)	Not very likely to join (%)	Not at all likely to join (%)
1998 BSAS	15	26	30	29
2001 BWRPS	19	31	30	20

Base: 653 (BSAS98) and 660 (BWRPS01) non-union workers.

Results are not directly comparable because the wording of the questions is slightly different. The BSAS asks 'how likely would you be to join a union if one were available at your workplace?', while the BWRPS asks 'how likely would you be to join a union if a group of workers at your workplace formed a union and asked you to join?'

latter (BWRPS01) question may elicit more positive responses than the former. Second, both surveys are based on relatively small samples, implying that there is likely to be a margin of error of ± 3 per cent. Therefore, it would be more accurate to say that the percentage of non-union workers willing to unionize in 1998 was between 38 and 44 per cent, and the percentage of non-union workers willing to unionize in 2001 was between 47 and 53 per cent. Whichever figure is taken, these results suggest a sizeable union representation gap.

Belfield and Heywood (2002) also examined the representation gap, using data from the 1998 Workplace Employee Relations Survey (WERS). They measured the desire for union representation on the basis of who workers thought would best represent them in three specific circumstances: when they were seeking a pay increase, had a complaint about work, or were being disciplined. The list of possible representatives was themselves, co-workers, or a union. Belfield and Heywood found that 19.9 per cent of workers believed that a union would best represent them on at least one of these issues. This figure suggests that the union representation gap is lower than the results reported so far. The reason for this apparent discrepancy most likely lies in the difference between the measure of desire for union membership used in the BSAS and BWRPS, and the measure of desire for union representation used by Belfield and Heywood. It is possible for individuals to believe that they could represent themselves more effectively than a union would, while still desiring union membership and representation, because they believe that a union either provides additional insurance or is generally desirable.

A conservative estimate, based on the figures from the BSAS and BWRPS, would suggest that if those workers who are willing to join a union actually joined, somewhere in the region of 3.5 million workers would become union members. However, for this support to be converted into new members via new recognition agreements, unions will need to focus their organizing efforts on concentrations of workers who want to join. Alternatively, if support for unionization is not concentrated, they will need to persuade more workers of the benefits of membership. In either case, an understanding of the factors associated with a willingness to unionize is important.

Theoretical frameworks for explaining willingness to unionize

The starting point for any consideration of the determinants of willingness to unionize must be the following observations from Bakke (1944: 2):

The worker reacts favourably to union membership in proportion to the strength of his [or her] belief that this step will reduce his frustrations and anxieties and will further his opportunities relevant to the achievement of his standards of successful living. He reacts unfavourably in proportion to the strength of his belief that this step will increase his frustrations and anxieties and will reduce his opportunities relevant to the achievement of such standards.

Kochan (1980: 142–9) developed this insight into a theoretical model similar to that represented by Model 1 in Figure 4.1. Factors that cause individuals to unionize can be divided into three areas. First, there are beliefs about unions, including the extent to which individuals believe that a union would improve the workplace (union instrumentality) in which they work and general beliefs about the role and value of unions in society. Second, there are perceptions of the work environment, including perceptions of equity at work and aspects of satisfaction with the job. Third, there are prospects for influencing the working environment and perceptions of the level of actual influence and the level of desired influence. Kochan (1979) tested this model against empirical evidence from a re-presentative survey of non-union US employees. His results show that instrumentality beliefs are the most important predictors of willingness to unionize; job dissatisfaction and pay inequity are also significant predictors (but only among white-collar workers), as is desire for influence (Kochan, 1979: 26). Kochan's work on willingness to unionize has aged well. However, more recent theoretical insights make it possible to improve on this framework.

It is a feature of Kochan's work (1979, 1980) that, although it is implied (through use of the Bakke quotation cited above) that factors such as job dissatisfaction and desire for influence will lead to a willingness to unionize, this is only the case if the worker also believes that a union would remove the cause of dissatisfaction, or provide a mechanism for securing greater influence. Another way of expressing this proposition is to say that we would expect (1) the relationship between desire for influence and willingness to unionize to be moderated by perceived union instrumentality, and (2) the relationship between job dissatisfaction and willingness to unionize to be moderated by perceived union instrumentality (these relationships are included in Model 2 of Figure 4.1). These propositions are not built into the model or tested formally by Kochan. It is also possible that job satisfaction or desire for influence may cause workers to be more likely to view union instrumentality highly. Premack and Hunter (1988) investigated this idea (known as a mediated relationship) and found

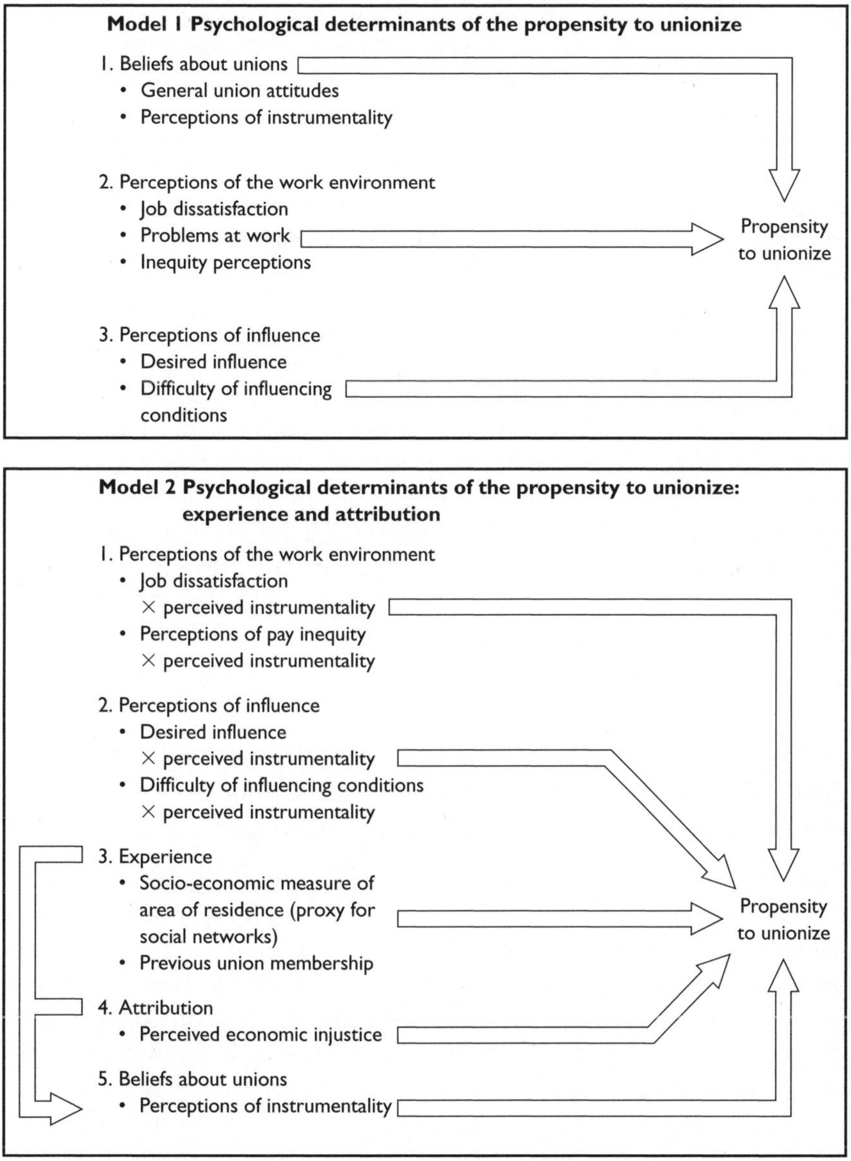

Figure 4.1 Two models of the determinants of propensity to unionize

that perceived instrumentality mediates the relationship between job satisfaction and willingness to unionize. Their results indicate the need to incorporate mediated relationships into a theoretical model of willingness to unionize. Model 2 of Figure 4.1 contains a number of hypothesized mediated relationships.

Proposition 1: Moderating and mediating relationships need to be incorporated into a theoretical model of willingness to unionize

Hartley's (1992) summary of the literature on the individual unionization decision draws attention to the potentially important role of family and social networks. Visser (2002: 416) finds some empirical support for this proposition. Bryson and Gomez make a similar point in Chapter 5, when they argue that union membership is an experience good. The essence of their argument is that an individual's assessment of the costs and benefits of membership are formed by the individual's own past experience and from the experiences of close friends and family. Most studies of the unionization decision have failed to include variables designed to capture these influences (in part because they are difficult to measure), but there appear to be good theoretical reasons for their inclusion.

Proposition 2: The role of past experience should be incorporated in models of willingness to unionize

Kelly (1998: 27–32) highlights the importance of ideological frameworks and attribution in creating the conditions in which individuals are prepared to act collectively. He argues that for people to want to act collectively, they need to attribute their grievances to an external source – in short, they must 'blame the system' (Kelly, 1998: 30). For example, individuals with left of centre views may regard the employment relationship as a form of exploitation by capitalists. Free-marketeers will see the employment relationship (free labour contract) differently. If individuals do attribute the cause of grievance to an external source, such as the market economy, they are likely to be more willing to act to challenge the source of grievance. Unionization is a key method for organizing opposition. It may also make individuals more inclined to perceive union instrumentality as high (because they are sympathetic to collective organization). Kochan's (1979) study may have inadvertently captured the extent to which individuals 'blame the system' through variables designed to measure general attitudes towards unions (favourable views about unions may be bound up with wider political beliefs that lead individuals to 'blame the system'), but it would seem preferable for the model explicitly to include the role of attribution.

Proposition 3: The way in which individuals attribute grievances should be included in a model of willingness to unionize

Model 2 in Figure 4.1 incorporates these propositions into a modified form of Kochan's model. Note that it is predicted that the impact of job dissatisfaction, perceptions of pay inequity, and issues regarding influence will be moderated by perceived union instrumentality. The relationship between variables that capture experience and attribution should be mediated by perceived instrumentality.

A further practical issue, raised by Freeman and Rogers (1999: 113), is whether management-initiated voice mechanisms (such as the type of information and consultation committees discussed in Chapter 8) affect willingness to unionize. Freeman and Roger's work suggests that workers who are covered by this type of arrangement are less likely to want to unionize. However, Gollan's (2001) case study of joint consultation in a British rail company found that frustration among parts of the workforce about the limitations of the committee actually increased demand for union representation. Therefore, we might want to differentiate between workers who work in companies with information and consultation committees, where the workforce feel that management is good at sharing power and responsibility, and those who work in companies such as that studied by Gollan, where there is a widespread perception that management is not very good at sharing power and responsibility with the workforce. It might be expected that workers in workplaces with a joint consultation committee and where management is perceived as being good at sharing power and responsibility would be less likely to want to join a union. On the other hand, workers in workplaces with a committee who do not perceive that management is bad at sharing power and responsibility may find the information and consultation committee an inadequate mechanism for developing influence, with the consequence that they may actually be more likely to want to unionize.

Data and methods

The 1998 British Social Attitudes Survey is the sixteenth of an annual series designed and conducted by the National Centre for Social Research. The survey is designed as a representative sample of British adults aged 18 and over. Overall 3,146 interviews were conducted, with a response rate of 59 per cent. Of these 1,408 were workers in employment, of whom 653 worked in workplaces without a union presence, which fall within the scope of this study (Jowell *et al.*, 1999). The strength of the British Social Attitudes Survey is that it questions workers on aspects of working life and industrial relations, while also providing detailed information on employees' social and political attitudes and socio-economic backgrounds, which may have an important bearing on their attitudes and actions towards trade unions (Bryson, 1999: 68–9). The weakness of the data stems from the breadth of subjects that the survey examines, which means that key variables are based on single items. This makes it impossible to test the reliability of the measures. However, the data can be used to test Model 2 (Figure 4.1).

Table 4.2 summarizes the variables used to operationalize the model. The role of experience is operationalized in two ways: first, by looking at whether the individual respondent has been a union member in the past, and second, by looking at the socio-economic characteristics of the area in which the respondent lives (this is done using socio-economic classifications of local authority areas developed from the 1991 census by the Office for National Statistics). These variables are derived from the type of housing stock prevalent in a geographical area, and the industries and occupations in which residents are employed. We can use these as a proxy for (a) the majority experience of employment; (b) the normative values and attitudes that this experience imparts; (c) social networks through which these values and attitudes are transmitted. The extent to which workers are likely to provide an external attribution for problems at work is proxied by a scale that measures the individual's perceptions of economic injustice. Once again, the components of this scale are summarized in Table 4.2.

The 2001 BWRPS is a one-off survey, commissioned by the TUC and designed by staff at the Centre for Economic Performance, London School of Economics. The fieldwork was carried out in the early summer of 2001 by BMRB International, using a random location sampling technique. The survey collected information from 1,355 British workers, 662 of whom worked in workplaces without a trade union. The survey investigates the perceptions and experience of work, and also contains supplementary

Table 4.2 Key variables used in analysis of willingness to unionize

Definition	BSAS	BWRPS
Perceived union instrumentality		
Do you think that a trade union would make your workplace better or worse? 1 = a lot worse, 5 = a lot better	2.99	3.14
General union attitudes		
Strong trade unions are needed to protect the conditions and wages of workers. 1 = strongly disagree, 5 = strongly agree		3.74
Job satisfaction		
BSAS: How satisfied are you with your current job? 1 = very satisfied, 4 = not at all satisfied	1.87	
BWRPS: My job is interesting and enjoyable: 1 = strongly agree, 5 = strongly disagree		2.02
Wage equity		
BSAS: Would you say that your pay was 1) on the high side, 2) reasonable, 3) on the low side, 4) very low?	2.42	
BWRPS: Do you have any experience of workers being paid unfair wages? (Yes or no)		0.21
Problems at work		
Do you have any experience of a) workers being disciplined or dismissed unfairly; b) preferential treatment for some workers by management; c) bullying by management of fellow workers; d) sexual or racial discrimination? (Yes or no)		0.24
Actual influence		
BSAS: The sum of: a) How much say do you have over the way in which your job is done? b) How much say do you have in future plans that would affect your job? 0 = none, 3 = a great deal	1.00	
BWRPS: The sum of how much influence over *either*: a) pace of work; b) deciding on how to work with new equipment; c) deciding on the types of perks offered to workers; *or*: d) deciding how to do your work and organize your job; e) setting working hours and breaks; f) deciding on pay rises for people in your workgroup. 1 = a little influence, 4 = a lot of influence		2.61
Desire for influence		
BSAS: Would you like more say over a) the way in which the way you do your job; b) future plans that will affect your job. 0 = no, 1 = yes to one, 2 = yes to both	0.76	
BWRPS: The sum of how important is it for you to be able to influence *either*: a) pace of work; b) deciding on how to work with new equipment; c) deciding on the types of perks offered to workers; *or*: d) deciding how to do your work and organize your job; e) setting working hours and breaks; f) deciding on pay rises for people in your workgroup. 4-point scales, 1 = not at all important, 4 = very important.		3.05
Perceived economic injustice		
Three-item scale a) big business benefits owners at the expense of workers; b) given the opportunity, management will try to get the better of workers; c) ordinary working people do not get a fair share of the nation's wealth.		
5-point scales, 1 = strongly disagree, 5 = strongly agree	2.51	
Previous union membership	0.29	

(Weighted *n*: 482, BSAS; 376, BWRPS)

demographic information. These data were used to test Model 1 (Figure 4.1). It is important to note that there are differences between the BSAS and BWRPS in the instruments used to measure concepts like job satisfaction and desire for influence; these differences are set out in Table 4.2. In particular, the BSAS job satisfaction measure is likely to include an assessment of job satisfaction based on extrinsic and intrinsic aspects of job satisfaction, while the BWRPS measure refers specifically to intrinsic aspects only.

The impact of information and consultation committees on willingness to unionize can be investigated using the question:

> Where you work, is there a committee of management and workers who meet regularly to consult over workplace issues? These committees could be called works councils, joint consultative committees or staff forums.

A further question asks:

> If you were asked to rate the performance of management at your workplace on a scale similar to school grades – A for excellent, B for good, C for fair, D for poor and F for failure – what grade would you give your management for willingness to share power and authority with workers in the workplace?

The latter question can be used to investigate whether the impact of information and consultation committees on willingness to unionize is contingent on the extent to which management is perceived as sharing power.

Regression analysis was used to operationalize Models 1 and 2. It is important to understand that cross-sectional data like the BSAS and BWRPS can highlight statistically significant relationships between variables, but cannot be used to test for causality. Consequently while causality is assumed in the models being tested, it is possible that the arrow of causality runs in the opposite direction when the relationship is statistically significant. To check that the two data sets were consistent in areas where direct comparison was possible, simplified versions of the models containing just those variables that were consistent across both data sets were estimated. Key results for variables common to both surveys (e.g. perceived union instrumentality) were consistent. If results had not been consistent, it would have raised serious doubts about the validity of the measures in this study. These simplified models were also used to investigate differences in the impact of demographic, job and workplace characteristics, with all other characteristics held equal.

A further set of models with interaction terms between desired influence and perceived instrumentality and between job dissatisfaction and perceived instrumentality tested for the moderating relationships predicted in Model 2. The mediating relationships predicted in Model 2 were tested using the procedure explained in Baron and Kenny (1986: 1177). It is possible that willingness to join a union and perceived union instrumentality are different expressions of an underlying and unmeasured union orientation variable. If this is the case, the results could be biased. This issue was investigated in more depth in Charlwood (2002: 477). The results reported there suggest that this type of bias is not a significant problem.

Results

The key results are reported in Table 4.3, and are broadly consistent with both of the theoretical models set out in Figure 4.1. In Model 1, experience of problems at work, low levels of influence and desire for influence are all positively associated with willingness to unionize, as are perceived union instrumentality and general beliefs about unions. However, the association between job dissatisfaction and increased willingness to unionize is not statistically significant.

Results also provide broad support for Model 2 proposed in Figure 4.1. Dissatisfied workers are more likely to want to unionize, as are workers who are not resident in the most prosperous areas of the country, those who perceive economic injustice, and those who perceive union instrumentality to be high. However, while the relationship between former membership and willingness to unionize is positive as expected, it is not statistically significant. The relationship between desire for influence and willingness to unionize is small and negative.

Interaction terms (not reported in Table 4.3) were introduced to the model to test the hypothesis that the relationship between desired influence and willingness to unionize is dependent upon perceptions of union instrumentality. There was partial support for this hypothesis: workers who desire more influence and perceive union instrumentality to be high are significantly more likely to want to unionize than those workers who desire influence but who perceive union instrumentality to be low. However, the relationship between job dissatisfaction and willingness to unionize was not moderated by perceived instrumentality. The tests for mediating relationships found evidence that the relationships between willingness to unionize and perceived economic injustice, and

Table 4.3 Determinants of willingness to unionize

Change in probability of …	BWRPS–Model 1		BSAS–Model 2	
	being very likely to join a union	being very unlikely to join a union	being very likely to join a union	being very unlikely to join a union
Perceptions of work environment				
Job dissatisfaction	0.100	−0.017	0.036	−0.051***
Pay equity perceptions	−0.011	0.008	0.005	−0.002
Experience of other problems at work	0.052*	−0.046*		
Perceptions of influence				
Desire for influence	0.033**	−0.029**	0.010	−0.016
Level of influence	0.037**	−0.033**	0.001	−0.002
Past experience				
Socio-economic area of residence (ref. Prosperous England)				
Mining, manufacturing and industry	—	—	0.072**	−0.100**
Coast and services	—	—	0.078	−0.102**
Education centres and outer London	—	—	0.137*	−0.150*
Inner London	—	—	0.056	−0.061
Rural areas	—	—	0.076**	−0.101**
Urban fringe	—	—	0.041	−0.101
Former union membership	—	—	0.035	−0.050
Perceived economic justice	—	—	0.040***	−0.075***
Beliefs about unions				
General beliefs	0.083***	−0.063***	–	
Instrumentality perceptions	0.122***	−0.084***	0.132***	−0.142***
Predicted P	0.202	0.184	0.147	0.305
Observed P	0.205	0.187	0.149	0.309
Percentage of respondents correctly predicted by model	48.4		47.5	
Weighted n	354		477	

Controls: Age, gender, ethnic minority, region, highest educational qualification, current union member, occupation, broad industry, job tenure, workplace size

* statistically significant at the 10 per cent level or better; ** statistically significant at the 5 per cent level or better; *** statistically significant at the 1 per cent level or better.

willingness to unionize and experience variables, were partially mediated by perceived instrumentality; however, the size of the mediating relationships was small.

Does Model 2 perform better than Model 1? The answer to this question can be deduced by looking at the extent to which there was empirical support for the hypotheses set out in the theory section, and by comparing the predictive accuracy of the two models (i.e. the percentage of workers who have their answer to the question about willingness to unionize correctly predicted by the model). There is some weak support for Proposition 1; desire for influence is moderated by perceived instrumentality, but job dissatisfaction is not. There is evidence that the impact of perceived economic injustice and experience on willingness to unionize are partially mediated by perceived instrumentality, but the size of the mediation is small. The socio-economic variables perform as predicted, but the relationship between previous union membership and willingness to join is not statistically significant (further analysis revealed a statistically significant association between former membership among manual workers, but not among non-manuals). Therefore there is some support for Proposition 2. The chosen proxy for the way in which individuals attribute grievances (perceived economic injustice) performed as expected, so there is also support for Proposition 3.

Despite empirical support for Propositions 2 and 3, Model 2 has slightly less predictive power than Model 1, but this difference is so small as to make the models equally valid. The similarity between the models can be attributed to the fact that perceived instrumentality is the most important predictor of willingness to unionize, and this measure is the same in both. In Model 1, the second most important predictor is the general union attitudes variable. The perceived economic injustice variable in Model 2 performs in a similar way. In practice there is likely to be considerable overlap between perceived economic injustice and general union attitudes; both are likely to be bound up with an individual's general political outlook. Overall, these results suggest that future researchers need to take care in developing accurate measures of the way in which individuals attribute grievances that separate out the impact of general attitudes towards unions. Variables like job dissatisfaction and desire for influence have a lesser influence on willingness to unionize; the exact size of the effect varies according to the instrument used to measure it.

Table 4.4 investigates the relationships between information and consultation committees and willingness to join a union. The second column summarizes the 'mean willingness to unionize' scores for workers

Table 4.4 The impact of information and consultation committees on willingness to unionize

	Mean willingness to unionize score (1 = very unwilling, 4 = very willing)
Management is perceived as being excellent at *sharing power and authority with workers*	
Information and consultation committee	2.37
No information and consultation committee	2.18
Management is perceived as being good at *sharing power and authority with workers*	
Information and consultation committee	2.40
No information and consultation committee	2.44
Management is perceived as being fair at *sharing power and authority with workers*	
Information and consultation committee	2.47
No information and consultation committee	2.52

Management is perceived as being poor or
  failures at sharing power and authority with
  workers	

Information and consultation committee	2.81
No information and consultation committee	3.02

(Weighted *n* = 398, source: BWRPS)

according to how well they rate managements' willingness to share power by whether or not there is an information and consultation committee. As expected, the key difference in willingness to unionize is between those who believe management is excellent or good at sharing power and who are less likely to want to unionize, and those who believe that management is poor or very poor at sharing power and who are more likely to want to unionize. There is little difference between workers in a workplace with an information and consultation committee and workers in a workplace without an information and consultation committee. Once controls are added, it is impossible to reject the hypothesis that willingness to unionize does not vary among these groups. These results suggest that an increase in joint consultative committees will not in itself lead to a decrease in the desire for unionization on the part of the non-union workforce. Such arrangements are only (weakly) associated with a reduced desire for unionization if workers perceive management to be good at sharing power with the workforce.

Finally, most results for the associations between individual, job and workplace characteristics, and willingness to unionize differ across the data sets or, if results do point in the same direction, they are not consistently statistically significant. This suggests that individual, job and work-place characteristics have little bearing on willingness to unionize. Occupation provides an exception to this rule; workers in craft and skilled, personal and protective services, operative and assembly, and unskilled occupations are more likely to want to unionize than managerial occupations. This finding contrasts with that in the USA, where ethnic minority workers are consistently more willing to unionize than their white counterparts.

In summary, results from Model 1 are broadly comparable with the results reported by Kochan (1979: 26). Dissatisfaction and desire for influence appear to play a relatively minor part in determining willingness to unionize, compared to general union attitudes and perceived union instrumentality. Given these results, the prominence given to job dissatisfaction as a trigger to unionization in the literature seems rather curious. However, Model 2 does not provide a better theoretical framework. Perhaps theory in this area could be developed through a two-stage model where attitudes towards unions predict willingness to unionize and another set of variables predict attitudes. However, the question of how attitudes towards unions are developed is not well understood. This is an area where further research would seem fruitful.

Practical implications

What are the implications of these findings for trade unions and managers interested in understanding the factors that are likely to make a worker willing to join a union? This question is answered by examining the willingness to unionize of four types of workers that the TUC has identified as target groups for recruitment. These results are then placed in the context of the wider debate about union organizing prospects. It is important to consider these results in the light of this debate, because successful union-organizing campaigns that result in recognition agreements are the key mechanism by which willingness to unionize among non-union employees can be converted into new union members.

The four types of workers were defined on the basis of groups of workers identified by TUC General Secretary John Monks (Monks, 2001) as important targets for British trade unions. Box 4.1 introduces the four workers and gives the probability of being willing to unionize for each worker, these being calculated from the BSAS data, using regressions run on separate samples for manual and non-manual employees.

Box 4.1 *Targets for recruitment*

Supermarket Sue, a woman in her early 50s, is married with teenage children and lives in a prosperous market town in the Midlands. She left school at sixteen with basic qualifications. She has centrist political views. Once her children started secondary school, she began part-time work as a sales assistant at a large out-of-town supermarket. The supermarket was built on land once occupied by a unionized factory. She has now worked there for just under five years, and recently started working full time. She is satisfied with her job, has never been a union member, and does not think that a union would make much difference to her workplace. Sue has a predicted probability of being willing to unionize of 0.36.

Cleaner Mandy is a woman in her mid-30s, a single mother of a teenage son, and lives in a former mining town in South Yorkshire. She left school at sixteen with basic qualifications. Employment opportunities are limited; she considers herself lucky to work full time as an office cleaner, employed by a small contract-cleaning firm. She is paid at minimum wage rates, and her employer often demands that she works unpaid overtime. Despite this, she is broadly satisfied with her job. She is not much interested in politics, although her views are broadly centrist. She has never been a union member and does not think that a union would make much difference to her workplace. Despite this, she is fairly well disposed towards unions; her father was once a miner and she enjoys regular nights out in the local Trades and Labour Club. She has a predicted probability of being willing to unionize of 0.68.

Time-served Tony is a married man in his late 30s. He lives and works in a post-war new town in the southeast of England. He is a skilled fitter in a large non-union factory on a green-field site. A generation ago he would have been a union member as a matter of course, but entry into the labour market coincided with the early 1980s' recession and government policies, which restricted the ability of unions to organize new workplaces. As a consequence, he has never worked in a unionized factory and has never been a union member. Politically he is a *Sun*-reading centrist. He is satisfied with his job, believes his wages are reasonable, and does not think that a union would make much difference to his workplace. Tony has a probability of being willing to join a union of 0.17.

Hi-tech Harry is a single man in his late 20s. Educated to degree
level, he has a well-paid job as an information systems engineer for a
medium-sized services company. He lives an affluent lifestyle in one
of the wealthier parts of the country. He likes his job and likes the
pay; he is not much interested in politics, but has centrist political
views. He has never been a union member and does not think that a
union would make any difference to his workplace. Harry has a
probability of being willing to join a union of 0.08.

Of the characteristics described in Box 4.1:

- Supermarket Sue should be a prime target for unions, according to
  John Monks, since he claims that workplaces like hers contain 'large
  numbers of people doing similar jobs who want to be represented to
  their employers on a collective basis' (Monks, 2001). However, Sue's
  fairly low probability of being willing to unionize suggests that
  Monks' hopeful claim may prove false in reality.
- Cleaner Mandy represents workers caught up in what Monks called
  the 'rough end' of the labour market. Pay is low, employment is insecure, and the employer has the whip hand. Despite (or perhaps
  because of) these conditions, Mandy is likely to be willing to join a
  union. However, the insecure nature of Mandy's work is likely to
  mean that unions will find it extremely difficult to organize Mandy
  and workers like her.
- Time-served Tony is a skilled factory worker and as such represents
  the bedrock of the traditional union constituency. However, Tony has
  a low probability of being willing to unionize, which suggests that
  unions cannot assume that traditionally unionized groups of workers
  will return to the unions now that the law offers unions the opportunity to organize them. It is worth noting that a worker with similar
  characteristics to Tony, but an operative with an assembly job in a
  traditional union area, would have a significantly higher probability of
  being willing to unionize.
- Hi-tech Harry is, according to the TUC focus group research cited by
  John Monks, the type of worker who is unlikely to perceive the need
  for a union because 'unions are for blue-collar workers with problems,
  not white-collar workers with opportunities'. However, unions need
  to find ways of appealing to workers like Harry because he works in
  the type of job and type of industry where employment is set to grow
  most strongly (Monks, 2001). Harry's unionization probability

suggests that the views expressed by the TUC focus group participants were generally representative of younger workers in non-manual jobs in private services. Consequently, unions will find it extremely difficult to grow through organizing the expanding private services sector.

It is important to bear in mind that the key factors that will change these probabilities are perceived union instrumentality, perceived economic injustice, the area in which a worker lives and, in the case of non-manual workers, job dissatisfaction. Unions are unlikely currently to affect the political views of individuals. However, they may be able to change employees' perceptions of the way in which their workplace is managed and the way in which they perceive trade unions. Indeed, Bronfrenbrenner's (1997) research in the USA suggests that the strategy and tactics of unions in organizing campaigns are likely to have a critical influence on unionization decisions. She found that the greater the number of 'aggressive organizing tactics' used by trade unions, the greater the likelihood of union success. Presumably this is because higher-intensity union campaigns are more effective in persuading workers that a union will improve their conditions than others. However, just as union tactics can have a positive (for unions) impact on unionization outcomes, employer tactics can have a negative impact. Even if unions appeared to have a natural majority in many workplaces (and these results suggest that support is not concentrated enough for this to be the case, except perhaps in the traditionally heavily-unionized mining, manufacturing and industry areas), Bronfrennbrenner's work suggests that militant anti-union tactics by employers can corrode support for unionization.

Union decline in the USA since Kochan's (1979) results provides a warning to unions that desire for unionization among a significant proportion of the workforce will not in itself lead to a revival in union fortunes. In the USA in the 1980s, political changes made it harder for unions to win certification elections, and unions responded to this tough political and economic climate by cutting back on organizing activity (Farber and Western, 2002). So, despite the preferences of non-union employees, unionization rates fell because employers were more powerful than unions, and they were prepared to use this power to stop unions winning certification elections (Logan, 2002).

Gall and McKay (2001: 98–102) have found significant evidence of management intent to use aggressive anti-union tactics in the UK. Even in workplaces that had not self-consciously imported aggressive style anti-union tactics, Dundon (2001: 14–15) found that fear of an adverse management reaction had a powerful inhibiting effect on workers' desire for unionization and that managers were projecting anti-union views in order to deter workers from unionizing. In addition, Diamond and Freeman (2000) found evidence for an 'incumbency effect' – in general non-union workers like the workplace they have, and consequently value preserving the comfortable aspects of the status quo. If unionization seems likely to jeopardize what workers feel they already have, then support will fall away. Monks' optimistic prediction that workers in non-union supermarkets and call centres will desire collective representation has yet to be proven in practice. The weight of the research evidence discussed above suggests that it is likely to prove false if employers adopt aggressive anti-union tactics.

The other context in which it would be very difficult for a union to win would be a workplace where workers express high levels of satisfaction with their jobs. Consequently the results of this study provide empirical support for the idea that employers who want to remain union-free can kill union organizing attempts with kindness (i.e. by addressing issues of grievance and causes of discontent) or with fear. If management does adopt fear or kindness tactics successfully, unions may find that the only option open to them is to adopt strategies of organizing away from the workplace, either through communities (Wills, 2001) or virtually through the Internet (Diamond and Freeman, 2002b: 579). Writing elsewhere in this book, Kochan reaches a similar conclusion. He argues that organizing-based union strategies will not result in union revival, and that if present trends continue, unions will only be able to grow if they transform the way in which they operate.

Bronfrennbrenner (1997) is less pessimistic. She advocates that unions adopt the 'organizing model' as the best set of union strategies and tactics for overcoming militant employer opposition and persuading workers of the benefits of unionism (the organizing model can be defined as both a philosophy of trade unionism that emphasizes the building of collective identification and organization among workers, and a set of best-practice tactics and methods (Heery *et al.*, 1999: 39–40)). The TUC is also encouraging unions to adopt this approach (TUC, 1999a). However, research by Heery *et al.* (2000: 997) suggests that only around half of British unions are adopting elements of this approach, and only two small unions have adopted it wholeheartedly. British unions are also less radical in the organizing tactics that they use compared to their US counterparts. Carter (2000: 132–3) found that even in a union that had endorsed the organizing model, political divisions and entrenched behaviours meant that it was not always practised at the local level. Moreover, the organizing model is resource-intensive. Heery *et al.* (2000: 990–1) found that the overall level of resources devoted to organizing was low – probably too low to bring about a large influx of new members. To reiterate the point made by Machin in Chapter 2, unions are not running fast enough to keep up with the expanding new economy, perhaps because they are cowed by the difficulties and risks involved. A significant minority of non-union employees want unions. If unions are to reach these workers, they will need to overcome entrenched behaviours that act as barriers to organizing by pursuing fresh thinking and internal reform. Reform needs to be backed by increased investment in organizing activity.

Despite Kochan's pessimism about the ability of an organizing-based approach to union growth and renewal, more widespread adoption of organizing-model tactics and philosophy by British unions may result in membership gains because current organizing activity is comparatively limited in scope and ambition. Kochan's argument suggests that this in itself will not be enough to revive union membership, and other forms of innovation will also be necessary.

Conclusion

This chapter has investigated the level of support for unionization among workers in non-union establishments in Britain. Depending on the question asked, somewhere between two-fifths and one-half of these workers say that they would unionize if a union were available to them. The theoretical framework developed by Kochan (1980) was found to be applicable to Britain – the determinants of willingness to unionize among British workers now are remarkably similar to the determinants of willingness to unionize among the US workers questioned by Kochan (1979). This model was contrasted with a second model that included variables that capture the previous experience of the worker and the way in which a worker attributes problems at work. In practice there was little to choose between these models. By far the most important influence on willingness to unionize in both was perceived union instrumentality; job dissatisfaction is relatively unimportant. Management-initiated voice mechanisms such as consultation committees appear to have no impact on willingness to unionize.

The results of the research were used to generate predicted probabilities of being willing to unionize for four representative workers. These results suggest that unions cannot assume automatic support from workers in the traditional union constituency of male manual workers in manufacturing, or in the growing private services sector. To win recognition agreements, unions will need to persuade workers that the union will make their workplace better. Management will be able to resist union-organizing campaigns if they adopt aggressive anti-union tactics that cause workers to believe that unionization will make the workplace worse. If current trends continue, lack of investment in organizing and conservative union tactics suggest that unions will be unable to do this on a large enough scale to affect aggregate union membership levels.

Acknowledgements

I am grateful to Katarina Thompson and Wayne Diamond for help and advice with the BSAS and BWRPS respectively. The BSAS data was originated by the National Centre for Social Research and distributed by the ESRC data archive at the University of Essex. I would also like to thank the editors and many colleagues who have provided helpful comments on previous versions of the work reported in this chapter at seminars at the CEP, LSE Industrial Relations Department and the International Conference on Union Growth 2001 at the University of Toronto.

Chapter 5

Buying into union membership

Alex Bryson and Rafael Gomez

Over the past twenty years, trade unions in Britain, Canada and the USA – three countries sharing similar labour market institutional frameworks – have had a difficult time maintaining, let alone advancing, membership rates (Figure 5.1). There are two principle reasons for this. First, unions have been unable to attract new members, as is evidenced by the growing proportion of all employees who have never been members (see Chapter 2). Indeed, union density decline in Britain can be almost entirely explained by

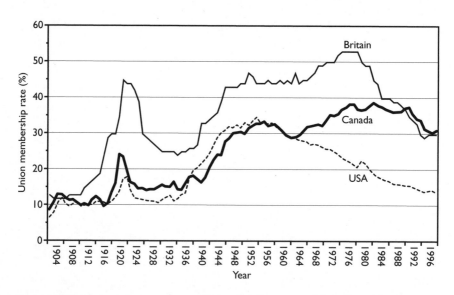

Figure 5.1 Union membership rates in Britain, Canada and the USA, 1900–2001

Sources: US source data from Troy and Sheflin (1985). US and Canada data from Bain and Price (1980, Tables 3.1 and 4.1). Supplemented for the US with Bureau of Labor Statistics (BLS) data and for Canada with CALURA (various issues) and Labour Force Survey (LFS various waves). British data from Booth (1995, Table 2.1) and supplemented with British Social Attitudes Surveys (BSAS) (various waves using authors' calculations).

a lack of uptake on the part of new labour-market entrants rather than by an outflow of existing members (see Box 5.1, Figure 5.2). This points to a key feature of unionization: that increasing the flow of members into unions is far more difficult than maintaining the existing stock.

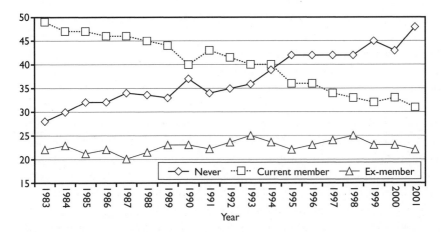

Figure 5.2 The rise of never-membership, 1983–2001

The data are BSAS 1983–2001. In all years except 1994 and 1997 those who were not current members of a union were asked: 'Have you ever been a member of a trade union or staff association?' Figures are percentage of employees in the whole economy. Figures for 1994 and 1997 for never- and ex-membership are interpolated as the mid-point between adjacent years.

Box 5.1 *The case of never-membership in Britain*

- The decline in union density since the early 1980s is almost wholly accounted for by the rise in never-membership (see Figure 5.2). Between 1983 and 2001, union density fell from 49 to 31 per cent. Ex-membership remained virtually static, but the rate of never-membership rose from 28 per cent to 48 per cent.
- In the period 1999–2001, never-membership rates in Britain were highest among young workers (78 per cent), those in non-unionized workplaces (66 per cent), low earners (57 per cent), private sector employees (55 per cent), and those in the south of England (52 per cent).
- Multivariate analysis (Bryson and Gomez, 2002a) reveal that compositional change in the workforce accounted for around half the rise in never-membership over the period. The remainder is due to an increase in never-membership rates for all types of worker.

(Source: BSAS 1983–2001)

The second reason for the reduction in trade union density relates to the nature of trade union membership itself. Employees in all three countries typically have to be organized for the purposes of collective bargaining before becoming members. However, since the benefits of trade union membership are often collective in nature, free-riding is a particularly acute problem. Labour economists have focused on the question of how unions overcome this (Booth, 1985; Naylor, 1989; Booth and Chatterji, 1995). Their proposed solution involves the use of so-called 'club or incentive goods', which are simply benefits that are targeted exclusively to due-paying members. The availability of incentive goods, however, offers an incomplete explanation for why workers join unions. This is because most incentive goods require sampling before determining their quality, and as such the incentive approach fails to note that joining a union is a decisional problem akin (but not identical) to the one involved in purchasing a good with an uncertain payoff. Products or services whose value can only be fully determined after purchase are referred to in the economic literature as 'experience goods' (Nelson, 1970).

This chapter focuses on how the notion of unions as experience goods can be incorporated into the traditional cost–benefit model of trade union membership. The distinctiveness of the experiential framework is two-fold. First, the model points to the risk involved in joining a union for the first time. Risk enters the decision-making process because the quality of union membership is only imperfectly observed before purchase. Imperfections in knowledge make joining less likely because employees are obliged to spend time acquainting themselves with the value of union membership before purchase. The cost of acquiring information about an experience good is therefore higher than an equivalent search good, i.e. a good whose quality is observable upon simple inspection. Equally important, because information gathering is costly, the experience model predicts that individuals will be less inclined to change their purchasing decision once it has been made. Thus, membership status is predicted to be highly persistent.

The structure of the chapter is as follows. First, insights from consumer theory and industrial organization are incorporated into the traditional union membership literature, in what is termed the experience model of trade union membership. Second, it is demonstrated how the experience model can synthesize a number of well-established and recent empirical findings about union membership into a singular framework. Third, applications of the experience model to union membership data are illustrated by countries sharing similar decentralized institutional frameworks, namely Britain, Canada and the United States. Finally, the experience model is applied to union-organizing strategies.

The traditional worker-choice model of union membership

The question as to why individuals join unions has been the subject of considerable academic scrutiny for several decades (Olsen, 1965; Farber, 1983; Booth, 1985; Naylor, 1989). From an instrumental perspective, an individual joins a trade union when the net benefits are positive. The key problem for unions, under this framework, is how to overcome the free-riding behaviour of prospective members. For the researcher, the central question is, why do individuals participate in organizing drives and pay union dues when joining is not compulsory?

According to labour economists, the answer lies in the ability of unions to provide benefits that exclude non-members (Booth and Chatterji, 1995). In most cases, these private advantages are of the incentive-good variety (Arulampalam and Booth, 2000: 291). Applied to the union case, incentive goods include such things as personal protection from unfair dismissal, the provision of family-friendly policies, access to individual grievance procedures, private pension advice, and positive reputation effects arising from compliance with the 'social custom' of union membership (Booth, 1985: 254).

While incentive goods solve the free-rider problem, they do not account for how workers learn about the quality of these private incentives in the first place. The incentive-good solution also does not account for the durable nature of union membership (i.e. the fact that union members have longer job spells with a single employer), nor the informational asymmetries that incentive goods generate between supplier and customer (i.e. the fact that unions have more information about the quality of their services than potential members). A more accurate portrayal of how and why workers become unionized needs to accommodate the hard-to-observe nature of most union-provided benefits, especially for new labour-market entrants (i.e. first-time buyers). The argument advanced below is that because incentive goods require purchase or sampling before determining their quality, they should be classified as experience goods and subjected to the same theoretical treatment. Table 5.1 describes the experience good concept and this potential link to the union membership question.

Table 5.1 Evidence for the experience-good model of trade union membership

Feature	Empirical evidence	
	Product market	Labour market
1. *Durability:* Product has long shelf-life. Infrequently purchased.	*Porter (1976):* Infrequently purchased items increase demand for pre-purchase information in keeping with experience model.	*Freeman and Medoff (1984):* Tenure is longer for unionized workers. *Bryson et al. (2002):* Union jobs exhibit longer tenure than non-union jobs (USA, Britain).
2. *Brand loyalty:* Purchase 'stickiness' is more common among experience goods than search goods. People remain loyal to their brand despite similar (often less costly) alternatives.	*Klemperer (1995):* First-mover advantages and existing market share in experience-good markets are strongest predictors of future market share.	*Bryson and Gomez (2002a):* Workers who sample membership stick with it. Ex-membership rate has remained constant in Britain since 1983. *Machin (2002):* De-recognition is rare. Majority of union density decline in Britain due to lack of uptake on the part of new workers and workplaces.
3. *Post-purchase satisfaction:* Once sampled, experience goods exhibit higher levels of satisfaction than search goods.	*Greer (1992: 117–47):* Reviews evidence on higher consumer ratings of experience goods once purchased.	*Diamond and Freeman (2000):* Identify the 'incumbency effect'. Workers initially exposed to either unionized or non-union forms of employee voice remain more favourable to those forms (Britain). *Bryson and Gomez (2002b):* Desire for unionization increases with exposure (Britain, Canada, USA).

4. Switching costs: Once purchased, experience goods generate informational advantages and other frictions, inducing higher switching costs.

Klemperer (1995): Many instances of where switching costs appear in product markets settings.

Freeman and Medoff (1984): Quit rates are lower for unionized jobs (USA).
Fernie and Metcalf (1995): Union recognition associated with reduction in quits (Britain).
Arulampalam and Booth (2000): The persistence of union status in a longitudinal study of British youth.
Farber and Krueger (1993); Riddell (1993); Bryson and Gomez (2002c): There is significantly more frustrated demand than over-supply of unionization, a condition that is hard to explain without switching costs (Britain, Canada, USA).

5. Personal referrals: Experience goods commonly promoted via informal advertising channels, social networks, and word-of-mouth of referrals.

Rees (1966): Employees are like 'experience goods' for employers. Tend to be hired on the basis of personal referrals.
Reinstein and Snyder (2000): Strong evidence for movie reviews affecting box-office intake.
Kotler (2000): Most products with high experience good qualities (auto repair, movies, employees) tend to be promoted via social networks and personal referrals.

Machin and Blanden (2002): Strong inter-generational transmission of union status independent of industry and occupation (Britain).
Gomez et al. (2002): Strong social network effect (having a family or peer group who is supportive of unionization) associated with greater desire for unionization (Canada).
Charlwood (2002): Socio-economic characteristics of the community where a person lives have significant effects on desired unionization (Britain).

The nature of trade union membership: a consumer choice perspective

Three assumptions drawn from the theoretical perspectives employed in industrial organization and consumer behaviour underpin the consumer model of experiential choice (Lambin, 1997: 120–5). These disciplines have much to offer the experiential model of union membership, since they each have a long history of integrating risk and informational asymmetries into individual decisional models. Three assumptions underpin the consumer model of union membership, and these are depicted in Figure 5.3.

Assumption 1: there is a market for employee voice

For employees, unions are but one way to satisfy a generic demand for non-wage or voice benefits at the workplace. Generic demand, in the parlance of consumer theory, is a need that is an inherent requirement of natural or social life. Voice at work – defined in the same manner as the original formulation found in Freeman and Medoff (1984: 8) – is here taken to be such an inherent requirement.

The generic demand for voice is situated within a solution market, defined as a market where specific customer groups seek a solution or

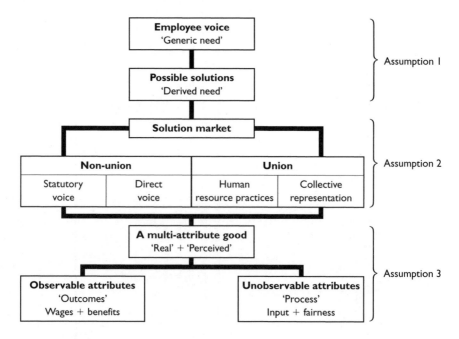

Figure 5.3 The consumer choice framework and union membership

assortment of solutions to meet a particular demand or to perform a certain function (Lambin, 1997: 229). Consumers within a given solution market require the same function or need, but the solution used to satisfy that demand can vary. This means that any given solution is subject to partial substitution by another. Figure 5.3 depicts how, in the union membership case, partial substitutes for employee voice exist between representative/collective channels offered by unions (union voice) and potential non-union forms of voice. These non-union voice mechanisms include voluntary joint-consultative committees without union input supplied by management (non-union representative voice), collective channels such as works councils offered by the state (statutory voice), and non-union forms of direct two-way communication between management and employees (direct voice).

Several features of these non-union voice substitutes are of importance. As with union voice, they are multi-attribute products that contain both easy-to-observe characteristics (the search dimension) and hard to observe characteristics (the experiential dimension). However, in contrast with their union voice substitutes they require no formal fee and, with the exception of statutory voice, are generally not independent from management. Individuals may also partake of union and non-union voice simultaneously (though the focus of this chapter is on whether an individual partakes of union membership).

The assumption of a solution market for voice has two added implications for unions. First, under this market for voice assumption, the workplace is akin to a storefront where workers can inspect, purchase and be supplied with voice. The question of whether unions can bypass the workplace (and hence avoid employer opposition) by supplying their voice services via different distribution channels such as the Internet can therefore be accommodated using this framework. Second, the assumption implies that consumers are not interested in forms of voice per se, but care only about the solution to a problem that a particular form of voice is likely to provide (Lambin, 1997: 243). In the realm of consumer theory this may seem obvious (e.g. a consumer attending a concert is interested in hearing the music and not in the ticket that grants entry to the hall), but in the consumer choice model of unionism the assumption has an important implication. It implies, somewhat controversially perhaps, that employees are attracted to unions for the benefits that they provide, as opposed to any intrinsic desire for unionization itself.

Assumption 2: the market for voice is regulated but contestable

The second assumption builds on the observation that in systems where decentralized workplace recognition prevails, the market for employee voice is contestable. Unions compete to win the allegiance of workers against other voice mechanisms. Under such systems, employees have scope (albeit circumscribed) to choose a particular type of voice mechanism. If an employee desires unionization he or she can apply for a job in a firm with union recognition or, if employed in a non-unionized setting already, can seek to organize the workplace for the purposes of collective bargaining. Conversely, if an employee prefers to negotiate individually with an employer, he or she will choose either to apply for work in a non-unionized firm or refuse to cooperate in an organizing campaign.

Assumption 3: employee voice and union membership are multi-attribute products

The existence of a contestable market for union voice is premised on a third assumption: that the provision of voice can be modelled as a product or service with a number of attributes. This approach is drawn from the multi-attribute product model of consumer choice (Lancaster, 1966). The multi-attribute model assumes that consumers evaluate a product or service along several dimensions, which can be real or perceived (Jagpal, 1999: 54–60). The notion that employee voice is a multi-attribute product appears indirectly in most standard labour economic models, when they recognize the wage and non-wage aspects of union benefits (Farber, 1983: 1417–18). For unions, therefore, the multi-attribute model is analogous to the union wage premium being only one (observable) attribute among many (mostly unobservable) others that union membership can provide.

These three assumptions suggest (among other things) that unions are in competition with other voice mechanisms in attempting to gain the allegiance of workers. To the extent that employers can match both the wage and non-wage aspects of unionized employment, then even workers with favourable attitudes towards unions will have less incentive to purchase unionism since the demand for unionization is contingent on the relative benefits that it can provide to members.

The experience model of union membership

Union membership as a search good: the single attribute case

The purchase of a particular good is a function of decisions made independently by consumers and producers. Similarly, the determination of union status is a function of decisions made separately by workers, unions and employers. Initially, consider an employee choice model where unions have only one function: they positively affect the wage received by unionized workers. As there is a cost associated with union membership, such as the membership fee and costs of participation in union activity, then the worker becomes unionized when benefits outweigh costs and otherwise remains non-union.

The model above is identical to the framework advanced by Farber (1983, 2001) and used by many labour economists. If we assume that the size of the wage premium is known to workers before the hiring decision or is learnt as workers go through the search process, then a unionized job that only affects the wage is akin to a search good with a single attribute – the wage premium. This means that union quality can be evaluated before purchase without the need for prior sampling. Union membership is therefore a search good when the gross benefit is known to workers before purchase, for example when the wage premium is identifiable before applying for a job.

Two key implications emerge from the single-attribute (search-good) case. First, since union benefits are easily identifiable by workers, any exposure to union membership should have no significant effect on the willingness to join or remain in a union. This proposition should hold, irrespective of labour market experience and prior knowledge of unions. However, empirical evidence casts doubt on this particular proposition. Studies from Britain and Canada indicate that direct and indirect exposure to unions has a significant effect on both existing and desired union membership status (see Figure 5.4a and feature 3 of Table 5.1). Simply put, the willingness to join a union rises after sampling membership at work or after an employee has experienced unionism by proxy through social interactions at home or with friends who have experienced unionism. The phenomenon of preferring unionism after having been exposed to it through the workplace has even received a specific label, the 'incumbency effect' (Diamond and Freeman, 2000).

A second implication of treating union membership as a search good is that switching out of union status or between unionized and

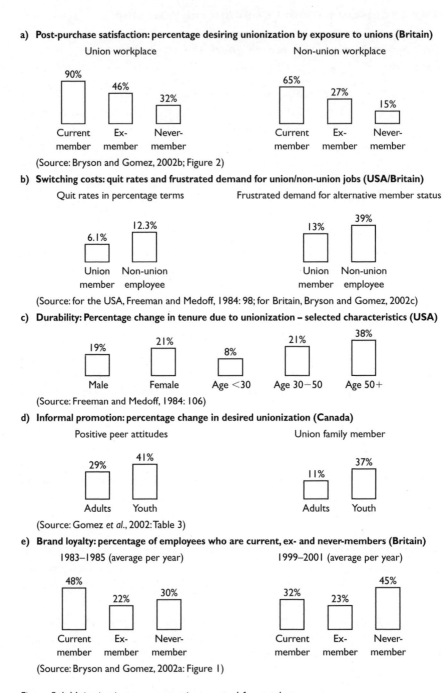

a) **Post-purchase satisfaction: percentage desiring unionization by exposure to unions (Britain)**

Union workplace

90% Current member
46% Ex-member
32% Never-member

Non-union workplace

65% Current member
27% Ex-member
15% Never-member

(Source: Bryson and Gomez, 2002b; Figure 2)

b) **Switching costs: quit rates and frustrated demand for union/non-union jobs (USA/Britain)**

Quit rates in percentage terms

6.1% Union member
12.3% Non-union employee

Frustrated demand for alternative member status

13% Union member
39% Non-union employee

(Source: for the USA, Freeman and Medoff, 1984: 98; for Britain, Bryson and Gomez, 2002c)

c) **Durability: Percentage change in tenure due to unionization – selected characteristics (USA)**

19% Male
21% Female
8% Age <30
21% Age 30–50
38% Age 50+

(Source: Freeman and Medoff, 1984: 106)

d) **Informal promotion: percentage change in desired unionization (Canada)**

Positive peer attitudes

29% Adults
41% Youth

Union family member

11% Adults
37% Youth

(Source: Gomez et al., 2002: Table 3)

e) **Brand loyalty: percentage of employees who are current, ex- and never-members (Britain)**

1983–1985 (average per year)

48% Current member
22% Ex-member
30% Never-member

1999–2001 (average per year)

32% Current member
23% Ex-member
45% Never-member

(Source: Bryson and Gomez, 2002a: Figure 1)

Figure 5.4 Unionization as an experience good for workers

non-unionized jobs should be a relatively low-cost decision, or no different to the cost of switching between any two non-union jobs. This is so because learning and uncertainty play such a small role in determining quality before the purchase of a search good (Klemperer, 1995: 515–20). Thus if union membership is a search good, then those who desire membership (but who are not organized) should have no reason to remain a non-member, and vice versa. However, if a significant number of workers do not conform to these predictions, it should be considered whether workers are simply irrational or attribute their frustrated demand for voice to substantial switching costs from changing their union status.

The empirical evidence again points away from the search-good case. As demonstrated in Figure 5.4b and Table 5.1 (feature 4), there is a significant number of non-union workers who desire union membership and a smaller (though still significant) proportion of union employees who desire to be non-union. The presence of frustrated demand amongst both groups of workers (union and non-union) indicates that the search-good model of union membership requires amending. One obvious way to amend the model is simply to argue that unionization is more like an experience good with a number of attributes, most of which are hard to observe.

Union membership as an experience good: the multi-attribute case

A model that includes the wage premium as well as the non-pecuniary or incentive benefits that union membership provides is thus a more accurate depiction of union status determination. The experience model of union choice does not require a major transformation of the standard cost–benefit model presented above, and can be adapted from an approach used in Farber and Western (2001). Initially each worker is allowed to have a benefit derived from union employment that includes the observed wage premium and all the hard-to-observe aspects of union voice. Then, as in the search-good case, the net value to the worker of being unionized is some function of benefits minus costs. A worker desires unionization if this function is positive, and does not otherwise.

Even though attributes apart from the wage have been added to the cost–benefit model, it is still only applicable to unionization in the case where membership quality is perfectly observed. This is so because the concepts of risk and switching costs have not been formally introduced in the formulation above. Membership is risky because it delivers a payoff that is observable only after unionization has been sampled, and hence there is always a chance that joining a union will not deliver its expected return and will leave the worker stuck with his original decision. Risk also emerges, in part, because union membership is infrequently purchased (membership renewal can be treated as automatic until such time as an employee switches jobs or enters a managerial role). Consistent with this last conjecture, Figure 5.4c and Table 5.1 (feature 1) display how union membership does display more durability, in the sense that unionized workers have longer job spells with a single employer than comparable non-union counterparts.

Second, once purchased, union membership should confer an informational advantage to the purchaser, since the worker would have to undergo a costly search process to find a comparable voice substitute. This means that there is a cost to switching out of union voice. Examples of switching costs applied to the union case include: the transaction cost of quitting a job with a unionized employer and starting work in a job that is non-union; the learning cost incurred by switching to a new work environment; the uncertainty about the quality of work environment with the untested non-union employer; and, in the case of a worker in the recognized workplace, the uncertainty of transgressing the social custom of unionism by abandoning union membership. Empirical evidence is consistent with the switching cost assumption, since it is well established that both union workers and unionized workplaces (all else equal) exhibit lower quit rates (see Figure 4b, left, and Table 5.1, feature 4) and that frustrated demand for alternative membership status exists amongst both union and non-union employees.

Adding the risk and switching-cost elements to the initial search model produces the following experiential version of the standard cost–benefit framework:

1 A worker will desire unionization if the net benefit is positive, and will remain unionized, even if gross benefits fall, so long as the cost of switching away from membership outweighs the benefits of finding a new form of voice.

2 A union will successfully organize a given worker when the probability of a successful payoff from joining a union is greater than the ratio of costs (which includes both direct costs and switching costs) over benefits.

3 A critical value for the probability of a worker desiring unionization is defined by the experiential model, which means that unions will successfully target workers for whom the probability above is greater than some threshold.

With this framework in mind, it is possible to begin to consider differences in labour market experience, managerial opposition, or the effectiveness of union-organizing tactics in determining the union status of workers. These factors can affect any of the elements of the experience model – the uncertainty of trade union membership quality, the benefits and costs of membership, and the costs of switching away from trade union voice. The implications arising from changes in each are considered below.

Implications of the experience-good model

Changes in the uncertainty of union membership quality

A change that makes workers more certain of the returns derived from joining a union is represented by an increase in the probability of accurately assessing the expected returns from membership. This makes the effectiveness of union organizing higher, by increasing the number of workers for whom the critical threshold is higher than the ratio of costs over benefits.

A decrease in the risk associated with the quality of incentive goods can occur when the experiential properties of unionism are revealed to workers. Thus workers with past experience in unionized environments should have, *ceteris paribus*, higher perceived valuations of gross benefits, as should workers who have been exposed to the benefits of unionization through social interactions either at home or in the community. Such a proposition is consistent with the empirical evidence (see Figure 5.4d and Table 5.1, feature 3, which show how desire for membership is positively related to exposure).

Changes in the gross benefits of membership

A change that reduces the actual return to unionization for workers is represented by a reduction in gross benefits. Following Farber and Western (2001), a reduction in the benefit of union membership could result either from militant employers unwilling to negotiate improvements in compensation and benefits, or from poor negotiating on the part of the union. Recent evidence indicates that the union wage premium has fallen in Britain and the USA (see Chapter 2; Hirsch *et al.*, 2002; Blanchflower and Bryson, 2003). From a signalling perspective, the inability of unions to deliver a union wage premium may be construed as a sign that their effectiveness as employee representatives has diminished.

Changes in the costs of becoming a union member

An increase in costs arises when a change occurs that makes it more difficult to become or remain a union member but keeps fixed a worker's
assessment of the potential benefits derived from unionization. This can
happen for a number of reasons. For employees already unionized, this
may include increases in the cost of membership dues, or participation in
industrial action. The most obvious cost increase for non-members is an
increase in managerial opposition to unionization for workers seeking to
organize.

Changes in the costs of switching away from union voice

A change that makes it more costly to leave a unionized job is represented
by an increase in switching costs. Though switching costs make union
membership more durable, they also make it harder for a worker to be
successfully organized for the first time because the gross benefits have to
be greater than the direct costs of joining, plus the costs of switching after
having joined. Switching costs may also not be static over the worker's life
cycle, and can be positively correlated with tenure and age of worker.
Indeed this could explain why older union members are more likely to
remain unionized even if the gross benefits of unionization begin to fall,
whereas younger workers are more likely either not to pay dues in recognized workplaces or to bypass union jobs altogether (see Chapter 3).

This proposition is corroborated by the fact that union members are
brand loyal. Brand loyalty in this instance is related to the fact that the
decline in union density in Britain (the only country for which we have a
consistent series) has been due to a lack of uptake on the part of new
labour market entrants and not because of a marked increase in current
members leaving their unions (see Figure 5.2, Figure 5.4e and Table 5.1,
feature 2, which highlight evidence of how people remain loyal despite
having alternatives to choose from).

Conceiving of unionization as an experience good creates an interesting
set of problems. For example, are workers with high labour-market knowledge and low switching costs more likely to favour union voice? Do
workers engage in low-cost sampling of jobs in order to discern the quality
of employee voice provision? Can a worker be duped into applying for (or
remaining in) a non-union job with poorer quality voice provision, believing that the employee voice is of higher quality than an otherwise similar
unionized job? Here we concentrate on the implications of the experience
model for union-organizing strategy.

Experience goods and union-organizing strategy

What mechanisms exist to aid unions such that individuals will be willing to pay membership dues, or join a union if a workplace is non-unionized? The so-called 'three Ps' of promotion, pricing and placement are marketing's answer to the problems brought about by the selling of experience goods. Because union membership can be viewed as a multi-attribute product partly made up of experiential characteristics, the three Ps are therefore applicable to the design of an optimal set of union-organizing strategies.

Union promotional strategies

Information theory suggests that knowledge about the potential benefits of experience goods is optimally disseminated via personal recommendations rather than through formal advertising channels (Stigler, 1961: 213). Mechanics and doctors do not generally advertise their services on television – indeed, we tend to be suspicious of any who do. Instead, they acquire their patient lists and customer base through personal referrals or by word-of-mouth. This is because trustworthiness is highly correlated with reputation, and a personal referral is akin to someone staking his or her reputation on the product in question. Thus when attributes are hard to observe before purchase, personal recommendations become the preferred channel by which potential customers are informed about product quality (Reinstein and Snyder, 2000).

The information asymmetries generated by experience goods are replicated in the union case, as seen in the strong intergenerational transmission of union status observed in British panel data (Machin and Blanden, 2002). Sons and daughters of union workers are 20 per cent more likely than are comparable individuals raised in non-union households to become union members later in life. This effect is independent of occupation, region and industry. The finding that the willingness of British youth to join a union is significantly related to the socio-economic characteristics of the area in which that individual resides is also broadly congruent with the social network basis of the experience model (see Chapter 4). Similarly, in the Canadian case, having a social environment consisting of friends and relatives who support unions makes the probability of desiring unionization higher, as compared to those lacking such social networks (Gomez et al., 2002). The positive effect of a social circle that is supportive of unionization is twice as large for those with less labour-market experience (Gomez et al., 2002). Older workers therefore tend to rely on their accumulated labour-market experience to form opinions about unionization, whereas young workers with less labour-market experience rely on social networks and personal referrals. This is consistent with the experience model, since it implies that those with a lower degree of certainty regarding the potential benefits of unionism will be influenced to a greater degree by external indicators of quality, such as friends or relatives being union members.

The lesson for unions is therefore a simple one: although they may not be able to affect the familial and social patterns involved in the intergenerational transmission of union status, they may be able to replicate some of the same processes that make such transmission possible. In other words, unions could segment and target new labour-market entrants in much the same way as do firms selling experience goods. Positive initial exposures to a product – via advertising or sponsorship – are a favoured approach used by many firms selling experience goods (Kotler, 2000). Perhaps a less costly way of targeting new labour-market entrants is by the expansion of existing paid summer internships in organizing academies and union head offices. These policies replicate the processes that make individuals who are raised in union households more likely to become members later in life, irrespective of their chosen region, occupation or industry.

A more general segmentation strategy – one with appeal to old and young employees alike – would lower the uncertainty associated with the purchase of union voice through some targeted form of formal promotion. Promotion could, for example, make the experience properties of unionism – such as the fostering of family-friendly practices, which until now have been largely underreported (see Chapter 6) – more visible to the non-member. In order to achieve optimal dissemination to prospective members, tailoring product endorsements or reviews from trusted and well-known public personalities to the union membership case is another possibility. It is well established that most consumers are more likely to purchase a good that is recommended by someone they identify with and trust (Kotler, 2000: 234). What, for example, would the effect be of famous performers (e.g. footballers or actors) extolling the virtues of their own unions and unionism more generally? Such a promotional policy could very well demonstrate the relevance of membership to workers who would normally have perceived little or no use in unionization.

Union pricing policies

Pricing in the union context is more complicated than in the case of a typical good, since union membership has a direct cost that mirrors a price, and an indirect cost (based on such things as managerial opposition) that is harder to quantify. Indirect costs are hard for unions to alter, but membership fees could be lowered or even eliminated for first-time users in order to encourage the sampling of union services. Firms operating in experiential markets (from software companies to film distributors) do this by offering free samples and limited previews of their products or services. Unions could do the same by cross-subsidizing their services to attract new members, by offering certain services freely to workers who have traditionally been unlikely to purchase membership, or by targeting these same workers with non-uniform 'pay-as-you-go' service fees.

Economists refer to this as price discrimination, and, rather than conceiving of such differential pricing in negative terms, it can enhance consumer welfare when the total supply of a good or service is expanded. The idea is that while uniform pricing allows customers with higher reservation prices to pay much less than they would otherwise, it also forces certain customers with lower reservation prices out of the market. Unions that adopt differential pricing strategies, so long as they ensure that segments of non-union workers with lower demand schedules are supplied with benefits, can therefore enhance welfare for workers generally.

A final issue related to pricing involves the cost of switching once union membership has been purchased. Switching costs are good at keeping workers locked in, and as such account for the persistence of union membership following periods of membership expansion. However, switching costs work in the opposite direction during long periods of membership-rate decline. Specifically, they can make attracting new workers more difficult since the gross benefits of membership have to be greater than the direct costs of joining, plus the anticipated costs of switching after having joined. Switching costs therefore lead to inertia and an in-built acceptance of the status quo.

In circumstances such as these, unions in Britain have the option of lobbying government to permit once again automatic due payments within recognized workplaces as a means of changing the current non-due-paying system. The law could still retain the freedom of workers to opt out of paying dues, but the presence of switching costs would ensure that free-riding would be much less than the current one-third of workers who are covered but are not paying dues. The fact that such agency shop systems prevail in Canada and a majority of US states where union density is relatively high, explains the relative absence of the free-rider problem in workplaces with automatic due-payment systems.

Union distribution policies

Distribution channels for most goods are usually improved with better in-store placements, with more numerous outlets in lucrative locations, and by the combining (or in marketing terminology the bundling) of two or more complementary goods and services. For unions, the former strategy involves making their presence and services more accessible within workplaces where unionization is already available, and opening up new distribution channels in workplaces where the union movement has been historically unsuccessful. It may also be possible to bypass the workplace altogether and market union services directly to employees. This is the direct or relationship marketing method that has been used by many new companies, such as low-cost airlines, to great success. Such companies offer their services via the Internet at a lower cost than if they would have distributed their services through a retailer or vendor. Freeman and Rogers (2002) have recently coined the term 'open-source unionism' to describe similar (though more nascent) attempts by unions to target their services directly to prospective employees.

In terms of bundling strategies, unions in all three countries have the opportunity to piggy-back their services onto other voice mechanisms. This can be done by being the enforcers of procedural justice in companies that claim to offer progressive human resource management polices. In Britain at least, unions also have an opportunity to introduce their services via proposed statutory works councils, which compel employers to form an elected council of worker representatives and to consult with these workers over major workplace decisions (see Chapter 8).

Conclusion

This chapter's premise is that joining a union confers certain advantages – such as the enforcement of procedural justice or the encouragement of the use of benefits such as family-friendly policies – that are hard to observe before entering the labour market, and near impossible if the employee has never sampled union membership. Only workers who have actually been employed in unionized jobs or who have access to reliable information about unions can form an accurate assessment of whether benefits outweigh any of the potential costs. If workers never sample union membership, they may be more inclined to free-ride in workplaces where unions are present and less likely to organize in workplaces lacking any union presence.

Consequently, unions have the difficult task of recruiting workers based on a set of benefits that are hard to observe to the first-time buyer. Their task therefore is to convince employees that the experiential benefits of membership are of high quality. This is especially relevant if the largest and most visible benefit, the wage premium, has declined over the past decade, as recent British and American research suggests. The fall in the observable wage mark-up and the hard-to-observe nature of union voice may therefore be key factors in explaining why unions have been unable to organize new workers and new workplaces over the last two decades.

Chapter 6

What do unions do for women?

Helen Bewley and Sue Fernie

The first workplace described in Box 6.1 illustrates the conditions typically experienced by female workers in sectors where women constitute the vast majority of the workforce. Four-fifths of the workforce is female in the private healthcare workplace where Jane finds her first job, and also in her second (and rather more attractive) job in public education. More generally, almost half the workforce is female, and women full-timers are more likely than men to be union members. The Department of Trade and Industry (DTI) points out that the number of people working more than 60 hours per week rose from one in eight in 2000 to one in six in 2002, and the biggest rise in this group was amongst women, from 6 to 13 per cent (DTI, 2002).

Box 6.1 *A working woman*

Jane's first job[1] was with a typical employer of a predominantly female workforce. She was employed as an ancillary worker in a long-established private care home with between 10 and 24 workers, although the establishment was part of a larger organization. Jane's employer did not recognize a union, and Jane herself was not a union member, but her employer did use human resource management (HRM) methods. She was regularly appraised on her performance, and, although her employer had few competitors, her most recent pay rise prior to leaving the workplace was about average for similar workers in her locality. Her employer had a formal written policy on equal opportunities, but no formal family-friendly policies. Workers were not paid for any time they needed to take off at short notice to deal with family problems. Jane worked 30 hours a week for £116.88.

Dissatisfied with her lack of access to family-friendly policies in her job with a typical employer, Jane sought alternative employment[2] in order to maximize her access to equality of opportunity. Her new employer is an educational establishment in the public sector. This employer recognizes a union, has a human resources plan, trains supervisors in personnel management, and uses HRM methods in recruiting staff. Union membership is high, and Jane has joined the union. Again a majority of the workforce is female, but this workplace is much larger, with over 500 workers. More than half the workforce is highly skilled, and their most recent pay rise was above average for similar workers in the locality. Jane's new employer has a formal written policy addressing equality of treatment on the grounds of gender. The employer also collects statistics on posts held by gender, and monitors promotions by gender. Selection procedures are reviewed for indirect discrimination, and the employer measures the effect of the equal opportunities policies. Parental leave is offered to non-managerial workers, as is the opportunity to work from home or on term-time only contracts. Jane has the option of switching from full- to part-time employment, or to job-share. However, she is disappointed to find that even this most family-friendly of employers still does not provide a workplace nursery, financial help with childcare, flexible hours, or a $4\frac{1}{2}$-day week. Jane is pleased to see that there is at least some evidence of greater equality in her new workplace, though; over the past five years there has been an increase in the proportion of women managers, and Jane now earns £195.47 for her 30-hour week.

1 Based on the characteristics of a typical workplace where the majority of the workforce is female in the 1998 Workplace Employee Relations Survey (WERS98)
2 Based on the characteristics of a typical workplace most likely to offer family-friendly practices in WERS98

However, women still bear the brunt of domestic work and assume major responsibility for children. They spend an additional nine hours a week on household tasks compared to men (not including time spent on childcare) and where a husband and wife both work full time the woman performs 62 per cent of domestic labour, including time spent on childcare (Gershuny, 1997: 148). In addition, in the UK 1.2 million women care for an elderly parent (Institute of Management, 2001: 3). Women's earnings suffer from their absence from the labour market to have and rear children, and the poor provision of childcare places in the UK (currently only 8 places for every 100 children aged under five) does little to help them in managing their lives. For 30 years trade unions have campaigned for workplace nurseries with no great success – only 3 per cent of workplaces provided these in 2002.

In terms of education, 2002 was the third successive year that girls outperformed boys at both GCSE and A-level. In terms of degree-level qualifications, in 2001 56 per cent of women obtained either a first or upper second degree, compared with 49 per cent of men. It might not be too fanciful to suppose that this academic lead of women would be reflected in the workplace, in terms of pay and positions held. However, women make up only 18 per cent of all Members of Parliament, 30 per cent of managers, 37 per cent of lawyers, and 38 per cent of doctors. Conversely, men constitute only 5 per cent of receptionists, 10 per cent of nurses, and 19 per cent of cleaners. In 2001, women working full time in the UK earned, hourly, 83p for every £1 earned by men. Women working part time earned, hourly, 59p for every £1 earned by full-time males – a figure virtually unchanged for 30 years (EOC, 2002).

Though the legislative route to equality at work may not be exhausted there are other approaches that can be used in tandem to effect greater change in the workplace, such as employer initiatives, local authority action programmes, and local and national action by trade unions, sometimes in partnership with employers. Much of the closing of the full-time gender pay gap in the early years after the Equal Pay Act came into effect (1975) was due to the high level of collective bargaining coverage at that time. It is the unions' role as monitors, law enforcers and proactive partners in employment that is considered here.

This chapter assesses the impact of trade unions in monitoring existing equality legislation and in promoting family-friendly working by incorporating equality issues into the bargaining agenda. First, the Labour government's policies vis-à-vis equal pay and work-life balance are set out, and the general approach of employers and unions towards equality in the workplace is explored. The position of women within the British union movement is then described, and the actual steps taken by a number of unions to further equality of opportunity for their members. Finally, a comparison is made between workplaces that recognize a trade union and those that do not, which leads to the finding that trade union membership has much to offer women in terms of the availability of family-friendly working and the existence of equal opportunities policies.

The state as catalyst for change

The Equal Opportunities Commission (EOC)'s Equal Pay Taskforce, which reported in February 2001, found that there had been insufficient coordinated and concerted commitment from employers, trade unions and the government to closing the gender pay gap. One of their recommendations was that the Equal Pay Act be amended to require employers to carry out regular pay reviews to check for gender inequalities in pay systems. Hepple *et al.* (2000: 3) also suggest that one way to overcome weaknesses in the present law and procedures is the introduction of pay equality plans that place a positive duty on employers to provide pay equity – compulsory pay audits, and remedying any gaps through negotiation with worker representatives. The government chose not to accept the Equal Pay Taskforce's recommendation for compulsory pay audits, but instead decided to encourage employers, via the recommendations arising from the independent review of women's employment and pay carried out for the government by Denise Kingsmill and the Chancellor's 2002 budget, to undertake voluntary pay reviews. Employers have actually had this opportunity since the 1997 EOC Code of Practice, which recommends pay reviews, but have chosen not to take up this invitation to any great extent. EOC research shows that only one in five larger organizations have made use of this code (Morrell *et al.*, 2001: 37), and most firms confidently stated that there was no gender pay gap in their organization without having ever carried out a review (Equal Pay Taskforce, 2001: 10).

The other main cause of gender pay inequality – the unequal impact of family responsibilities – continues to form the second main plank of both the government's and the trade unions' policies towards women. The Labour Government has started to address this unequal impact via its manifesto commitments to strive towards highly productive workplaces through fairness and partnership at work. The Working Families Tax Credit, proposals on a national childcare strategy, the enactment of the European Directive on parental leave, and encouragement to conduct pay audits, have been welcome moves for working parents. Improved maternity rights legislation now results in two-thirds of women returning to the same employer after childbirth, thus increasing job tenure and subsequent pay and promotion rates. Legislating for parental leave has created an opportunity to increase men's role in the domestic sphere. The Employment Act 2002 has provisions for paid paternity and adoptive leave, better maternity pay, and a clause that imposes a duty on employers to consider requests from parents with young children to work flexible hours.

Other policies designed to improve rights at work (e.g. for part-time workers, temporary workers and the low paid, and also the working time regulations) might also have an impact on the gender pay gap. For example, the Part-time Workers Regulations give part-timers the right to the same hourly rates as equivalent full-timers, if the part-time female can find a full-time male in a comparator job. Three-quarters of those paid the national minimum wage (NMW) are women, and in 2000 the Low Pay Commission (LPC) reported that, in the year to April 1999, the gap in the average hourly pay of women relative to men narrowed by 1 per cent, consequent on the introduction of the NMW – the largest reduction for a decade. The Equal Pay Taskforce suggested that the LPC should have a specific remit to narrow the pay gap when recommending the level at which the NMW is set.

Employers' behaviour can also impact on the gender pay differential. In the 1970s, employers' strategies for reducing inequality were primarily based on equal opportunity-type arguments, supported by the need to comply with anti-discrimination legislation. Hepple *et al.* (2000: 27) suggest that the main feature of the equality legislation of the 1970s was a negative duty to prevent discrimination, rather than a positive and explicit duty to enforce equality. The late 1980s and early 1990s saw a switch in favour of arguments founded upon business interests as a rationale for equality action. Some employers recognized that equality or diversity management measures could serve their interests in competing in the labour market. The management of diversity fitted in well with management trends such as human resource management (HRM), flexibility, and the business case for equality, and was seen as part of a strategic approach to human resources, compared to the reactive compliance route of the earlier equal opportunities perspective. For example, 12 per cent of Ernst and Young's 7,500 UK staff are on flexible working schedules in an attempt to recruit and retain the right calibre of staff (Allan and Monkcom, 2001: 17). Of course, it is worth remembering that the numbers of employers who have such a strategic approach is very low – for example, Employers for Work-Life Balance, whose aim is to share best practice and establish a 'one-stop shop' with information for employers on work-life issues, consists of 22 business leaders. Moreover, the cyclical nature of equal opportunities provision has been well documented (see, for example, Breugel and Perrons, 1998).

As for the Trade Union Congress (TUC), in 2001 it amended its constitution to ensure that unions are committed to the promotion of equality within the workplace, including pushing for improved rights to family-friendly employment policies. This move is accompanied by a TUC equality auditing process to monitor and encourage progress. The TUC also launched a scheme, funded by the government's Union Learning Fund, to train 500 equal pay representatives by August 2002 in order to tackle the gender pay gap in the workplace. The main aim of this pilot scheme was to equip union activists and ordinary members with the skills necessary to work in partnership with employers in carrying out pay reviews. In practice it seems that the Kingsmill recommendations, together with a partnership approach, have formed the basis for a revitalization of many trade unions' moribund equal-pay campaigns.

The TUC has emphasized the need for a partnership approach to flexible working, as exemplified by its *Changing Times* (a TUC guide to work–life balance and a fortnightly bulletin) and the use of DTI funding for such initiatives via the Challenge and Partnership Funds. The TUC states that 'achieving work–life balance requires unions and management to work together in partnership', and gives several examples of organizations who have negotiated innovative work practices with their staff. Within this it differentiates 'flexibility' (where management can impose forms of work organization on workers who have no opportunity to object) from 'positive flexibility' (where workers have more autonomy and choice in work–life issues, indicating a considered approach to work–life balance; Morris, 2002).

Besides the TUC commitment to equality and work–life balance, there is evidence of a changing approach to equality of opportunity within many unions. Unions have a history of being active in this field, as many important equal pay cases have been brought to tribunals (and won) by unions over the last 30 years. However, there is now evidence to show that equal pay issues are moving away from the domain of legal or equalities officers and becoming a more central part of trade unions' work. Campaigning on equal pay is slowly turning into campaigning on pay. In addition, in some unions the term family-friendly is giving way to work–life balance and is achieving greater prominence. This change in emphasis suggests an increasing recognition of the need to expand access to these policies to all workers with caring responsibilities, and a growing belief that such practices can benefit those without a caring role.

The position of women within British trade unions

Between 1991 and 2001, union density fell much faster amongst men than women. Union density amongst male workers stood at 41 per cent in 1991 compared with 29 per cent in 2001, whereas female density, which was 32 per cent in 1991, had only fallen by 4 percentage points by 2001 (Brook,

2002: 343). Although female union density is still 1 percentage point lower than male density, this is explained by the fact that women are more heavily concentrated in part-time work, where union density for both men and women is lower. In fact, union density is higher amongst women than men for both full-time and part-time workers. Of women in full-time employment, 33 per cent are union members, compared with 31 per cent of men, while union density is 22 per cent amongst female part-time workers, compared with 12 per cent for male part-time workers (TUC, 2002). It is also notable that among full-time workers union density fell by 10 per cent to 32 per cent from 1991 to 2001, while density amongst part-time workers remained at around 20 per cent throughout this period (Brook, 2002: 346).

Almost half of all women who work are part time, and women hold 80 per cent of all part-time jobs. Many of these jobs are unskilled, have little scope for progression, and are low paid. In the past, trade unions showed little interest in part-time workers; their strategies either marginalized or excluded them completely – in part this explained the lower level of union membership amongst this group. However, this is changing as unions realize that they must target women, and therefore part-time workers, to stem the flow of falling membership. Most unions now have a policy on the recruitment and retention of part-timers, often based on banded sub-scriptions. Some negotiate national agreements containing clauses relating to pro rata equality for part-timers. Conley et al. (2001) note that an extension of the traditional union agenda to incorporate the interests of part-time workers seems most likely to occur when women officers have taken up the cause, but also comments that none of the unions they studied had participatory structures specific to part-timers. However, Walters (2002), using qualitative data gained from 50 part-time women workers in the retail sector, found that women have, on the whole, favourable attitudes to trade unions, regarding them as highly relevant and desirable. Therefore there appears to be potential for unions to increase their membership amongst part-time workers, although the fact that in 1998 40 per cent of women did not know who their union representative was indicates the problem faced by unions in seeking to translate expressed support into membership.

Table 6.1 shows the proportion of women at various levels in the five largest unions, which account for around half of all union members. Although two-fifths of TUC-affiliated members are women, only nine of the TUC's 69 affiliated unions have a woman in the top position. Most of these are very small unions with fewer than 9,000 members. However, there has been some growth in women's representation at senior levels in

Table 6.1 Characteristics of the five largest unions

	UNISON	TGWU	GMB	Amicus	USDAW
Total membership (millions)	1.2	0.9	0.6	0.4	0.3
Women as proportion of:					
Members (per cent)	72	21	38	32	60
National executive committee members (per cent)	64	33	38	33	59
National full-time officers (per cent)	48	6	17	20	63

the largest unions, including at national executive committee level and in TUC delegations, where the majority of the top ten unions now have women in a proportion similar to that of their membership. It has been argued by Heery and Kelly (1988: 502) that the presence of women role models in top union positions has an impact on the extent to which those unions espouse women's concerns. A 1994 survey of 3,000 new members of Manufacturing, Science, Finance (MSF), showing that women were twice as likely as men to support union negotiation of career breaks and three times as likely to support union backing for job-sharing, provides further evidence that this is likely to be the case (Kirton and Healy, 1999: 37). However, none of the ten largest unions has a woman general secretary, and only four have any women at deputy general secretary level.

Given the importance to unions of recruiting and retaining female workers, is there any evidence that trade unions are embracing 'women's issues' as part of their mainstream bargaining agenda, and, if so, how successful have they been? This can be examined in two ways: first, by considering the various policies on equal pay and family-friendly practices adopted by a selection of Britain's largest unions, and second, by analysing the 1998 Workplace Employee Relations Survey (WERS98) (Department of Trade and Industry, 1999a) to assess the impact of trade unions on women's employment experiences.

Selected trade unions' policies on equal pay and family-friendly working

The Kingsmill Report on women's pay and employment provided a fillip to unions' action on equal pay, and nowhere is this more apparent than in the case of MSF/Amicus. Following the Kingsmill recommendations, MSF wrote to thousands of employers asking them to conduct pay reviews.

By May 2002 only 80 had agreed, many of these being in the engineering industry. Several large employers in the finance sector – where women earn 57 per cent less than men – have also agreed to conduct reviews. The union is now threatening to name and shame those employers who refuse to carry out pay reviews. This is likely to have an impact upon those companies who wish to be an employer-of-choice – especially in the finance sector, for example, where large organizations, worried about recruitment, copy each other's personnel policies.

MSF has a top-down approach to the pay question, meaning that it is based on policies that are made at conference (as opposed to local action) and given a high profile in the union, with resources being allocated to dissemination to members. It is one of the eleven unions participating in the TUC pilot project to train 500 workplace equal pay representatives, and is incorporating targets on equal pay reviews into its performance management for regional officials. In terms of work–life balance, in addition to monitoring the statutory requirements on maternity leave and hours of work, MSF aims to have work–life balance clauses inserted into national agreements and has been successful in promoting work–life balance in the NHS Whitley Council Scotland agreement via the Partnership Information Network.

Another union with a top-down approach to equality, GMB, won the first ever equal pay for work of equal value case (Hayward v. Cammell Laird 1988) and has continued to win compensation for thousands of members for unequal pay, sex discrimination and sexual harassment. In 2001 the union agreed to place equal pay centrally on its bargaining agenda, to give this a high priority in each region, and to train officers and activists. By May 2002 GMB had trained 80 equal pay representatives – the highest number trained by any union. The equalities department expanded in 2002, and the GMB is one instance where cases previously handled by the legal department are now being dealt with by an equalities committee. In the public sector, female ancillary workers have been compared with male maintenance workers at NHS Trusts, and in the private sector the GMB campaigned to raise the lowest rate of pay for female jobs to the lowest rate of pay for male jobs – a factor that was so important in the success of the Equal Pay Act. Continually raising awareness of equality in the union and making women's issues integral is an aim. Membership is growing by 1 per cent per annum and 50 per cent of new members are women, mostly employed in the public sector. Also, the number of young female officers is increasing.

Flexible working arrangements have been the subject of much negotiation between GMB and various employers, and the union cites a number of examples where a positive approach to flexibility from both the unions and the employer has created clear business benefits. Pringle, a manufacturer of woollen products, previously an inflexible employer, was persuaded of the benefits of flexible hours in the retention of valued staff. The union has worked for some time with Asda, the supermarket chain, on issues relating to flexibility, staff retention and morale, and family-friendly working practices. Arla, a dairy manufacturer and milk processing firm with 2,000 workers has, through the partnership arrangement with union shop stewards, modernized its working practices and introduced an annualized hours scheme that both meets business needs and introduces valuable benefits to family life.

Contrary to many other unions' approaches, the Union of Shop, Distributive and Allied Workers (USDAW), organizing mainly in retail, employs a bottom-up approach to equality issues – that is local or regional officers identify a problem/opportunity at branch level and then build up a campaign in order to secure certain benefits in the workplace. Equal pay representatives are trained, via the TUC route, to identify problems in the workplace and to encourage the employer to undertake reviews. The union sees equal pay as still being a major issue despite a successful tribunal case in 1989 where a woman checkout operator at Sainsbury, the supermarket chain, claimed equal pay with a male warehouse worker. However, the leadership still see low pay as the problem, because of occupational segregation, not unequal pay.

USDAW has achieved reasonable success in ensuring compliance with legislation on family-friendly practices, but has made little improvement on statutory minima. However, the retailer Littlewoods, as the 1999 Parents at Work 'Employer of the Year', is an exception – many improvements, including five days' paid carers' leave, ten days' paternity leave, enhanced maternity arrangements and a workplace nursery, have been secured. The union is experiencing an upturn in membership, with women constituting 60 per cent of members. There is no specific campaign for part-timers; being two-thirds of the membership, these workers are regarded as mainstream. In recent years USDAW has signed 40 new negotiating agreements, and its enthusiasm for partnerships is epitomized in its relationship with Tesco, the nation's largest private employer, covering nearly 100,000 members.

Finally, the public service union UNISON is the largest union, with women making up 72 per cent of its membership. In 2000, a survey of its members revealed that 78 per cent regarded obtaining equal pay as the most important thing the union could do for them. The 'Getting Equal' campaign in local government, where 70 per cent of workers are women, aims to identify possible equal pay claims and to persuade the employer that such cases would cost more than the implementation of non-discriminatory pay structures. As regards work–life balance, in January 2002 UNISON prioritized this issue. The UNISON work–life balance website says 'It's about working to live, not living to work', and money has been specifically allocated for work–life balance campaigns, which used to be paid for out of the equalities budget (UNISON, 2002). Concerns about possible resentment of family-friendly policies by co-workers with no family responsibilities have been widely reported (Kodz *et al.*, 2002: 37), and so UNISON hope that by emphasizing that work–life balance has something to offer everyone, this issue will unify the membership and not just appeal to specific interest groups. Although national guidelines have been established, officers believe that the union cannot dictate work–life balance policies at national level, but that only individual branches can be responsive enough to negotiate on these issues. UNISON has received DTI Challenge Funding to help raise the profile of work–life balance at branch level. The London Borough of Merton and the Wirral and West Cheshire NHS Trust are two examples of UNISON's success in achieving innovative ways of working flexibly, while offering opportunities to both parents and those with no family responsibilities, using this funding.

What unions do for women in the workplace

So far we have considered whether unions have identified family-friendly concerns as a key bargaining issue. The policy descriptions above suggest that they have indeed realized that emphasizing issues of importance to women is a potentially powerful recruitment mechanism. But how successful are unions in actually negotiating policies of benefit to women within individual workplaces?

WERS98 asked managers about their use of a range of equal opportunities and family-friendly policies. It also established whether a union was recognized within the workplace for the purposes of negotiating pay and conditions. Table 6.2 shows that workplaces with union recognition were almost twice as likely to have a formal written policy that specifically addressed equality of treatment on the grounds of gender than those without. Workplaces with a recognized union were more than twice as likely to collect statistics on the career progression of men and women, four times as likely to monitor promotions by gender, and more than three times as likely to review selection procedures to identify indirect discrimination. A unionized workplace with an equal opportunities policy was

Table 6.2 Union recognition and the incidence of equal opportunities policies and family-
friendly working for non-managerial workers

	Proportion of workplaces (unless indicated otherwise)[1]	
	Union recognition	No union recognition
All workplaces	38.9	61.1
Equal opportunities policies:		
Formal written equal opportunities policy on gender	82.1	42.3
Statistics collected on posts held by gender	40.6	15.4
Monitor promotions by gender	20.6	5.4
Review selection procedures to identify indirect discrimination	36.9	9.9
Measure effects of equal opportunities policy on workforce	20.4	4.8
Family-friendly policies:		
Parental leave	54.5	21.8
Working from home	15.3	10.9
Term-time only contracts	24.2	10.0
Switching from full- to part-time employment	58.2	37.8
Job-sharing	48.8	15.4
Workplace nursery or nursery linked with workplace	6.3	1.4
Financial help with childcare	5.9	2.6
No family-friendly policies (from the seven policies above)	22.2	47.5
Take-up of these policies:		
No workers take them up	35.5	36.4
A small proportion take them up	51.7	51.2
Up to a quarter take them up	8.8	6.1
A quarter or more take them up	3.9	6.3
Flexitime	26.8	12.2
4½-day week/9-day fortnight	4.5	1.5
Change in proportion of women managers over past 5 years:		
Gone up a lot	11.1	9.6
Gone up a little	25.2	22.8
Stayed the same	61.2	61.8
Gone down a little	1.3	3.4
Gone down a lot	1.2	2.4
Paid leave for time off at short-notice (Survey of Employees Questionnaire (SEQ))	47.1	40.9
Number of hours worked per week (SEQ)	34.0	36.5
Weekly pay of female workers (SEQ)	£174.43	£154.30

1 From all workplaces with ten or more workers. WERS98 Management and Employee questionnaires, with probability weights.

four times more likely to measure the effects of such a policy than a non-unionized workplace.

As for family-friendly working, Table 6.2 shows that unionized workplaces were much more likely to provide flexible working and help with childcare than non-unionized ones. Indeed, 48 per cent of non-unionized workplaces reported that they offered none of a list of seven benefits. However, it is important to control for the characteristics of the workplace in seeking to observe the relationship between the use of equal opportunities or family-friendly policies and trade unions. While workers were more likely to have access to equal opportunities and family-friendly policies in workplaces with union recognition, unions were also more likely to be recognized in larger workplaces. Smaller employers may simply be less able to afford equal opportunities and family-friendly policies than larger employers, and so whether the employer offers such policies may be determined by size rather than union recognition. As the WERS98 dataset contains information on management practices, workplace size, sector, the gender composition of the workplace and many other establishment characteristics, the following analysis controls for a wide range of factors likely to influence access to equal opportunities and family-friendly policies.

Union recognition and the incidence of equal opportunities or family-friendly policies and outcomes

Table 6.3 shows the relationship between a range of equal opportunities policies and union recognition or HRM practices, controlling for a range of factors including private/public sector, size, and the proportion of women employees. The Table provides a statistical representation of workplaces identical in every respect except one, namely the features listed to the left. The baseline figure indicates the proportion of workplaces that offered a particular equal opportunities policy from all workplaces with ten or more workers. It is against this baseline that we compare the impact of the workplace having union recognition or any of the HRM practices listed.

Recognizing a union for the purposes of negotiating pay and conditions raised the likelihood that a workplace had a formal written policy that addressed equality of treatment on the grounds of gender by 20 percentage points. Also, a workplace with union recognition was 13 per cent more likely to collect statistics on posts held by gender than an identical workplace without recognition. Recognizing a union raised the likelihood that the workplace reviewed selection procedures to identify indirect discrimination and monitored promotions by gender. Therefore, unions are associated with a greater likelihood that a workplace has a number of equal opportunities policies and that it monitors them, regardless of any other characteristics of the workplace or employer.

Looking at Table 6.4, parental leave was far more likely to be available in workplaces with union recognition, and the opportunity to switch from full- to part-time employment was on offer in 50 per cent of workplaces with union recognition against 37 per cent of those without, despite these workplaces being the same in every other key respect. Union recognition was also associated with a greater likelihood that workers received financial help with childcare. Looking at the likelihood that a workplace offered no family-friendly practices from a list of seven, this was far less likely where managers recognized a union. Therefore, there is strong evidence to link union recognition with the availability of at least some family-friendly practices.

So far we have concentrated on whether employers offer formal equal opportunities and family-friendly policies, but more interesting is the extent to which these policies actually have an effect on women's experiences at work. Table 6.5 demonstrates that their take-up is not strongly associated with the employer recognizing a union, although it is important to note that where one or more family-friendly practice was in place, at least one worker took his or her entitlement in almost all workplaces (97 per cent). There is also no evidence to suggest that employers were more likely to report an increase in the proportion of women managers over the previous five years where they recognized a union. In addition, they were no more likely to offer paid time off at short notice to deal with unexpected caring responsibilities. However, workers in establishments with a recognized union worked an average of 90 minutes less each week than their colleagues in non-union workplaces – a factor of great importance to women given their dual responsibilities.

Turning to other factors associated with access to equal opportunities and family-friendly policies and outcomes, there is some evidence that employers are more likely to offer equal opportunities and family-friendly policies where they use certain personnel practices such as HRM recruitment methods (personality or performance tests, or recruitment based on skills, qualifications, experience or motivation rather than references, availability, recommendation or age), training supervisors in personnel management, and having a human resources plan (a formal strategic plan covering employee development and forecasts of staffing requirements prepared by someone responsible for employee relations; Fernie and Gray,

Table 6.3 Association between use of equal opportunities policies and union recognition or HRM practices[1]

	Marginal effects associated with recognition or HRM practice[2]				
	Formal written equal opportunities policy on gender	Statistics collected on posts held by gender	Monitor promotions by gender	Review selection procedures to identify indirect discrimination	Measure effects of equal opportunities policy on workforce
Union recognition	0.200***	0.133*	0.042*	0.142**	0.019
Guaranteed job security for largest occupational group	0.179**	0.009	0.013	0.013	0.099
Supervisor trained in personnel management	0.136**	0.099*	0.033*	0.041	0.192***
Human resources plan[3]	0.163***	0.012	0.026	0.130***	0.091**
HRM recruitment methods[4]	0.083	0.097**	0.056***	0.240***	0.084*
Formal off-the-job training for largest occupational group	0.023	0.073	0.008	−0.034	0.073*
Most workers in largest occupational group (LOG) trained in a job other than their own	−0.073	−0.055	0.024	0.080*	0.067
HRM communication methods[5]	0.014	0.076	0.013	0.023	0.038
Performance pay[6]	0.216***	−0.055	−0.013	0.077	−0.071**
Performance appraisal for most workers	0.119**	0.025	0.010	0.032	0.077
Some workers on fixed-term or temporary contracts	0.047	0.117**	0.062**	0.066	0.017
Baseline: probability workplace has policy[7]	0.447	0.281	0.047	0.227	0.168
Sample size	1,471	1,479	1,479	1,479	1,478

*, significant at the 0.10 level; **, significant at the 0.05 level; ***, significant at the 0.01 level.

1 From all workplaces with ten or more workers. WERS98 Management questionnaire, with probability weights.

2 Results control for all policies listed in the above table and also whether workplace is in public or private sector, gender composition of workforce, whether workplace is less than ten years old, whether more than half workforce is in managerial, professional or technical occupations, number of competitors, size of most recent pay increase compared to similar workers in locality, size of workforce and major group industrial sector.

3 Formal strategic plan that covers employee development and forecasts of staffing requirements, with someone responsible for employee relations involved in preparation of the plan.

4 Use of personality or performance tests in recruitment, or recruitment based on skills, qualifications, experience or motivation but not references, availability, recommendation by another employee, or age.

5 Consultative committee of managers and workers that discusses a range of issues; quality circles; and regular briefings for some of the workforce.

6 Individual or group performance pay, profit-related pay, deferred profit-sharing, or employee share ownership.

7 Probability of the policy being offered in a public sector workplace without union recognition or any of the HRM practices, with the average gender composition, where the workplace is ten or more years old, where less than half the workforce are in managerial, professional or technical occupations, with few competitors, an average recent pay increase, between 200 and 499 workers, and in the manufacturing sector.

Table 6.4 Association between availability of family-friendly practices and union recognition or HRM practices[1]

| | Marginal effects associated with recognition or HRM practice[2]: | | | | | | | | | |
	(1) Parental leave	(2) Working from home	(3) Term-time only contract	(4) Switching from full- to part-time employment	(5) Job-sharing	(6) Workplace nursery or nursery linked with workplace	(7) Financial help with childcare	No family-friendly policies (from 1–7)	Flexitime	4½-day week/ 9-day fortnight
Union recognition	0.196***	-0.036	-0.013	0.123*	0.088	0.007	0.002**	-0.190***	0.104	0.047
Guaranteed job security for largest occupational group	-0.027	-0.065	-0.037	0.153*	0.209***	-0.002	0.450×10^{-3}	-0.132*	-0.019	-0.068
Supervisor trained in personnel management	0.091**	0.104***	0.146**	0.001	0.109**	0.006*	-0.148×10^{-4}	-0.094*	-0.072	0.103*
Human resources plan[3]	0.056	0.074	0.168***	0.089	0.041	0.003	-0.214×10^{-3}	-0.003	0.061	0.057
HRM recruitment methods[4]	0.068	-0.002	-0.025	0.025	0.090**	0.040***	$0.003***$	-0.002	0.116**	0.002
Formal off-the-job training for largest occupational group	0.108**	0.007	-0.019	0.054	0.020	0.001	0.315×10^{-3}	-0.107*	-0.069	0.197***
Most workers in LOG trained in a job other than their own	0.048	0.020	-0.059	0.117*	-0.007	-0.003	0.381×10^{-3}	-0.088	-0.066	-0.076
HRM communication methods[5]	0.129***	-0.099***	0.007	-0.090	0.041	0.004	-0.203×10^{-3}	-0.015	0.029	-0.004
Performance pay[6]	-0.039	0.027	0.069	0.125*	0.068	0.006	$0.001*$	-0.066	-0.068	-0.073
Performance appraisal for most workers	-0.005	0.123**	0.034	0.089	0.089*	-0.002	0.187×10^{-3}	-0.040	0.035	0.068
Some workers on fixed-term or temporary contracts	0.061	0.067	-0.004	0.016	0.042	0.293×10^{-3}	0.001	0.025	0.204***	0.037
Baseline: probability practice offered[7]	0.249	0.205	0.254	0.374	0.181	0.005	0.328×10^{-3}	0.410	0.247	0.215
Sample size	1,479	1,479	1,479	1,479	1,479	1,479	1,479	1,479	1,481	1,481

*, significant at the 0.10 level; **, significant at the 0.05 level; ***, significant at the 0.01 level.

1 From all workplaces with ten or more workers. WERS98 Management questionnaire, with probability weights.
2 Results control for all policies listed in the above table and also whether the workplace is in public or private sector, gender composition of workforce, whether workplace is less than ten years old, whether more than half workforce is in managerial, professional or technical occupations, number of competitors, size of most recent pay increase compared to similar workers in locality, size of workforce and major group industrial sector.
3 Formal strategic plan that covers employee development and forecasts of staffing requirements, with someone responsible for employee relations involved in the preparation of the plan.
4 Use of personality or performance tests in recruitment, or recruitment based on skills, qualifications, experience or motivation but not references, availability, recommendation by another employee, or age.
5 Consultative committee of managers and workers that discusses a range of issues; quality circles; and regular briefings for some of the workforce.
6 Individual or group performance pay, profit-related pay, deferred profit-sharing, or employee share ownership.
7 Probability of the practice being offered in a public sector workplace without union recognition or any of the HRM policies, with the average gender composition, where the workplace is ten or more years old, where less than half the workforce are in managerial or technical occupations, with few competitors, an average recent pay increase, between 200 and 499 workers, and in the manufacturing sector.

Table 6.5 Association between equal opportunities or family-friendly outcomes and union recognition or HRM practices[1]

| | Marginal effects associated with recognition or HRM practice[2] | | | | |
| | | | Survey of employees | | |
	Any take-up of family-friendly policies	Increase in proportion of women managers over the past five years	Paid leave for time off at short notice	Working hours per week (fraction of an hour)	Weekly pay of female workers
Union recognition	−0.025	0.005	0.014	−1.498**	£5.02
Guaranteed job security for largest occupational group	−0.001	−0.241***	0.044	0.466	−£3.05
Supervisor trained in personnel management	−0.019	−0.018	−0.022	−0.140	£1.71
Human resources plan[3]	0.009	0.041	0.008	0.453	−£0.63
HRM recruitment methods[4]	0.004	0.083*	0.037*	0.672	£8.43**
Formal off-the-job training for largest occupational group	−0.019	−0.055	0.009	0.271	£4.63
Most workers in LOG trained in a job other than their own	0.004	−0.012	−0.002	−0.137	−£6.64*
HRM communication methods[5]	0.014	0.045	0.027	0.245	£6.55*
Performance pay[6]	0.008	0.123**	0.055**	1.005*	£1.76
Performance appraisal for most workers	0.010	0.074	0.066***	1.415***	£4.35
Some workers on fixed-term or temporary contracts	0.011	−0.013	0.089***	1.573**	£12.88***
Baseline[7]:	0.974	0.543	0.520	35.423	196.28
Sample size	1,091	1,477	17,743	18,399	18,168

*, significant at the 0.10 level; **, significant at the 0.05 level; ***, significant at the 0.01 level.

1 From all workplaces with ten or more workers. WERS98 Management questionnaire, with probability weights.

2 Results control for all policies listed in the above table and also whether workplace is in public or private sector, gender composition of workforce, whether workplace is less than ten years old, whether more than half workforce is in managerial, professional or technical occupations, number of competitors, size of most recent pay increase compared to similar workers in locality, size of workforce and major group industrial sector.

3 Formal strategic plan that covers employee development and forecasts of staffing requirements, with someone responsible for employee relations involved in preparation of the plan.

4 Use of personality or performance tests in recruitment, or recruitment based on skills, qualifications, experience or motivation but not references, availability, recommendation by another employee, or age.

5 Consultative committee of managers and workers that discusses a range of issues; quality circles; and regular briefings for some of the workforce.

6 Individual or group performance pay, profit-related pay, deferred profit-sharing, or employee share ownership.

7 Probability of characteristic, or average number of hours worked, or average weekly pay for female workers, in a public sector workplace without union recognition or any of the HRM policies, with the average gender composition, where the workplace is ten or more years old, where less than half the workforce are in managerial, professional or technical occupations, with few competitors, an average recent pay increase, between 200 and 499 workers, and in the manufacturing sector.

2002). However, these HRM practices do not exhibit the consistently positive relationship with the incidence of equal opportunities and family-friendly policies that is observed in the case of union recognition. Therefore, having a recognized union in the workplace seems to offer workers a greater likelihood of access to equal opportunities and family-friendly policies.

The typical union workplace

Table 6.6 shows the difference in the incidence of equal opportunities and family-friendly policies, and in outcomes, between the typical workplace with union recognition, the typical workplace without recognition, and the typical workplace where the employer does not recognize a union and does not have any sophisticated HRM practices such as a human resources plan, performance pay, performance appraisals and training supervisors in personnel management. This means that rather than just looking at the impact of various workplace characteristics on the likelihood that an equal opportunities or family-friendly policy or outcome will exist, we compare the overall impact of the characteristics of certain types of workplace.

Looking first at the availability of equal opportunities policies, the incidence of these is far higher in the typical workplace with union recognition than in workplaces without recognition, or without either recognition or HRM practices. In total, 88 per cent of workplaces that recognized a union had a formal written policy that addressed equality of treatment on the grounds of gender, against 43 per cent of workplaces without union recognition and just 13 per cent of workplaces without recognition or HRM policies. Statistics were collected on posts held by gender in over a third of typical unionized workplaces, compared with 19 per cent of those without recognition, and 13 per cent of those without HRM practices or recognition. Only 0.5 per cent of employers who did not recognize a union monitored promotions by gender, yet 18 per cent of employers who recognized a union claimed to do so. In 37 per cent of workplaces with union recognition the employer reviewed selection procedures to identify indirect discrimination, but this occurred in just 6 per cent of non-union workplaces and even fewer establishments (0.6 per cent) without HRM practices or recognition. Finally, 7 per cent of typical employers who recognized a union measured the effects of their equal opportunities policies, against 0.2 per cent of workplaces without union recognition. Therefore, Table 6.6 suggests a union effect in the establishment and monitoring of equal opportunities policies.

Table 6.6 Equal opportunities and family-friendly policies and outcomes for typical workplaces[1]

	Proportion of workplaces (%) (unless stated otherwise):		
	Union recognition[2]	No union recognition[3]	No union recognition or HRM practices[4]
Equal opportunities policies:			
Formal written equal opportunities policy on gender	88.0	43.3	12.9
Statistics collected on posts held by gender	35.2	18.6	12.5
Monitor promotions by gender	17.8	0.5	0.2
Review selection procedures to identify indirect discrimination	36.5	5.7	0.6
Measure effects of equal opportunities policy on workforce	6.8	0.2	0.2
Family-friendly policies:			
Parental leave	42.1	18.2	22.1
Working from home	16.2	2.3	1.0
Term-time only working	21.6	4.8	1.8
Switching from full- to part-time employment	35.6	40.7	15.7
Job-sharing	54.1	7.2	1.6
Workplace nursery or nursery linked with workplace	3.2	0.1	2.6×10^{-3}
Financial help with childcare	3.9	3.1	0.1
No family-friendly policies (from the seven policies above)	37.2	57.4	73.3
Flexitime	10.0	6.9	8.2
$4\frac{1}{2}$-day week/9-day fortnight	1.8×10^{-2}	2.0×10^{-2}	1.6×10^{-2}
Outcomes:			
Any take-up of family-friendly policies (from the list of seven policies)	50.8	75.1	48.2
Increase in proportion of women managers over the previous five years	22.4	56.1	17.4
Paid leave for time-off at short notice (SEQ)	29.4	36.4	23.1
Number of hours worked per week (SEQ)	30.3	31.8	27.3
Weekly pay of female workers (in pounds) (SEQ)	200.37	181.38	154.71

1 Based on regression analysis of data from WERS98 Management and Employee questionnaires.
2 Features of typical union workplace: union recognition, appraisal, workers on fixed-term or temporary contracts, HRM recruitment methods, 61 per cent of workforce female, education sector, 10–24 workers, few competitors, public sector.
3 Features of typical non-union workplace: no union recognition, appraisal, performance pay, HRM recruitment methods, private sector, 46 per cent of the workforce female, many competitors, 25–49 workers, wholesale and retail sector.
4 Features of typical non-union, non-HRM workplace: no union recognition or HRM practices, private sector, many competitors, 49 per cent of the workforce female, 10–24 workers, wholesale and retail sector.

Considering the availability of family-friendly practices in typical work-places, we see that workers are more likely to have access to these practices where their employer recognizes a union for the purposes of negotiating pay and conditions. In total 42 per cent of such workplaces offered at least some non-managerial workers the right to take parental leave, with only 18 per cent of establishments without union recognition and 22 per cent of establishments without HRM practices or recognition granting this right. Workers were also far more likely to be allowed to work from home, be on term-time only contracts, job-share where a union had recognition.

Workplaces with union recognition were the most likely to provide a workplace nursery and financial help with childcare, and to allow workers to be employed on flexitime. Union recognition was strongly associated with the employer offering at least one family-friendly practice, with just under two-thirds of all employers who recognized a union having at least one family-friendly policy, against 43 per cent of employers without union recognition. A total of 73 per cent of employers who did not recognize a union or have any of the HRM practices considered here did not offer any family-friendly practices.

The only family-friendly policy less likely to be offered in a workplace with union recognition, as opposed to the non-union recognition work-place, was the right to switch from full- to part-time employment. Of employers who did not negotiate pay and conditions with a union, 41 per cent allowed workers to reduce their hours, compared with 36 per cent of employers who did recognize a union and 16 per cent of employers who did not recognize a union or use any HRM practices. Offering a $4\frac{1}{2}$-day week was rare in all the types of workplace considered. However, it is clear that workers are more likely to have access to the vast majority of the family-friendly practices examined if they are in a workplace where a union is recognized for the purposes of negotiating pay and conditions.

Finally, we consider whether, given the strong link between the incidence of equal opportunities and family-friendly policies and union recognition, the typical workplace with union recognition is more likely to be associated with outcomes that are favourable to women. The union effect is not so obvious here. Table 6.6 demonstrates that workers were more likely to take their entitlements to family-friendly policies in the typical workplace without union recognition, and managers were far more likely to report an increase in the proportion of women in managerial posts where no unions were recognized but the employer had some HRM policies. Workers were most likely to be given paid leave for time off at short notice where a union was not recognized for the purposes of negotiating pay and conditions, with 36 per cent of these employers allowing workers to take this paid time off against 29 per cent of workplaces with recognition and 23 per cent of workplaces without recognition or HRM practices. However, unions are associated with the best outcome for women in terms of female weekly pay. Female weekly earnings were at their lowest in a workplace without union recognition or HRM policies at £155, whilst they stood at £181 for a woman in a workplace without union recognition and £200 where a union negotiated pay and conditions. While take-up of family-friendly working was relatively low in unionized workplaces, workers were less likely to have access to paid time off at short notice and these establishments failed to match the increase in the proportion of women managers in workplaces without recognition, the fact that female workers could expect to earn more in the typical union workplace compared with the typical non-union or the typical non-union, non-HRM workplace is significant. Also, although an increase in the proportion of female managers over the previous five years was less likely in a unionized workplace than in a workplace without union recognition, cross-tabulations show that unionized workplaces had a higher proportion of female managers overall.

Campaigning on equal opportunities and family-friendly policies – prospects for the future of trade unions

The government predicts that in the next ten years the total number of workers in employment will grow by 2 million. It is estimated that around two-thirds of the new jobs will go to women, and also that around two-thirds of all the new jobs will be part time. Nonetheless, by 2010 more than four-fifths of male workers and over half of women workers will still be working full time. This is despite the fact that the Department for Education and Employment Work–Life Balance Baseline survey, carried out in Spring 2000, found considerable demand for reduced hours and flexible working amongst both male and female workers not currently offered (or using) these arrangements (Hogarth et al., 2001: 26). Cully et al. (1999: 74) point out that the increase in the diversity of the workforce over time, in particular due to greater female participation, makes it increasingly important for employers to adapt to the needs of these new workers if they are to recruit and retain staff. As the demand for flexible working arrangements by both workers and employers looks set to continue to grow in the coming years, negotiating flexible working patterns will become a key collective bargaining issue for trade unions.

Unions may push employers to adopt work–life balance policies as a mechanism for recruiting workers and perhaps ultimately as a platform from which to seek recognition. If unions are making widespread use of this strategy, they could have a greater impact on access to equality of opportunity than that estimated by our concentration on workplaces that have already granted recognition. One way of assessing whether unions are likely to be successful in recruiting or retaining union members by campaigning on equal opportunities and family-friendly issues is to look at the level of union density in workplaces that offer these practices. It is possible that where an employer has equal opportunities and family-friendly policies in place, workers feel less need to join (or to remain in) a trade union, so union density levels could be lower. However, our analysis of WERS98 showed union density to be generally higher in workplaces that both recognized a trade union and offered equal opportunities and family-friendly policies than where the employer recognized a trade union but did not offer these policies. An alternative source of information, the LFS 2000, indicates that workers using non-standard working practices – flexitime, job-sharing, term-time only working – were more likely to be union members than those without access to such practices. For example, full-timers with term-time only contracts had a much higher union density (74 per cent) than any other group. Returning to WERS98, it is also the case that where the employer made use of a number of HRM policies in addition to providing individual equal opportunities and family-friendly policies and recognizing a union, density was higher still for the vast majority of equal opportunities and family-friendly policies. Therefore, it does not appear to be the case that the use of HRM practices or access to equal opportunities policies reduces the perceived need to join, or remain in, a union.

Other analysis shows that workplaces that offer a range of family-friendly practices are far more likely than others to report above average outcomes on a range of economic indicators, such as productivity and financial performance (Gray, 2002). This suggests the possibility that unions could make a case to the employer for offering family-friendly practices to workers and then exploit their success in negotiating these policies in seeking to recruit new members. However, the type of policy on offer is critical. Where the practices available reduce the presence of the worker in the workplace by cutting their hours from full to part time, or through term-time-only contracts or homeworking, the employer is much less likely to have above average performance than where they offer policies that facilitate work–life balance whilst maintaining greater workplace visibility. This alternative set of practices consists of flexitime, $4\frac{1}{2}$-day weeks, financial help with childcare, or a workplace nursery. This high-lights the fact that besides negotiating access to equal opportunities and family-friendly policies for workers, unions can also serve an important purpose in representing workers who experience disadvantage resulting from their use of family-friendly policies. Skinner (1999: 433) finds that part-time workers are often unable to attend training that takes place away from the workplace or outside their working hours. A similar problem could arise in relation to those who work at home or on term-time-only contracts. Also, Lewis (1997: 16) found that part-timers are sometimes thought to lack commitment to their employer, reducing their likelihood of promotion. Therefore in their voice capacity (see Chapter 5) unions have a significant role to play in drawing attention not only to the demands of working parents for increased flexibility but also to the prob-lems that workers with family responsibilities face in using these practices, and in alerting employers to the barriers that prevent their workplace from benefiting fully from the practices they offer.

Conclusions

Employers who recognize a trade union for the purposes of negotiating pay and conditions are more likely to have a number of equal opportuni-ties policies than those that do not. Union recognition is also strongly asso-ciated with the provision of parental leave, financial help with childcare, and the right to switch from full- to part-time work. Evidence that the use of equal opportunities policies and access to some family-friendly practices in workplaces with union recognition results in equality of outcomes such as increased take-up of the practices is less apparent, but recognition is associated with a shorter working week, and female workers in a typical unionized workplace can expect to be better paid than their counterparts in a typical non-union workplace. Moreover, a greater proportion of man-agers are female in workplaces with union recognition.

Given the recent changes to the TUC constitution and the strategies developed by a number of unions, we would expect that the association between union recognition and the greater incidence of equal opportunities and family-friendly policies is at least in part due to unions playing an active role in lobbying employers for such policies. As workers are more likely to have access to equal opportunities and family-friendly policies where there is union recognition than where the employer uses sophistic-ated HRM practices, it seems that union representation is critical to workers in gaining access to such practices. Unions also have a role to play in advocating and securing cultural change in the workplace, ensuring that commitment to the employer is measured in terms of outputs rather than inputs (such as visible time spent in the workplace) and that problems experienced in taking entitlements to family-friendly practices are identified and eliminated.

As we have seen, unions benefit women workers, both because employers who recognize unions are more likely to have equal opportunities policies and because women's greater responsibility for the family means that they have more to gain from the higher incidence of family-friendly policies in workplaces with union recognition. This being the case, the question remains whether unions can be successful in persuading women that they are active on their behalf. As we have seen in Jane's case (see Box 6.1), female workers in a union workplace not only have higher pay but also have better access to certain family-friendly working arrangements. This is a key recruitment and organizing tool to secure a future increase in trade union membership, especially now that women constitute half of the workforce and men show little sign of sharing domestic work equitably.

Chapter 7

The impact of the trade union recognition procedure under the Employment Relations Act, 2000–2

Stephen Wood, Sian Moore and Keith Ewing

Recognition of trade unions by employers is vital for union membership in decentralized industrial relations systems such as in the UK. The introduction of the statutory recognition procedure in the Employment Relations Act 1999 (ERA) both provides trade unions with a legal route for achieving recognition and transforms any negotiations about recognition that they may have with employers, since both sides know that the union can resort to the legal machinery. It is thus possible that a statutory procedure can stimulate recognition agreements if employers become more willing to sign agreements, knowing the alternative is union recognition imposed by the state. While it was not an explicit objective of the Labour Government to promote recognition, as it was keen to appear not to be prejudging the value of trade unions, it was concerned to design a procedure that would encourage the voluntary settlement of disputes over recognition without recourse to the legal procedure. Any evaluation of the ERA procedure must examine whether the procedure is working in this way. This chapter thus analyses how the recognition procedure has operated in its first two years in order to assess whether it can provide a right to union recognition that facilitates voluntary recognition with the result that the statutory procedure is de facto used as a last resort.

The analysis is based on data from four sources. First, we conducted a survey of 400 private sector employers in July 2000, to coincide with the introduction of the ERA. It concentrated on the employers' experience of union activity. Second, we drew on semi-structured interviews with the general secretary or a senior national officer responsible for recognition in seventeen TUC-affiliated trade unions, which were conducted between February and August 2000. These centred on trade union strategies in relation to recognition and recruitment. Third, we carried out a postal survey of all unions and staff associations listed in the Annual Report of the Certification Officer 1999–2000. This was undertaken in December 2000, just after the procedure had been introduced, and was also concerned with the approach of the unions to recognition and the statutory procedure. Fourth, we analysed information on the cases that have gone through the ERA procedure. This has been gained from a variety of sources, including documents made publicly available on the web site of the Central Arbitration Committee (CAC), the body responsible for administering the procedure, observations of CAC hearings, interviews with CAC officers about details of the ERA procedure, and interviews with trade union officials involved in cases. The chapter opens with the background to the introduction of the statutory procedure, a description of it, and the extent of its use so far. The remainder of the chapter assesses the operation of the procedure by focusing on whether the procedure: (1) provides recognition where the majority of a workforce wants it; (2) proves to be workable, with reference in particular to possible employer resistance and judicial review of the CAC's use of its powers; and (3) has stimulated trade union recognition, and particularly voluntary recognition.

Origins and purpose of the statutory recognition procedure

The ERA procedure was introduced in the context of the long-term decline in union membership, collective bargaining coverage and new recognition agreements. The expectation amongst trade unionists was that a new statutory system, if based on learning from past failures, could help arrest this decline. The last procedure, under the Employment Protection Act 1975 (EPA), had been fraught with political and legal problems during the five years of its operation (1975–80) and its use was largely confined to the traditionally unionized industrial areas of the economy, though its occupational coverage extended to the growing white-collar workers in these sectors. However, its effect on union membership was not insubstantial (Wood, 2000: 134–6). The period 1975–80 was a relatively successful period for union recruitment. Membership increased by over 11 per cent, and by over 3 per cent in each of 1976 and 1977, making these the only two years in the century with such gains. While the statutory procedure alone cannot account for such trends, state support for trade unionism (which extended beyond this procedure to include legislation that facilitated closed shop agreements and that established the Advisory Conciliation and Arbitration Service (ACAS) – the body charged with operating the EPA procedure – having a duty to promote collective bargaining) did appear to be having a positive effect on recognition activity. This conjecture is further supported by the subsequent decline in both union membership and recognition after

1980 when the EPA procedure was repealed, though again the changing nature of state support for union recognition is only part of the story.

The number of new recognition agreements declined gradually throughout the 1980s and the first part of the 1990s. The scale of employer derecognition of trade unions was limited, with the newspaper publishing and the petroleum and chemical sectors being particularly affected (Claydon, 1996: 161). However, largely because of the failure of unions to recruit in new workplaces between 1980 and 1998 (see Chapter 2), the proportion of private sector establishments with over 24 employees that had a recognized union had fallen from one-half to one-quarter, whilst total union membership dropped by a quarter between 1970 and 1990. The decline in the public sector was confined to the 1990s and was not so sharp, as trade union density fell from 99 per cent in 1984 to 87 per cent in 1998 (Millward *et al.*, 2000: 96).

As the programme of Conservative labour legislation and the decline in union recognition were gaining momentum in the mid-1980s, trade unions began to campaign for a new statutory recognition procedure. Unions such as the National Union of Journalist (NUJ) and Graphical, Paper and Media Union (GPMU), which had been affected most by derecognition, were particularly prominent in this campaign. The TUC (1995) outlined the basis for a statutory scheme in its *Your Voice at Work*, published in 1995. The major employers' bodies (e.g. the Confederation of British Industry, the Institute of Directors, and the then Institute of Personnel and Development) expressed a principled opposition to any statutory scheme. The Labour Government nonetheless produced a White Paper, 'Fairness at Work' (Department of Trade and Industry 1999b), which outlined a statutory recognition procedure that mirrored the TUC's proposals in many respects though it omitted a number of key aspects.

In 'Fairness at Work', the Labour Government presented three main objectives that it was aiming to achieve (DTI, 1999b: 23–5):

1 'to provide for representation and recognition where a majority of the relevant workforce wants it';
2 to introduce 'a procedure that will work';
3 to 'encourage the parties to reach voluntary agreements wherever possible'.

By 'a procedure that will work', the government appeared to mean one that would be acceptable to both sides of industry and could be operated in a way that is likely to withstand (a) employer tactics calculated to undermine trade union support, and (b) any judicial review of the agency charged with the responsibility of administering it.

The Prime Minister made it clear in his foreword to 'Fairness at Work' that the recognition procedure was to be part of a lasting industrial relations settlement that he wanted to achieve in his first term of office – a settlement that was designed to maintain and extend peaceful employment relations. The White Paper stressed that the parties should find voluntary solutions to their problems over representation, and that the statutory recognition procedure should only be used as a last resort where reaching an agreement outside of the statutory procedure 'proves impossible'. Even once inside the procedure, there are opportunities for the parties to decide their own arrangements. The Labour Government's emphasis on choice in industrial relations means that the ERA is not aimed at promoting collective bargaining per se – as the EPA was – but rather, that it is concerned to support its development where this is what the majority of workers want. The underlying rationale is that 'each business should choose the form of relationship that suits it best', but that this should be tempered by an extension of this freedom to employees to choose union representation.

The statutory recognition procedure

The CAC is responsible for handling recognition claims. This allows ACAS to continue its normal conciliation work in the area of union recognition without its being directly involved in the statutory procedure (as occurred under the EPA in the 1970s). To trigger the new procedure, a trade union must formally approach the employer for recognition; if the employer rejects the request or fails to respond, the union may refer the case to the CAC. For such an application to be valid the application must be made in writing, the union must be independent, and the employer must employ at least 21 workers. The design of the ERA procedure reflects the lessons that had been learnt from the EPA procedure (Ewing, 1990; Wood, 2000). The latter system gave wide discretion to ACAS to decide the criteria for the acceptance of applications, to resolve disputes about bargaining units, and the circumstances in which a union should be recognized. However, it failed to impose either a duty on employers to cooperate with ACAS in the conduct of its inquiries, or strong sanctions on employers who refused to bargain with a union once ACAS had recommended recognition rights for the union. The procedure was, on the admission of the Chairman of ACAS, rendered unworkable by employer resistance (most notoriously at Grunwick Processing Laboratories) and the decisions of the courts that challenged ACAS on a number of key points – in the process demonstrating the judges' suspicion of the procedure (Simpson, 1979: 82).

Under the ERA procedure, the criteria for the acceptance of applications are much tighter. An application can be accepted only if at least 10 per cent of the workers in the proposed bargaining unit are union members, if there is not already a collective bargaining agreement covering some or all workers in the proposed bargaining unit, and if the CAC is satisfied that a majority of the workers in the bargaining unit are likely to be in favour of recognition. The requirement to demonstrate baseline support before a claim can proceed was designed to deter insubstantial claims (DTI, 1999b: 24). Once the application has been accepted, there is a twenty-day period for the employer and union to agree the bargaining unit. If the parties are unable to reach an agreement the bargaining unit will be determined by the CAC, with the main consideration being the need for the unit to be compatible with effective management. Other factors that the CAC has to consider include the views of the employer and union, existing national and local bargaining arrangements, the desirability of avoiding small fragmented bargaining units, and the characteristics and location of workers. If the unit decided by the CAC or agreed by the parties differs from that proposed by the union, the application must be reconsidered against the acceptance criteria.

Where a majority of the bargaining unit are not union members, the CAC will then order a ballot. If the union has a majority of the bargaining unit in membership, the CAC may grant recognition without a ballot. The CAC may, however, still order a ballot when it:

1   deems that it is 'in the interests of good industrial relations' (Trade Union and Labour Relations (Consolidation) Act, 1992 (TULR(C)A), Schedule, A1, para. 22(4) (a)) to hold a ballot;
2   is informed by a significant number of union members that they do not wish the union to represent them for collective bargaining; or
3   has evidence that leads it to doubt that a significant number of union members want the union to bargain on their behalf.

Where a ballot is ordered, the union is entitled to have access to the workforce and there are legal duties on the employer to cooperate in the conduct of the ballot. The union must secure a majority in favour of recognition, but also the support of at least 40 per cent of the workers in the bargaining unit. If recognition is granted, the parties are expected to reach agreement on a method for conducting collective bargaining. If the parties are unable to reach an agreement, the CAC may assist and ultimately determine a legally enforceable bargaining procedure that is limited to pay, hours and holidays. Adherence to this imposed procedure is enforced by an order of specific performance, in which non-compliance means contempt of court with the possibility of unlimited fines and imprisonment.

The number of applications to the CAC made within the first two years of the procedure was small, and Figure 7.1 shows the progression of these cases. Of the 158 distinct applications, 132 cases were decided or withdrawn in the first two years; of these 40 resulted in statutory recognition, and in a further 45 cases the application was withdrawn at some stage because the employer and the union had reached a voluntary agreement or desired to enter into voluntary discussion. Thus 64 per cent of the completed cases passing through the CAC procedure resulted in recognition or discussions on recognition. Of the 36 ballots completed by the CAC within its first two years, unions won 24 (67 per cent) and the outcome of four others was unknown by the end of the period). The case study in Box 7.1 illustrates how the procedure worked in a typical case that went right through the procedure.

So far the size of the proposed bargaining units has tended to be small. Of the 129 cases where we have information, the median unit proposed had 91 workers, with 29 per cent having 50 or fewer workers, 26 per cent having between 51 and 100 workers, 24 per cent having between 101 and 250 workers, and only 21 per cent with over 250 workers. In addition, CAC applications have tended to be in a limited number of industrial sectors. A majority of both applications and successful cases have been in manufacturing or in areas where trade unions traditionally have had a strong presence, such as in transport, print and newspapers.

The provision of a right to be recognized

Our main concern in considering the operation of the procedure is to assess the extent to which the government's objectives are being realized. The achievement of the first objective – providing workers with a right to recognition where a majority of the relevant workforce want it – has from the outset been limited by aspects of legislative design that mean that certain workers cannot use the procedure even if there is majority support for a particular union. An application may be invalid because the employer employs twenty or fewer workers, or it may be inadmissible because the employer has already recognized a trade union, even though the union may be neither the union of the workers' choice nor independent. In the first two years, three cases were dismissed by the CAC as invalid: *GPMU and Keely Print Ltd*, TUR 1/98[2001], on the first ground, and *Prison*

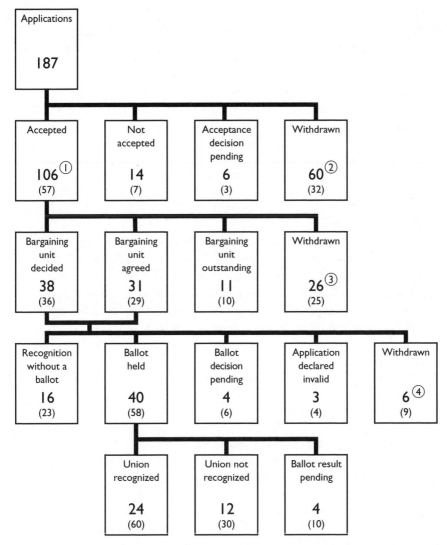

Figures in brackets are percentage of cases that reached the stage of the procedure represented by the row.

The applications declared invalid followed a change in the bargaining unit from the unit proposed by the trade union

1. The CAC determined at the admissibility stage that two applications were in associated companies and subsequently dealt with them as one application

2. 29 were withdrawn and resubmitted; 22 were withdrawn because the parties were discussing or had reached a voluntary agreement; 3 were withdrawn by the union and not resubmitted; we have no information on the remaining 6

3. From our research we know that 21 applications were withdrawn at this stage as the parties were discussing or had reached a voluntary agreement, in 3 cases no agreement had been reached, and in 1 case the company closed. We have no information on the remaining cases

4. 3 were withdrawn because the parties were discussing or had reached a voluntary agreement; in the other 3 cases no agreement had been reached

Figure 7.1 Progress chart of applications to the CAC for recognition: June 2000–May 2002

Box 7.1 *Recognition for the Transport and General Workers Union at The Snack Factory*

Background

The Snack Factory opened at Skelmersdale in 1989. It produces crisps and other snacks and is owned by Longulf Limited, a Saudi Arabian company. The TGWU has had members at the company since 1989 and a campaign for recognition was launched in November 2000. The workers in the union's proposed bargaining unit were unskilled process operatives, around 60 per cent of whom were women.

The application

The employer did not respond to the initial approach by the TGWU for recognition in November 2000. A formal letter under Schedule A1 of the recognition procedure was sent on 10 July 2001. The employer subsequently met with the union and stated that it did not believe that there was support for recognition amongst the workforce. The T&G suggested that ACAS become involved but the company declined. The union then referred the application to the CAC on 25 September 2001 claiming that it should be recognized for collective bargaining for all hourly-paid production and ancillary operatives.

The admissibility check

The CAC was satisfied that the application was valid and then had to determine whether it was admissable. In its application the union stated that over a twelve-month period it had 149 members out of a proposed bargaining unit of 274 workers. The employer questioned this, saying that during this period 40 workers had left the business and the union had not adjusted its membership figures.

The CAC undertook a membership check. The employer provided a list of workers in the proposed bargaining unit and the union a list of union members, both supplying these on the basis that they would be treated in confidence and not passed to the other party. Union members constituted 36.9 per cent of the bargaining unit (97 members out of the 263 workers listed by the employer). Thus the CAC was satisfied that at least 10 per cent of the proposed bargaining unit were members of the union

The employer stated that there was no support for trade union recognition and that the existing Joint Consultative Committee was functioning well. The union's application mentioned that an internal survey conducted by the employer had confirmed that the majority (88 per cent) of hourly-paid employees in the proposed bargaining unit would support the claim for recognition and negotiating rights in a ballot. Since the employer produced no contrary evidence, the CAC placed great weight on the internal survey, and concluded that there was no evidence that those who had joined the union had done so for reasons that would not point to support for recognition. The CAC was thus satisfied that the majority of workers constituting the relevant bargaining unit were likely to favour recognition for collective bargaining and, satisfied that there was no existing collective bargaining agreement covering these workers, accepted the application.

Bargaining unit

However, the parties did not agree on the bargaining unit. The union's proposed bargaining unit consisted of all hourly-paid staff (a slightly different description to that originally given), numbering approximately 263. The company argued that the bargaining unit proposed by the union was inappropriate and would hamper effective management. It proposed a bargaining unit covering all employees in the business (around 340 people) except directors.

A hearing was held in November 2001. The employer argued that anything other than the whole company would be divisive and would hamper flexibility between the hourly-paid and salaried groups of workers, particularly as management had been working towards an integrated system of employee involvement through a participative management structure. The Consultative Committee set up in July 2000 was based on the idea of the company as a team, and it was proposed that this Committee would deal with negotiating issues. The employer also feared that adopting the union-proposed bargaining unit would mean that the remaining employees (e.g. engineers) would be free to submit applications for separate recognition agreements, perhaps involving other unions, and that this would lead to fragmented bargaining with small units to the detriment of effective management, and would further undermine team working and the achievement of the company's philosophy and vision.

The union argued that the company did make distinctions between the workers in its proposed bargaining unit and its other employees, for example in pensions, sick pay and holidays. The hourly-paid workers had approached the union for an independent collective voice, but salaried staff had not. It also pointed out that the company's Consultative Committee was not a negotiating body.

The CAC agreed that the union's proposed bargaining unit was based on the reality of existing management organization and practice at The Snack Factory, and was therefore compatible with effective management. The company had always treated all groups of employees differently and the union's proposed bargaining unit was based on a clearly identifiable and distinct group of employees. It covered the vast majority of workers and was not in itself a small fragmented unit. Collective bargaining on pay, hours and holidays for all hourly-paid workers would not of itself prevent the transfer and flexibility of employees. Further, even if those employees currently outside the union-proposed bargaining unit chose to be represented by a union, there would be no need for this necessarily to lead to the entry of other unions or to fragmented bargaining.

Ballot

The CAC, having found that the union had less than 50 per cent membership in the bargaining unit, decided to arrange a secret ballot in which the workers in the bargaining unit would be asked whether they wanted the union to conduct collective bargaining on their behalf. The CAC asked for the views of the parties on the form of the ballot; the employer's preference was for a postal ballot and the union for a workplace ballot. The CAC judged that in the interests of good industrial relations a postal ballot would be the most appropriate. A formal Access Agreement was agreed between the union and employer. Under the terms of this the union held two workplace meetings for employees, one for the night shift and one for the day shift, each lasting 30 minutes. In addition individual employees were entitled to consult on matters relating to the ballot for up to 15 minutes with nominated workplace union representatives. Ballot papers were issued at the end of January.

The ballot result, reported to the CAC in mid-February, was that 205 out of 263 eligible employees voted, 1 paper was spoilt, and 183 – representing 89.7 per cent of the valid vote and 69.6 per cent of the bargaining unit – had supported union recognition. The CAC thus declared that the union be recognized by the company as entitled to conduct collective bargaining on behalf of all hourly-paid production and ancillary operatives employed by it. A method of bargaining was agreed between the parties on 6 August 2002, but this was limited to pay, hours and holidays.

Officers' Association and Securicor Custodial Services Ltd, TUR 1/5[2000], and *ISTC and Bausch & Lomb Ltd*, TUR 1/8[2000], on the second. Two applications (*TGWU and Kwik-Fit, Edinburgh*), TUR 1/179[2002], and *AMICUS* and *Kwik-Fit GB*, TUR1/181[2002], were not accepted because the proposed bargaining units overlapped and both unions had at least 10 per cent membership. However, within these boundaries the CAC may further limit the extent to which the procedure can provide representation through the way it exercises its discretionary powers when making the three key decisions:

1   whether a majority of the proposed bargaining unit would be likely to favour recognition;
2   whether the bargaining unit proposed by the union meets a number of statutory criteria, the overriding one being compatibility with effective management;
3   whether to order a ballot when the union has majority membership, on one of the three permitted grounds.

Admissibility

The test of 10 per cent membership has not presented any great difficulties for the CAC in the cases dealt with in the first two years. Decisions on whether a majority of the workers are likely to support recognition have been made on the basis of the level of membership, letters or petitions by the workers in question, or a recent ballot of the workforce. In some cases a union will claim that a majority are likely to support recognition on the basis of membership alone, even though it has less than half the workforce in membership. The CAC has not adopted a rigid rule for deciding on whether support for collective bargaining is likely, such as a given level of current membership. An application where membership was as low as 16 per cent has been accepted while one with 66 per cent has been rejected, the latter on the grounds that although ten of a bargaining unit of fifteen were union members, seven had written to the CAC opposing recognition for collective bargaining. No case thus far has been accepted with a membership of lower than 35 per cent without there being other evidence about the support for collective bargaining. The CAC has allowed for the difficulty the union has had in gaining access to the workforce when interpreting this other evidence. Consequently, even though the petitions have recorded lower than 50 per cent support, the CAC has accepted some cases: for example, at GE Caledonian it concluded that the 43.8 per cent support

Table 7.1 Cases where the CAC has determined the bargaining unit

Employer response to the union's proposed bargaining unit	CAC decision			
	Supported union's proposal	Variation of union's proposal	Employer supported	Distinctive bargaining unit
Employer argued to include additional occupational group(s)	18	2	3	2
Multi-site employer argued to include more sites	3		5	
Multi-site employer argued to included less sites	1			
Other (employer did not submit evidence)	1			
Total (%)	23 (65)	2 (6)	8 (23)	2 (6)

of the workforce was affected by anti-union conduct that had been carried to 'extreme lengths' (*AEEU and GE Caledonian Ltd,* TUR1/120/[2001]).

The bargaining unit

In 35 (51 per cent) of the cases that reached the bargaining unit stage the CAC needed to determine the appropriateness of a bargaining unit, as there was no agreement between the parties on what it should be. Table 7.1 shows that the CAC supported the union's proposed unit or a variant of it in 25 (71 per cent) of these. In all but 2 of the 35 cases (94 per cent) where the employer attempted to challenge the union's application, it proposed an expanded bargaining unit based on including either more occupations or sites than were in the original application. This may have the effect of diluting union strength by including groups of workers among whom there is little evidence of support for the union. Nonetheless, in all but three of the 25 cases where the employer sought to include more occupations, the CAC resisted this argument on the basis that the terms and conditions of the occupational group proposed were distinctive. In one of the three exceptions, the application by the NUJ at the *Staffordshire Sentinel*, the CAC ordered that the bargaining unit include both journalists and editorial staff, even though the NUJ does not (and has no power under its rules) to recruit the latter.

The trade unions have had more difficulties where the employer has sought to extend the bargaining unit to include all sites in the company, as in five of eight cases the CAC ruled that the bargaining unit should embrace workers sharing the same distinct terms and conditions on all sites in the organization. In four of the five cases, the union could not subsequently demonstrate sufficient support for recognition amongst the workers on the other sites that the CAC included in the revised bargaining unit (the fifth had not been revalidated by the end of the period studied). In these cases the application was either ruled by the CAC as no longer valid (*ISTC and Hygena*, TUR1/33[2001]), or the union withdrew the case (*GPMU and Getty Images*, TUR1/104[2001] and *TGWU and Maxims Casino*, TUR1/105[2001]), or a majority did not vote for recognition (*BFAWU and Seabrook Potato Crisps*, TUR1/54[2001]). In the one case, where the union supported a company-wide bargaining unit but the company argued for less sites to be included (*BALPA and Ryanair*, TUR1/70[2001]), the CAC ruled in favour of the union.

CAC-ordered ballots

The Committee ordered a ballot in 9 of the 27 cases where it was demonstrated that the union, on application, had majority membership. All three criteria have been invoked. In addition, the CAC has ordered ballots when there has been an apparent decline in the number of union members from the time when the application was made to a level of below 50 per cent. In two other cases, the union submitted that it did not want to claim recognition without a ballot.

The first criterion ('in the interests of good industrial relations') was invoked in two cases; in *GPMU and Red Letter Bradford Ltd*, TUR 1/12[2000], where relations between the union and the employer had been poor, a ballot was justified as an opportunity to 'clear the air'; whereas in *ISTC and Fullarton Computer Industries Ltd*, TUR1/29[2000], recognition was ordered on a membership of 51.3 per cent because a ballot would 'engender further antagonism and divisiveness detrimental to developing good industrial relations'. The second criterion (that a significant number of union members inform the CAC that they do not want the union to represent them in collective bargaining) was invoked in *UNIFI and Turkiye Is Bankasi AS*, TUR1/90[2001], when three members of the union wrote to the CAC stating they did not want the union to conduct collective bargaining on their behalf. The union submitted that these employees had done this under pressure from the employer; nonetheless the CAC considered that a ballot was necessary. Only 35 per cent voted in favour of recognition, despite a union membership level of 83 per cent at the time of the application. The third criterion was invoked in two cases. In *AEEU and*

Huntleigh Healthcare, TUR1/19/[2001] and *TGWU and Economic Skips*, TUR1/121/[2001], the CAC considered that membership evidence raised doubts as to whether a significant number of workers in the bargaining unit wanted recognition. In *Huntleigh Healthcare*, the CAC determined there should be a ballot because union membership had been granted on the basis of free membership.

In the remaining four cases, the CAC ordered a ballot when it judged that, at the point when the decision to ballot was made, the union no longer had majority membership. The reasoning is that the requirement for the CAC to be satisfied that a majority of the workers in the bargaining unit are members of the union (paragraph 22(1)(b) of the Schedule) is worded in the present tense. Thus for the CAC what matters is whether the union has a majority in membership at the time it takes the decision on whether to hold a ballot or grant recognition without a ballot. This is an area for concern, since majority membership can be fragile. Union membership in CAC cases is vulnerable to labour turnover, redundancies (a reality for a number of CAC cases), recruitment into the bargaining unit (possibly as an employer tactic), and employer pressure and intimidation.

A workable statutory recognition procedure

Employer conduct during the procedure

The procedure has scope for employers to influence the outcome of the process, first by allowing them to give evidence to the CAC on their view of the union's proposed bargaining unit and their perception of the likely support for trade unionism. However, the procedure also places few constraints on employers putting their case against the union to the workforce in order to influence the outcome. If the procedure is to test for majority support for the applicant union, the environment in which this is conducted must permit a true and fair measure of that support. There is a thin dividing line between employers putting their case to the CAC or the workforce and affecting the result by unfair practices. In a number of cases, it appears that the employer has genuinely wanted to test majority support for recognition and not to interfere with the process. In one CAC case that we observed, the employer did behave in a neutral manner during the ballot; the management simply responded to the claim by answering any questions posed by the CAC, while clarifying at the outset that it would accept the outcome of the ballot. In contrast, from CAC reports, our observations of CAC hearings, and interviews with union officials who have submitted an application to the CAC, there are a variety of ways in which employers have sought to discourage or defeat an application.

In some cases, employers have sought to gain the names of the union members and supporters, the implication being that they would act in some way on this information. The CAC has resisted this and developed a means of conducting a check on the membership by obtaining union membership names from the union and the names of workers in the proposed bargaining unit from the employer (Central Arbitration Committee, 2002: 11). In other cases employers have sought to control the CAC's use of its discretion so the procedure operates to their advantage. A good example of this is the practice of employers seeking to dilute the formal support for the union by expanding the bargaining unit into areas where union support is likely to be lower. As we have shown, the CAC has not always supported the union in such matters. In addition, there are still opportunities for the employer to manipulate the membership of the bargaining unit after its formal determination, and in at least one case unions have reported that employers have redefined the contractual status of employees in order to include them in the employees balloted. When ordering a ballot even though 50 per cent of the workforce is in membership, the CAC also appears to have been influenced by the employer's arguments. In *TGWU and Economic Skips Ltd*, TUR 1/121[2001], one of the reasons for ordering a ballot was 'the sincerely held view of the employer that the majority of the workers in the bargaining unit did not want recognition'.

We have also observed tactics in the process that display a strategy of opposition to the spirit of the process. Two stand out:

1   legalism, whereby the employer – with legal assistance – identifies and exploits technical legal points as a strategy of opposition;
2   litigation, whereby the employer challenges the CAC at every step, including admissibility, the bargaining unit, the need for a ballot and the form of the ballot.

The minimum effect of these approaches is to lengthen the case and to add to the costs for the union. The maximum effect is that the union is defeated on some technicality, as in *GPMU and Keeley Print*, TUR1/98-[2001], where it was ruled as a matter of law that a director is not a worker, with the result that the employer did not have 21 workers. The CAC is relatively powerless to do anything about such tactics: there is little that it can do but deal with the points raised if employers (or unions) who have chosen to be represented by counsel raise technical arguments about the meaning of a 'worker' or of a 'trade union member', or of an 'associated employer'. This is so even when these points may result in the termination of an application that, if tested, would have the support of the majority of the workforce.

Finally, the employer may threaten and intimidate workers so that any commitment to supporting the union dissipates. In one-third (12 of 36) of ballots union support has been lower than union membership was at the outset, and in some of these cases this may be explained by employer behaviour after the application was made or in the ballot period. Again, the CAC's powers are limited. It is true that employers must permit the trade union to have access to the workforce during the ballot period, and that employers are generally obliged to cooperate during the ballot process; and both access and employer conduct are governed by a Code of Practice that sets out minimum access conditions and advises the parties of the kind of behaviour that is not acceptable. Yet there is little regulation of employer behaviour before the ballot period, and intimidatory or disruptive behaviour during the ballot is difficult to prevent. Admittedly the CAC can impose recognition where the employer has failed to comply with the duty to cooperate during the ballot, without the need for a ballot to be held, but no such order has either been granted or contemplated. In two cases where the ballot was lost, an oppositional employer was able to limit the access granted to the union during the balloting period; other cases may also exist.

The courts and the statutory procedure

Employers may take their litigation strategy to the point where they challenge the CAC's decision in the courts. The steps that have been taken in the legislation to define and circumscribe the discretion of the CAC and to protect its autonomy do not guarantee immunity from judicial review. It is also the case that the introduction of the statutory recognition procedure coincided with the implementation of the Human Rights Act 1998, which gave the courts new powers to ensure that public authorities (including the CAC) respect the substantive and procedural human rights of the parties appearing before them. Four applications for judicial review were made in the first two years of the procedure; of these, employers made three and a trade union the other one (CAC, 2002: 18). Two cases were refused leave to be heard, and two were heard. It is nevertheless the case that the courts have approached the new procedure very differently from the way they approached the earlier procedure in the 1970s, where they appeared unsympathetic to the legislation. In *R (Kwik-Fit (GB) Ltd) v. CAC* [2002] Industrial Relations Law Reports (IRLR) 395, the Court of Appeal endorsed in 'strong terms' the view that 'the CAC was intended by Parliament to be a decision-making body in a specialist area, that is not suitable for the intervention of the courts' (p. 396). This is a sign that the courts may be willing to allow the procedure to work as intended and, crucially, to do so in a way that will enable workers to secure trade union recognition where this is in accordance with the wishes of the majority.

The two cases that have been heard have both supported the way that the CAC has been operating. The first, *Fullerton Computer Industries Ltd v. CAC*, [2001] IRLR 752, dealt with several concerns, including the refusal of the CAC to order a ballot where the union had only a slender majority of the bargaining unit (51.3 per cent) in membership – this being done on the grounds that a ballot 'would engender further antagonism and divisiveness detrimental to developing good industrial relations' (TUR1/29[2000]). The employer's challenge to this decision was unsuccessful, despite the fact that the court 'would have been inclined to take the view that a ballot has a stabilizing influence and might well improve industrial relations rather than to cause them to deteriorate' (p. 745) and that 'the reasoning' of the CAC 'might be said to be less adequate than might otherwise have been desired' (ibid.). Moreover, the court also disputed the decision of the CAC that a narrow majority was not an adequate reason for holding a ballot as, in the view of the CAC, this would raise the statutory threshold for automatic recognition. Nevertheless, the court was not inclined to challenge the decision of the CAC.

The other case involved the CAC's determination of a bargaining unit. In this case, *Kwik-Fit* challenged the CAC's rejection of its proposal for a single unit covering the whole country in favour of the union's proposal for a unit defined as being within the boundary of the London orbital road (the M25). In reaching this decision the CAC drew attention to the fact that, under the legislation, it is 'not required to decide on the most effective form of management, merely that what we decide is compatible with effectiveness' (TUR 1/126[2002]). This latter approach was endorsed by the Court of Appeal, which pointed out that in determining the bargaining unit 'the statutory test is set at the comparatively modest level of appropriateness, rather than the optimum or best possible outcome' (*R(Kwik-Fit (GB) Ltd v. CAC*, p. 396). However, the appeal judgment stressed that this does not mean the CAC can confine itself to the union's arguments. Its statutory requirement involves considering the views of the employer and thus, it concluded, the CAC has to consider alternative bargaining units to the extent that these are a part of the employer's argument in order to assess whether the union's proposed bargaining unit meets the statutory criteria. But once the CAC decides that the union's proposed unit is appropriate, 'its inquiry should stop there'.

These judicial review decisions are important, though they would not have undermined the procedure fatally had they gone the other way. If the employers had succeeded in the *Fullarton* case on the ballot point, the CAC would have been more likely to have ordered a ballot in cases where the union had only a slender majority in membership of the bargaining unit. The remarks of the judge in that case may in any event be enough to induce caution in future cases. If the employers had succeeded in the *Kwik-Fit* case, it would mean that the discretion of the CAC in bargaining unit disputes would have been significantly constrained and that the employer's voice in these cases would have been enhanced. This would have been particularly important in the case of multi-site employers, where the evidence suggests that, in most of the cases where the bargaining unit is disputed, the CAC has tended to prefer a larger multi-site unit rather than a single-site unit. The effect of *Kwik-Fit* is to remove doubt about the nature of the CAC's discretion, and may mean that it makes different decisions in the future in multi-site companies.

The effect of the statutory procedure on voluntary action

If the legislation were achieving its overt goal of encouraging the voluntary settlement of recognition disputes, we would expect that achieving recognition has become more significant for trade unions and that this is matched by their investing more resources into organizing and recruitment. We should also expect a significant change in the trend of voluntary agreements across the economy and that the majority of recognition disputes would be settled outside the procedure. If it were working perfectly, there would be no CAC cases. It is too early to test conclusively whether these expectations have been fulfilled, and any analysis is constrained by the limited data on recognition cases before the Act came into force. We will nonetheless examine the available data to provide an assessment of this aspect of the ERA procedure so far.

The statutory recognition procedure as a stimulant of activity

The union survey, referred to in the introduction, revealed that, in the three years between 1997 and 2000, unions have placed more emphasis on securing recognition. Discounting those for whom recognition is not significant (40 per cent of the sample), 61 per cent of unions claimed that by 2000 achieving new recognition agreements was more significant than it was in 1997. Two-thirds of these unions reported an increase in the number of recognition cases pursued between 1997 and 2000, and well over half reported greater success in securing voluntary recognition during this period. Nearly two-thirds of those recording greater success attributed it to the legislation, although two public sector unions said the change was linked more directly to the contracting-out of work and the transfer of undertakings law connected with this. Others put it down to union strategy and, specifically, the increased emphasis placed on recruitment and organizing in the light of the TUC's instigation of an Organizing Academy. Nonetheless, data from our interviews with union officials in 2002 concerning CAC cases have confirmed that the existence of the ERA procedure has increased their confidence of the union realizing a return on any enhanced investment that they may make in recruitment campaigns. As one union official put it, when discussing recruitment: 'The procedure has made all the difference. It has provided people with a reason to build membership, and the individual right to representation [also in the ERA – *authors' addition*] has given the union a way of being visible – the ERA is important as an organizing tool'. Consistent with this, the employer survey revealed an increase in union campaigns with the advent of the ERA procedure. Between 1995 and 2000, 12 per cent of workplaces were subject to a campaign – 41 per cent of which were in the first half of 2000, with 17 per cent in 1999.

The union survey confirmed that unions were not expecting to gain recognition ahead of recruiting members, so that a 'strategy of organizing the employer', as one General Secretary called it, was being pursued seriously by only one union, and this was not at the expense of its own organizing approach. It also revealed that unions for whom recognition is important were significantly more likely to be adopting a systematic approach to recruitment and organization. More specifically, they were more likely to target particular workplaces for both recruitment and recognition, to employ organizers or recruitment officers whose job is solely to recruit and organize, and to sponsor organizers from the TUC's Academy (Wood *et al.*, 2002: 224–7). These unions were significantly more likely to have a formal approach to the CAC procedure and to have an internal monitoring procedure to control the submission of CAC cases. The approach of not relying on employers is consistent with the results of the survey of employers, which revealed that the initiation of recognition discussion by employers is rare. Employers had initiated a minority of the discussions that led to new recognition agreements, which we observed between 1996 and 2000 or were live at the time of the survey, and these were largely in response to a union campaign or in anticipation of one. In some cases the employer had approached an alternative union to the one either pursuing recognition or thought by management to be contemplating a claim.

The statutory recognition procedure as a stimulant of agreements

The TUC has been monitoring recognition agreements since 1995 (TUC, 2002a). This is based on a survey of 75 per cent of the unions affiliated to the TUC, and thus is likely to underestimate activity, though recognition may not be important for those not included. The survey population is consistent over time, though there is no information on non-respondents to the individual surveys. The data are unfortunately collected in varying time periods. Table 7.2 reports the recorded voluntary recognition agreements from 1995–2001, and it can be seen that in the period November 2000–October 2001 the level of recognition agreements increased substantially from the levels for most of the second half of the 1990s. While it appears that the level was never above 100 per year in the latter period, post-the-ERA it was at 449 in the year November 2000–October 2001. It is difficult to gauge the precise effect of the ERA, since the reporting period immediately prior to its implementation extends from November 1999 to October 2000. It certainly cannot be assumed that all the additional cases beyond the norm for the 1990s (of below 100) were accounted for by cases that occurred after June 2000. It is noticeable that the increase in agreements began before the ERA, indicating that there was some shadow

Table 7.2 Voluntary recognitions: 1995-2001

Period	Number of new agreements
July 1995–December 1995	54
January 1996–June 1996	54
July 1996–December 1996	56
January 1997–June 1997	26
July 1997–February 1998	55
March 1998–November 1998	34
December 1998–October 1999	75
November 1999–October 2000	159
November 2000–October 2001	443 (plus 19 statutory and 25 semi-statutory through the CAC)

(Source: TUC Trends Surveys: TUC, 2002)

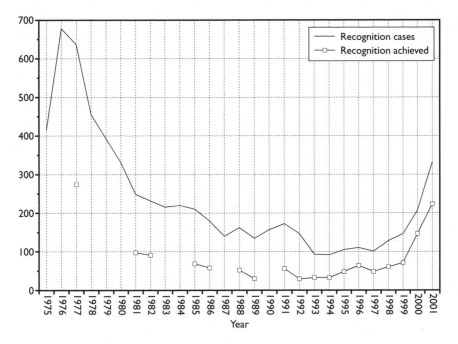

Figure 7.2 Completed recognition cases, 1975–2001

(Source: ACAS annual reports)

effect of the ERA prior to its implementation. Nonetheless, the main effect is post-the-ERA. However, even here there may be some pre-ERA shadow, as the initial discussions over recognition could well have begun before its implementation.

The second data source is the ACAS conciliation cases involving recognition disputes. Figure 7.2 records the ACAS conciliation activity in this area since its inception. It shows a gradual decline in cases from a peak of 697 to a low of 93 in 1994. There was a gradual increase from then on, with a substantial increase in 2000, taking the figure beyond 200 for the first time since 1985, followed by an even greater increase in 2001, when 339 cases were recorded. Moreover, the proportion of ACAS cases where recognition for collective bargaining was achieved has increased substantially since the early 1990s. From a low of 21 per cent in 1992 (when ACAS handled 148 cases the proportion was around 50 per cent each year between 1996 and 1999), in 2000 it was 70 per cent and, in 2001 it was 66 per cent of ACAS's conciliation cases that involved recognition.

The analysis of the TUC and ACAS data thus suggests that the ERA procedure did initially stimulate recognition on a voluntary basis, while the ACAS data suggest that it increased the chances of the unions achiev-ing recognition when recognition is in dispute, at least when they or the employer have involved ACAS. It does not of course follow that this initial effect will be maintained.

The statutory recognition procedure as a last resort

It is difficult to establish the proportion of recognition disputes that are settled outside the statutory procedure relative to those within. There is the initial problem of identifying the commencement of a recognition dispute. It could be when either a union or an employer makes a formal approach to the other party for recognition, or when a union campaign begins or an employee makes an approach to a union. Regardless of how defined, there is the problem that there is no available data set of such disputes. In the absence of this, we (1) compare the number of fresh voluntary recognition agreements that are determined by the CAC relative to the number of those settled voluntarily, using the TUC data; and (2) examine the disputes whose resolution involves state machinery, and thus compare the use of the CAC procedure with the use of ACAS conciliation.

Unfortunately the TUC's post-ERA data cover only the period November 2000 to October 2001. During this period, the TUC recorded 449 full and partial voluntary recognitions (of which 6 were semi-statutory, having initially been in the CAC procedure), while in the same period there were 90 distinct CAC applications by TUC-affiliated unions (and 6 by non-TUC unions) and the CAC awarded recognition in 17 cases (with around 24 cases withdrawn with a view to discussions on recognition). CAC cases thus represented 8.5 per cent of all new recognitions achieved by the unions reported to the TUC during that period.

The comparison of the use of the CAC procedure with that of the ACAS facilities reveals a similar picture. During the period June 2000 to December 2001 the CAC received 126 applications, which compares with 608 requests for conciliation over recognitions that the ACAS handled. However, there is likely to be some overlap between the two groups as ACAS may have been involved in some CAC cases before they entered the procedure (though this may have been before the period that our data cover) or even during it (as we observed happening in some cases, e.g. *Benteler Automotive*). Nonetheless, we can conclude that CAC cases represent no more that 21 per cent of all recognition disputes that involve a government agency.

In terms of the numbers of workers affected by the procedure relative to voluntary cases, again the impact of the CAC procedure has been limited:

10,567 workers are covered by the recognition orders that were made in the first two years of the scheme's operation. Of these, almost 4,000 are accounted for by the AEEU's successful recognition ballot at Honda (*AEEU and Honda*, TUR1/129[2001]). In addition we estimate that just over 8,000 workers are covered by agreements reached in the semi-statutory cases that were withdrawn from the CAC as the parties had reached or were discussing an agreement.

To put these figures in perspective, we estimate that the number of workers covered by recognitions with TUC-affiliated unions resulting from CAC cases (including semi-statutory agreements) represent 7.1 per cent of those covered by new recognitions (voluntary ones recorded by the TUC or through the CAC) during the period November 2000 to October 2001, the period covered by the TUC figures on voluntary recognition. Nonetheless, the increase in the number of recognitions is not insignificant relative to the number of 'ready-made' CAC cases when the ERA was implemented. On the basis of our employer survey in private sector workplaces with 50 or more employees, we estimated that while there was scope for recognition in 89 per cent of private sector workplaces (with 50 or more employees), i.e. 32,464 workplaces, in only 6 per cent (2,284) was there over 10 per cent union membership with no recognition and 0.5 per cent of workplaces (183) with more than 50 per cent membership (Wood *et al.*, 2002: 220).

Finally, the overall effect of the new recognitions is that the fall of membership (of 23,789) recorded by the TUC would, we estimate – on the assumption that 80 per cent of those in the new bargaining units had joined the union following recognition – have been nearly five times greater than it was. The fall (of 118,900) recorded by the Certification Officer for the same period (Certification Office for Trade Unions and Employers' Associations, 2002: 21) would likewise have been nearly double what it was. Put another way, the decline in membership of 0.35 per cent registered by the TUC would have been nearer to 1.65 per cent had the new recognitions not occurred, and that of 1.5 per cent recorded by the Certification Officer would have been 2.6 per cent.

Conclusions

The analysis of the first two years' operation of the CAC's procedure suggests that, within the terms of the government's initial objectives, it is working, albeit with some caveats. On the one hand, the procedure is providing a right for union recognition in the majority of cases where 50 per cent of the workforce wants it, and the CAC does not appear to be unduly constrained by the judicial review of its procedures and decisions. On the other hand, the experience of the first two years has highlighted problems with the procedure and its operation.

One problem relates to the CAC's approach to the bargaining unit, particularly in multi-site cases. Unless the CAC is consistently to take a different approach to the one adopted in the majority of such cases, the difficulties for unions in these cases could be insurmountable, with the result that the procedure will be confined in practice to small employers operating in a single location where bargaining units remain, as now, small. A second problem is that unions are vulnerable to a number of strategies adopted by employers that may defeat applications, and in these cases the CAC appears inadequately empowered to make an effective response. Employers are apparently free to recruit into a proposed bargaining unit before a ballot is held, with a view to diluting union strength, and unions have access to the workforce only during the balloting period. The employer has access to the workforce at all times, and there is little regulation, in practice, of hostile conduct (short of dismissal or discriminatory conduct directed at specific individuals) outside the balloting period. The failure rate in ballots of 33 per cent is likely to reflect such pressure and is significant, especially given that the cases have been through the admissibility tests.

In terms of the government's aim that the statutory procedure should encourage voluntary resolution of disputes and be used only as a last resort, the experience of the first two years suggests that there has been some success. From the outset, the unions, coordinated by the TUC, have been concerned to ensure that the CAC procedure was not discredited or made unworkable in its first years. Its ability to act as a device that influenced voluntary discussions clearly depends on its being perceived to be working. Ensuring that the voluntary route is pursued in the first instance is a vital part of this, the implication being that the unions will not submit CAC applications as a first move in a recognition campaign prior to their having secured a base of membership. Our survey of unions revealed that unions indeed only intended to use the procedure when they gauge that the employer is unwilling to discuss a voluntary agreement and are confident that they have sufficient support to win a ballot (Wood *et al.*, 2002: 227–8). They were thus not over-relying upon building up membership or support once they were in the CAC process. This approach is reflected in both the low number of cases that have gone to the CAC and their proportion relative to voluntary recognition agreements.

While the number of new recognition cases has increased, we cannot unequivocally attribute all the increase to the procedure and its impact.

Voluntary recognition did occur before the ERA. However, it does seem reasonable to suggest that the significant increase in the number of recognition agreements in recent years is due principally to the ERA. The factors that have been used to account for the union decline in the past two decades, such as product-market competition, the economic policies of the government and labour-market conditions, have not changed substantially in the past two years. Moreover, while it is not possible to separate the influence of the procedure itself from the government employment policy of which it is a part, there is little to associate the pursuit of partnership, a central plank of this policy, to the increased trade union recognition. Thus far it has had little impact on the behaviour of employers, and they certainly have not initiated recognition agreements with unions as a means of kick-starting a new partnership approach to employment relations.

More generally, our workplace survey confirmed that employers rarely initiate union recognition discussions and that, when they do, it is where union membership is approaching the level where a CAC case could be won and/or to exclude a particular union in favour of another. The main shadow effect of the law on employers, if there is one, is likely to be on their propensity to concede when faced with a level of membership that suggests the union might secure a CAC award. In the absence of any greater effect from employers, the impact of the legislation will depend on the extent to which the enhanced effort that unions are putting into organizing and recruiting extends well beyond the conventional terrain of unionism. This organizing effort must also ensure a solid base of membership prior to a recognition claim that is able to resist any attempt by the employers to undermine support for the union. Without this, the overall effect of the procedure will not be large. The legislation has clearly played a role in stimulating unions' organizing and recruiting activity, as unions now have greater confidence that there will be a return on any investment they make in recruitment. However, we should not under-estimate the considerable difficulties that unions still face, or the nature and scale of the investment that has to be made, in the recruitment, organization and servicing of members.

Chapter 8

Dilemmas in worker representation

Information, consultation and negotiation

Howard Gospel and Paul Willman

This chapter focuses on the mechanisms by which workers, unionized and non-unionized, are represented at work, and through which they obtain varying degrees of voice in employer decision-making. In addition to collective bargaining by trade unions, it highlights the mechanisms of information sharing and joint consultation. One argument is that an understanding of the interaction of these representative mechanisms is important for an appreciation of the present and likely future patterns of worker representation in the UK. Specifically, it suggests that forms of representation other than collective bargaining may in future prove more popular voice mechanisms – with both employers and employees – than they have in the past.

We can think about interaction between forms of representation in a number of ways. A basic perspective sees systems in terms of direct and indirect representation: the former occurs where the individual worker or group of workers is directly involved in decision-making, often around work tasks; the latter occurs where there is some sort of body through which employees express voice through representatives. Indirect forms of representation (the main focus of this chapter) may include collective bargaining through a union negotiating body, or joint consultation through works committees, or both. In these cases, representation can be exclusive or inclusive: in the former case the representative body acts only on behalf of certain employees (for example, union members); in the latter case the representative body acts for all employees. Another perspective sees systems of representation as rungs on a ladder: the first rung is where a worker might be represented by a fellow worker on an individual matter; the second rung is where there is provision of information and consultation for employee representatives covering a group of workers or the whole workforce; the third rung is where workers are represented by a trade union that bargains on their behalf (Ewing, 1990: 212; McCarthy,

2000). A similar perspective sees representation in terms of a rising hierarchy of forms, from information (where workers are informed by their managers) to consultation (where there is an exchange of views, albeit with management ultimately deciding) and to negotiation (where there is a measure of contestation and joint decision-making). The latter two perspectives imply both discrete representative categories and a hierarchy of their importance; both are increasingly questionable.

Further conceptual considerations need to be stated. Representation may exist on different types of issues, ranging from those that affect workers' immediate jobs (task-based) to those that are broader and more business-related (policy-based). Moreover, representation may be seen as either events-driven or process-driven. Where it is events-driven, it is triggered by a specific (usually employer-initiated) event, such as a reorganization of work or a plant closure; where it is process-driven, representation is part of an on-going process in which the representative body is more likely to be permanent and to have an agenda that is pro-active. There may be single or multiple channels of representation. Finally, of course, systems may be voluntary or statutory. In the latter two cases, the question arises whether these processes are likely to complement or conflict with one another.

The focus of this chapter is on workers and their representation, largely concentrating on the private sector. The data are drawn from various sources, in particular from the Workplace Industrial Relations and Employment Relations Surveys (WIRS 1980, 1984, and 1990 and WERS 1998) and the British Workplace Representation and Participation Survey (BWRPS), as designed by staff at the Centre for Economic Performance (CEP) (Diamond and Freeman, 2001).

The chapter structure is as follows. The first section places the development of representative systems in Britain in a broad historical perspective. The second section then maps the current situation – it deals with what British workers get. This is compared broadly in the third section with arrangements in three other major countries – the focus here is on what workers in these countries get. The fourth then deals with what British workers say they want. Finally, in the light of recent European developments, we speculate about what British workers are likely to get.

What did British workers get in the past?

Historically, employers unilaterally made most decisions on work matters. In some instances, usually job-related issues, skilled or strategically placed workers could unilaterally regulate certain aspects of their working lives.

From the late nineteenth century onwards, collective bargaining gradually developed. In some situations, to ward off collective bargaining, a minority of employers established joint consultative arrangements of various kinds (Gospel, 1992: 79–84, 99). However, unions were opposed to (or at least suspicious of) consultative committees, which they considered likely to undermine their appeal to workers and their ability to represent members.

During the First World War, both collective bargaining and joint consultation developed significantly at national and workplace levels. The Whitley Committee (1918) recommended that both should be further elaborated, with the former concentrated on pay and conditions, in particular outside the firm, and the latter on other matters, especially at the workplace. At the time, strong unions showed little interest in consultation; weaker unions accepted the proposals on multi-employer bargaining, but again showed little interest in joint consultation without collective bargaining. Equally, most employers were reluctant to accept workplace level representation, either by shop stewards or by other worker representatives. It was in Germany, at the time (in part drawing on British ideas), that a system of combined collective bargaining and joint consultation was introduced by legislation (Feldman, 1992). In Britain during the interwar depression, collective bargaining narrowed and formal joint consultation contracted. Subsequently, from the mid-1930s onwards and during the Second World War, with government support, both expanded (Milner, 1995: 79–87). However, at the end of the war, again neither employers nor unions were sufficiently committed to sustain the joint production committees that had been established (Hinton, 1994).

In the 30 years after the war, unions saw their membership and power grow and demanded collective bargaining in preference to joint consultation. As a result, in the private sector, joint consultation was overshadowed. This contrasted with the situation in continental Europe, where statutorily based employee consultation was firmly established in Germany, France and other countries, and operated alongside collective negotiations. In the late 1960s, the Donovan Royal Commission advocated exclusively collective bargaining for Britain: 'Collective bargaining is the most effective means of giving workers the right to representation in decisions affecting their working lives.' Approvingly, it quoted McCarthy as saying consultative committees 'cannot survive the development of effective shopfloor organization: either they must change their character and become essentially negotiating committees ... or they will be boycotted by shop stewards and fall into disuse' (McCarthy, 1967: 33; Donovan, 1968: 27, 54). When, a decade later, the Bullock Royal Commission reported on industrial democracy, it recommended union-based representation on company boards alongside collective bargaining. Bullock briefly mentioned German works councils, only to dismiss them, even though they arguably were a more important part of the German system than board level representation (Bullock, 1977: 42–3, 48, 126). Union support for 'free' collective bargaining, hostility to joint consultation, and opposition to non-union channels of representation prevailed.

A number of conclusions may be drawn from this broad historical survey. First, the paradox of the UK's voluntaristic system of 'free' collective bargaining was that it relied heavily on a framework of legal immunities and state support. It provided neither much of a ceiling on union aspirations, in favourable times, nor much of a floor in unfavourable ones. Second, in Wedderburn's terms, collective bargaining and joint consultation grew up in an interrelated and complex 'double helix' type relationship (1997: 30). At times they complemented each other; at other times the one subsumed the other. Third, in retrospect unions and employers missed a number of opportunities to build a system of employee representation based on interlocking collective bargaining and joint consultation. In the case of the unions, in the early 1970s they missed the opportunity to secure positive legal rights when they were strong. When, from the late 1970s onwards, the legal framework for the voluntaristic system eroded, the coverage of collective bargaining quickly shrank.

From the 1970s, a number of factors shaped representation in Britain. First, legal intervention steadily increased. Some of this was initially auxiliary to collective bargaining, such as the provisions for union recognition and for information disclosure introduced in the early 1970s. Some mandated forms of representation on specific issues, such as health and safety and, consequent on EU membership, collective redundancies and transfer of undertakings. These procedures initially gave legal priority to union representatives, but in their absence allowed for non-union representation (Gospel and Lockwood, 1999). Second, the political and legal context that favoured unions changed with the election of the Thatcher government in 1979. Through the subsequent years, immunities were removed and restrictions were placed on unions and their collective bargaining activities. Third, union membership and the coverage of collective bargaining began to shrink. Reasons for this are considered in other chapters in the book, but undoubtedly in part this was the result of an increasingly hostile legal and political environment (Freeman and Pelletier, 1990). Fourth, from the 1980s onwards, employers increasingly looked to alternative voice mechanisms, based in part on indirect representation via joint consultation, but more on direct communication and participation via direct workforce meetings, briefing groups and problem-solving circles (Forth and Millward, 2002: 3–7). In these circumstances, unions faced a dilemma about acceptance of new forms of consultation established by employers or introduced under EU directives. Slowly and unevenly, they began to re-concile themselves to events-driven and multi-channel representation (TUC, 1995). However, union conversion is still not complete.

The election of a Labour government in 1997 led to the re-introduction of law on union recognition and the reformulation of law deriving from European directives on representation in collective redundancies and trans-fer of undertakings. In the latter areas, priority in the choice of representa-tives is now vested in a descending order of, first, union stewards, followed by representatives of standing consultative committees, and last by repre-sentatives chosen ad hoc for the specific purpose. In the case of multi-national corporations, the government also implemented the European Works Councils Directive. This set two precedents. First, it established legally-based, standing, general consultative arrangements in Britain, albeit for a particular group of employees, those in transnational firms. Second, it treated representation as inclusive rather than exclusive, giving priority in the choice of representatives to the entire workforce and not to union members. Finally, from late 2001 the government has accepted the EU Directive on Information and Consultation rights in national level under-takings. Thus, in terms of the law and practice, Britain has moved decisively down a multi-channel road, but has been left with a fragmented system of information, consultation and representation (Gospel *et al.*, 2002).

What do British workers get?

In this section, successive WIRS surveys are used for two purposes: first, to look at the state of employee representation in 1998, the date of the last survey; and second, to assess patterns of change over the period from 1980 to 1998. Overall, we identify the story of a reduction in coverage of indirect representation. However, the pattern of change is complex.

We turn first to the pattern in 1998. In that year unions were recog-nized in 42 per cent of all workplaces, with a presence (i.e. membership but no recognition) in 11 per cent. In other words, around half of all workplaces had no union presence. In the private sector unions were recognized in only 24 per cent of workplaces, and within this sector the highest proportions of workplaces with union recognition were in recently privatized industries, such as utilities, transport and communications. Both organizational and workplace size are positively associated with union recognition (Cully *et al.*, 1999: 92).

However, recognition is not representation. In 1998, 22 per cent of workplaces had union representatives, 10 per cent had non-union representatives, and 5 per cent had both. In the private sector, these figures were 15, 10 and 2 per cent respectively. On the whole, non-union representatives were slightly more likely to be found in workplaces where there was a union presence but no recognition than in any other situation. Also, where they were found, there was a slightly higher number of non-union rather than union representatives per workplace (a mean of 4.7 as opposed to 3.7; Cully *et al.*, 1999: 96). Of course, overall it should be kept in mind that a majority of workplaces had no representatives of any kind.

In 1998, the coverage of joint consultative committees was not very different from that of collective bargaining in that 29 per cent of all workplaces had a workplace-level consultative committee. In the private sector, this was 26 per cent of all workplaces. However, in both cases a slightly lower percentage had a functioning committee, i.e. one which met at least three times a year (23 and 20 per cent respectively). However, the counterpart of this is that there is a decline in the scope of collective bargaining (Millward *et al.*, 2000: 138–83). Consultative committees can exist at various levels. Thus, in the private sector, 16 per cent of workplaces had a committee at workplace level, 18 per cent at a higher level, but only 8 per cent had both. Size effects here are complicated. Workplace size is positively associated with the existence of a workplace committee, but negatively associated with the use only of a higher-level committee. Organizational size is negatively associated with workplace committees, but positively associated with higher level committees or a combination of the two (Cully *et al.*, 1999: 99; Millward *et al.*, 2000: 109).

Union recognition and consultative committees appear to be associated in each size band. Thus overall, 38 per cent of workplaces with a recognized union had a committee, compared to 20 per cent of those where there was no union presence. In the private sector, these figures are 32 and 20 per cent respectively. On the basis of this, Cully *et al.* (1999: 100) conclude that 'union representation and indirect employee participation go hand in hand rather than being substitutes'. However, they also suggest that, in non-recognized workplaces where there is union presence, consultative arrangements do not appear to be a springboard for recognition (Cully *et al.*, 1999: 101).

Overall, the scope of joint regulation by any methods is modest. Table 8.1, which is for both private and public sectors, shows the balance of negotiation, consultation and information-sharing by issue in the minority

Table 8.1 The scope of negotiation, consultation and information provision by type of worker representatives: 1998

	Cell percentages			
Issue	Negotiates	Consults	Informs	None
Union representatives				
Pay or conditions of employment	38	13	17	32
Recruitment or selection	3	15	30	52
Training	5	29	24	42
Systems of payment	12	16	26	46
Handling grievances	18	54	13	15
Staffing or manpower planning	6	33	24	37
Equal opportunities	7	41	17	35
Health and safety	13	62	11	14
Performance appraisals	6	25	16	53
Non-union representatives – workplaces with no recognition				
Pay or conditions of employment	16	33	36	15
Recruitment or selection	2	33	32	33
Training	3	46	24	27
Systems of payment	4	20	48	28
Handling grievances	14	50	16	20
Staffing or manpower planning	3	36	40	21
Equal opportunities	10	45	23	22
Health and safety	18	62	19	1
Performance appraisals	2	48	19	31

(Source: Workplace Employee Relations Survey, 1998)

All establishments with 25 or more employees. The figures for union representatives are weighted and based on responses from 923 managers in workplaces with 25 or more employees, union recognition and a union representative on site. The figures for non-union representatives are weighted and based on responses from 134 managers in workplaces with 25 or more employees and without union recognition, but with non-union representative.

of workplaces where there is on-site representation. In workplaces where there are union representatives, bargaining is clearly dominated by pay and to a lesser extent by grievance handling. In these workplaces, aside from these two matters, consultation and information-sharing is the dominant joint process. The largest category overall is no joint regulation. In workplaces where there are non-union representatives and no union recognition, information and consultation are the dominant processes, but a surprising amount of negotiation is reported on health and safety and on pay and conditions. Again unilateral management regulation is a large category, but less so than workplaces where there are union representatives. The average number of issues over which negotiation occurred was similar at 1.1 for union representatives and 0.9 for non-union representatives. The average number of issues on which consultation occurred was 2.9 for union representatives and 3.7 for non-union representatives. Generally, the topics that score highest in terms of some sort of joint regulation are health and safety and grievance handling, both of course underpinned by statutory requirements (Cully *et al.*, 1999: 104–5).

In the private sector at least, the main form of workplace communication and participation is of the direct kind. Thus 35 per cent of workplaces have problem-solving groups, 35 per cent regular workplace meetings, and 43 per cent team briefing groups. Taking these three practices (problem-solving groups, workforce meetings, briefing groups), 75 per cent of all workplaces and 72 per cent of private-sector workplaces had one or more of these; the average workplace had 1.2, and the average private-sector workplace had 1.1 (Cully *et al.*, 1999: 64–9 and WERS98).

Turning to change in indirect representation over time, the main points to draw from Table 8.2 and from the survey of all the WIRS surveys (Millward *et al.*, 2000) are as follows. First, there is a major decline in union density and presence, in particular in the private sector, where recognition also halves across the period. The proportion of workplaces where collect-

Table 8.2 Union presence, density, and recognition, collective bargaining, and joint consultative arrangements, 1980–98

	Cell percentages			
	1980	*1984*	*1990*	*1998*
Union presence – by workplace				
All	73	73	64	54
Private manufacturing	77	67	58	42
Private services	50	53	46	35
Union density – by employees				
All	65	58	47	36
Private	56	43	36	26
Union recognition – by workplace				
All	64	66	53	42
Private	50	48	38	25
Collective bargaining predominant form of pay determination – by workplace				
All		60	42	29
Private manufacturing		50	33	23
Private services		36	29	14
Consultation: incidence of joint consultative committee – by workplace				
All – any consultative committee	34	34	29	29
Private	26	24	18	26
Union recognition	37	36	34	30
No recognition	17	20	17	18
All – any functioning consultative committee	30	31	26	23

(Source: Adapted from Millward *et al.* (2000), pp. 85–7, 96, 109, 186–91, 197)

ive bargaining was the dominant form of pay determination fell overall from 60 to 29 per cent between 1984 and 1998. In private manufacturing it fell from 50 to 23 per cent, and in private services from 36 to 14 per cent.

Second, the pattern of change in consultation is different. Overall, the decline is less marked than for the union-related variables. It is true that the relative proportion of workplaces with non-functioning consultative committees grows, but, as stated, there was also a 'hollowing out' of collective bargaining institutions. The overall and private-sector trends on consultation coverage are not as divergent as those on union variables; in fact, it will be noted that there is a rise in private-sector consultation coverage between 1990 and 1998. The percentage of private-sector work-places with a union representative fell from 41 to 17 per cent between 1980 and 1998, whereas those with a non-union representative (but no union representative) increased from 21 to 50 per cent. Both where there is union recognition and where there is presence, the incidence of union rep-resentatives has fallen, especially in the latter case. Non-union representat-ive numbers have risen in all cases. However, overall, fewer workplaces have any form of employee representative in 1998 because the decline in union representation has not been fully offset by the increase in non-union representation (Millward *et al.*, 2000: 115).

Third, we observe the growth of direct voice arrangements. Thus, regular meetings between senior managers and the workforce, problem-solving groups and briefing groups all increased significantly in the private sector. Between 1984 and 1998, the proportion of workplaces where there was union-only voice fell from 24 to 9 per cent; the proportion where there was both indirect voice (union and non-union) and direct voice fell from 45 to 39 per cent; but those where managers relied solely on direct arrangements rose from 11 to 30 per cent (Millward *et al.*, 2000: 127). In the case of briefing groups, in 1998 the increase was confined to work-places without a union and those without a consultative committee. In the case of regular meetings and problem-solving groups, these were more common where there was union representation and where there was joint consultation. Overall, according to Forth and Millward (2002: 22–3), direct communication practices do not seem to have been used to supplant indirect representation via trade unions, but there is some weak evidence that they may be used to exclude unions.

Finally, on the survival rate of arrangements, 85 per cent of private-sector workplaces recognizing unions in 1990 still had them in 1998. By contrast, the proportion of functioning committees to survive over the period was 63 per cent. The figure was a little lower for workplace-wide meetings (58 per cent), problem-solving groups (56 per cent) and briefing groups (42 per cent). Overall, therefore, despite its decline, union voice would seem to be more durable than non-union – but of course it has also been less likely to be established in new workplaces (see Chapter 2).

What do other workers get?

As part of the analysis of present and possible future UK patterns, it is useful to examine briefly forms of representation in three other major countries – the USA, Germany and France – chosen for lessons they may have for Britain.

The USA provides a useful comparison, given a common inheritance of a reliance on collective bargaining as the key form of employee voice. Historically, US unions sought joint regulation with employers through collective bargaining, though with limited success. On the other hand, a leading set of large employers established employer-dominated unions and non-union representative committees (Jacoby, 1985: 187–9; 1997: 20–34). With the New Deal, the 1935 Wagner Act outlawed the latter arrangements, and to the present date indirect representation without unions risks illegality. As a result, employers have been constrained in operating consultative committees that are not union-based. Unions have sought exclusively to bargain, and have not pushed for voluntary consultative committees or councils. The outcome is that collective bargaining coverage has shrunk and indirect forms of worker participation have not developed, while direct forms of employee involvement have grown.

Under the Clinton administration, the unions hoped to achieve changes in the legal framework that governs recognition for collective bargaining. Some of the research for the resulting Dunlop Commission touched on the possible desire on the part of US workers for joint consultative arrangements; however, proposals for legislative changes focused on the framework of recognition and collective bargaining law. As a counter, a group of employers promoted the so-called Team Bill, which would have promoted direct forms of participation. Neither set of proposals was passed into law. Thus, US unions remain dependent on organizing for collective bargaining. Union density in the USA has fallen to 9 per cent of the private-sector labour force, and on one prediction could fall to 3 per cent by 2010 (Freeman, 1995: 533).

Germany has provided a significant contrast with the UK for practioners and students of industrial relations. Unlike Britain, Germany went down the road of multi-channel representation – collective bargaining outside the firm, alongside legally-based joint consultation at the workplace and company levels, and representation on the supervisory board of companies. Our analysis of information disclosure and consultation in Germany (Gospel and Willman, 2002) shows that German unions have benefited from their relationship with works councils and vice versa. Works councillors tend to be union members, the union provides advice to the council, and this in turn gives the union influence. In law and practice, employees, through their works councils, receive more information and experience more consultation than their British counterparts. However, in recent years works councils have in some instances superseded unions, with more being discussed through the consultation process and with more deviations from nationally bargained agreements. For unions, this has presented the challenge and opportunity of developing new coordinating and servicing roles (Thelen, 1991; Turner, 1991; Mitbestimmung Kommission, 1998; Frick and Lehmann, 2001).

The German story is therefore usually seen as positive for union representation, where, on the whole, joint consultation and collective bargaining have complemented one another. Between 1980 and 1999 union membership fell from around 38 per cent in West Germany to 29 per cent for the whole of Germany; the coverage and scope of collective bargaining and joint consultation remains high, though with some shift towards decentralized dealings with works councils.

By contrast, the French story may be seen as a more negative one for unions. Historically, France also went down the road of multi-channel representation, with legally-based joint consultation alongside collective bargaining. Periodically, French governments have intervened in industrial relations to support consultative arrangements. Since 1945, the law has mandated the election of a *comité d'enterprise*. As further amended by the Auroux legislation in the early 1980s, the purpose of the *comité d'enterprise* is to ensure expression of the views of employees and to allow their interests to be taken into account in decisions. French employers are legally obliged to inform and consult employees over a wide range of matters (Gospel and Willman, 2002).

However, periodically French governments have needed to intervene to reinforce the system. In part, the more limited success of the French system is because *comité d'enterprise* have less extensive rights and are more employer-led than German works councils. In the main, it is because French unions are more fragmented, have less presence at the workplace, and consequently have been less able to use the law and institutions. Union membership has fallen from 18 per cent to 9 per cent between 1980 and 2000, and the scope of collective bargaining at workplace level is narrow. In France, it might be concluded that, on the one hand, there is evidence that joint consultation and collective bargaining have not complemented one another and the former has often come to substitute for the latter. On the other hand, French workers would undoubtedly obtain less in the absence of the *comité d'enterprise*, and arguably French unions have been able to maintain a foothold in many firms largely because of the role they play in these arrangements (Howell, 1992: 100–2).

Box 8.1 provides an example of representation in Europe, in the form of the European steel industry.

Box 8.1 *The European steel industry*

The European steel industry has undergone major restructuring in recent years, with far-reaching consequences for employment.

In early 1997 the major German steel maker, Krupp, launched a hostile takeover bid for its rival, Thyssen. The union IG Metall, representing workers in both workplaces, opposed the takeover. The works councils at both Thyssen and Krupp were able to mobilize their members against the takeover, in part on the basis of information achieved through the German co-determination and consultation system. Eventually, the takeover bid was dropped; later Thyssen joined Krupp in an agreed merger; and an agreement was reached with the union and works councils that there would be no redundancies as a result of restructuring. These arrangements are generally thought to have resulted in a better outcome for both labour forces and employment prospects in the two companies.

The major UK steel producer, British Steel, merged with the Dutch firm Hoogovens in 1999 to form Corus. There was little prior information provided to British workers on this, and little consultation. There was rather more information and consultation provided at the time in the Netherlands under a more extensive legally-based system of information and consultation.

In early 2001, following a change in its top management, Corus reassessed its production and location strategy in the light of the changing demand situation. In the case of Britain, it did this with minimal consultation with the union or workforce, and only after the decision to restructure had been taken by the company. Corus then announced 6,000 redundancies in the UK, again with little prior consultation, but in line with existing law. Further restructuring has continued, with the sale of different parts of the business. The provision of information to British workers has been limited; consultation has been in line with the minimal requirements of UK law, and the union has had little impact on the firm's planning.

Meanwhile, Corus's Dutch half, Hoogovens, was required by law to inform and consult its employees through its works councils in which the unions were closely involved. Under Dutch law, failure to inform and consult adequately could lead to a nullifying of management decisions. In the Netherlands the company accepted that the collective agreement with its unions and arrangements with works councils should stand, and job cuts have been less deep in the Dutch part of the company.

The German and Dutch stories regarding the steel industry are clearly more optimistic for employees than is the British story. In the former cases, information disclosure, joint consultation and collective bargaining complemented each other. In the British case, collective bargaining was severely constrained, and joint consultation and information provision was limited. However, there is an important sting in the tail of this story. It should be noted that in the Corus case there exists a company-wide consultative council in the form of a European Works Council. Yet though this improved information and consultation, it is not thought to have had a major effect on outcomes.

National systems are of course deeply embedded in national histories, and cannot be easily replicated. So, are there any lessons for British unions in these different national patterns? We would argue as follows. If British unions follow those in the USA, they may become ghettoized within the ever-shrinking perimeter of collective bargaining. On the other hand, there is a possibility that they could take advantage of works council-type arrangements, as in Germany. However, the French case shows this is no automatic route to success if they are unable to take advantage of such arrangements. Drawing on Germany and France, an obvious question is whether European-style representational arrangements can be successfully transferred to the UK. We have seen that there have been changes in UK practice towards mixed systems; joint consultation is of some interest to employers and of increasing interest to unions. A key question is: would British workers be interested in a move towards joint consultative arrangements and mixed systems of representation on European lines?

What do British workers want?

There are substantial difficulties involved in ascertaining what representation workers want. Workers may say they want one thing in everyday circumstances, but something else in more exceptional circumstances when confronted with a major change in contractual arrangements or when there are major redundancies. Here we draw on the BWRPS survey, which is more likely to reflect what workers want on an everyday basis.

As is often the case in such surveys, a majority of British workers report reasonably high levels of satisfaction in their jobs and of commitment to their employing organization. However, they are often critical of management – more so than suggested in a comparable US survey (Freeman and Rogers, 1999) – and a majority desire more say in decisions about work tasks, pay levels and organizational governance. In total, 38 per cent identify current problems with unfair and arbitrary treatment in areas such as rewards and discipline, and report favouritism and bullying. Despite this, 50 per cent of all workers reported that they do not go to anyone for help with work difficulties. This fairly high flow of problems in British workplaces is confirmed by the rapid increase in recent years in enquiries to the Advisory Conciliation and Arbitration Service and to Citizens Advice Bureaux and cases to industrial tribunals.

There would also appear to be a related representation gap. Table 8.3 suggests that most workers would prefer to deal with problems collectively rather than individually. The only area where there is a clear preference for individual remedies is promotion. However, in most cases the preference is for dealing with issues via a group of fellow workers rather than a trade union or staff association representative. Perhaps not surprisingly, union members show a stronger preference for collective solutions and prefer union representation rather than working through a group of fellow workers. The exceptions are again on matters of promotion and training, where union members would look more to a group of fellow workers. Non-union employees prefer fellow workers to unions as the method of collective action on all issues. It is notable that workers in situations where there is a recognized union and where there is both a union presence and a consultative committee would seem to have the highest preference for collective solutions.

Table 8.4 explores this further and shows that a majority (72 per cent) of employees think their workplaces would be better with some form of collective representation. This breaks down as 92 per cent of union members and 61 per cent of non-union members. However, in the case of union members it is striking that only 11 per cent favour a union on its

Table 8.3 Preferences of employees for dealing with workplace issues

Would you prefer to deal with this problem on your own or with …	Cell percentages							
	All employees	Union member	Non-union member	Only workplaces with union presence	Only workplaces with recognized unions	Only workplaces with WC or JCC	Both WC/JCC and union presence at workplace	Neither WC/JCC or union presence at workplace
Sexual or racial discrimination at work								
Group of fellow workers	72	78	68	78	78	70	76	63
Union or staff association rep.	67	84	58	72	77	56	83	54
Negotiating salary								
Group of fellow workers	65	81	56	73	74	60	82	44
Union or staff association rep.	53	80	38	73	77	38	72	31
Negotiating hours and conditions								
Group of fellow workers	71	81	65	73	75	67	80	62
Union or staff association rep.	52	76	38	69	73	39	68	34
Promotion issues								
Group of fellow workers	46	50	43	39	37	54	50	38
Union or staff association rep.	27	36	23	34	35	21	33	20
Workplace bullying								
Group of fellow workers	69	72	68	70	71	74	74	60
Union or staff association rep.	58	80	46	65	69	46	75	41
Training and skill development								
Group of fellow workers	67	73	65	66	63	73	71	59
Union or staff association rep.	30	36	26	40	41	28	30	23

(Source: BWRPS, 2001, Q35)

Sample was divided at random into two variants. One variant asked if the respondents preferred to solve specific problems on their own or with the help of a group of colleagues or fellow workers. The other variant asked if respondents preferred to solve problems on their own or with the help of a trade union or staff association representative. Each respondent could only choose either an individual or a collective solution.

Table 8.4 Employees' perceptions of the effects of having trade unions and works councils in their workplace

Do you think your workplace would be better off with ...	Cell percentages							
	All employees	Union member	Non-union member	Only workplaces with union presence	Only workplaces with recognized unions	Only workplaces with WC or JCC	Both WC/JCC and union presence at workplace	Neither WC/JCC or union presence at workplace
Trade union on its own	7	11	5	14	16	2	9	6
Works council on its own	21	6	29	11	10	40	9	27
Works council and trade union	44	74	27	60	63	24	72	20
Neither	24	5	34	11	8	31	9	43
Don't know	4	3	5	3	3	3	2	4

(Source: BWRPS, 2001, Q51)

own, whereas 74 per cent favour both a union and a joint consultative committee/works council. Non-members, wishes are more dispersed: 34 per cent want no form of representation, 29 per cent favour a joint consultative committee on its own, 27 per cent favour a joint consultative committee and a trade union, but only 5 per cent favour a union on its own. Workers in situations where there is already a union and a consultative committee are the group most in favour of dual-channel representation (72 per cent), but it is also striking that workers in situations where there is a recognized union or a union presence are also well disposed to dual representation. There is little preference for a consultative committee on its own, except where this already exists. All this suggests that many union and non-union members see the various institutions as potentially complementary.

Moreover, the survey shows that 82 per cent of workers would be in favour of legislation that required management to meet with employee representatives. Overall, union members are more favourably inclined to statutory works councils than are non-members (89 as opposed to 77 per cent). However, the belief in legislation is strongest (92 per cent) where there are already dual channels. In addition, there is a strong feeling that works councils should be elected by workers (72 per cent), have legal protection from possible discrimination by employers (75 per cent), and meet on a regular basis and not just at management discretion (89 per cent). However, the proportion favouring confidential information for employee representatives is relatively low (40 per cent in the case of union members and 33 per cent in the case of non-members).

Joint representation by a trade union and a consultative committee/works council would seem to have some pay-off in terms of satisfaction with information disclosure. Table 8.5 suggests that most workers feel very or quite well informed, with the lowest levels of satisfaction about future employment and staffing plans. There is no clear difference between union and non-union members, except that the former have an advantage in knowing what other people doing their job are earning, reflecting the union role in wage bargaining. Generally, workers in a situation where there was only a consultative committee/works council felt the best informed. This was followed closely by situations where there was both a consultative committee/works council and a trade union. Workers felt least well informed where there were no representative arrangements, but close to this were situations where there was exclusively a trade union. There are various reasons why union members may feel they receive less information – they may have higher aspirations that are unmet; management may feel more constrained to give information; and union representatives may

Table 8.5 Employees' perceptions of how well they are informed on key workplace matters

Cell percentages

	All employees	Union member	Non-union member	Only workplaces with union presence	Only workplaces with recognized unions	Only workplaces with WC or JCC	Both WC/JCC and union presence at workplace	Neither WC/JCC or union presence at workplace
Future employment or staffing plans for your workplace								
Very/quite well informed	63	58	65	49	48	72	66	61
Not very well/not at all	37	42	35	51	52	28	34	39
What other people doing your job are earning								
Very/quite well informed	62	71	56	61	64	60	72	52
Not very well/not at all	38	29	44	39	36	40	28	48
The financial performance of your employer								
Very/quite well informed	68	68	67	63	62	75	72	61
Not very well/not at all	32	32	33	37	38	25	28	39
Your job prospects with your employer								
Very/quite well informed	75	71	77	63	61	82	78	72
Not very well/not at all	25	29	23	37	39	18	22	28
The training you need to advance your career								
Very/quite well informed	74	76	73	69	69	84	81	63
Not very well/not at all	26	24	27	31	31	16	19	37

(Source: BWRPS, 2001, Q51)

not pass on information to members. However, it is significant that where there is both a union and a consultative committee/works council there is a high level of satisfaction with information disclosure.

In summary, there is a demand for more indirect representation and voice among British workers. However, among both non-members and members, there is not a strong demand for union voice alone. Consultative committees/works councils, especially legally-based, are clearly very attractive to both non-members and members, and are viewed as complementary to trade unions.

What are British workers likely to get – a new era in employment relations?

Finally, we turn to what representation British workers are likely to get. On union recognition, the research by Wood *et al.* (see Chapter 7) suggests that the present legal procedures will have a small direct effect and a somewhat larger indirect effect. However, the overall impact will be limited. On union membership, over the last few years there has been some increase in numbers but no increase in density, and it will be an uphill struggle for unions to maintain or increase momentum in recruitment. Even if recognition and density were to stabilize or increase, there seems little likelihood that the decline in the coverage of collective bargaining will be reversed in the short term, especially in the private sector, where employers' and employees' preferences are for forms of representation and participation other than collective bargaining (Millward *et al.*, 2000: 197–9). By contrast, on recent trends direct forms of information sharing and employee participation are likely to continue to increase.

So, what of indirect representation via joint consultation and its intersection with collective bargaining? Here, the passage of the EU Directive on Information and Consultation (2002/14/EC) is likely to play an important part in shaping future developments.

The Directive will affect large enterprises (over 150 employees) by early 2005, and will eventually cover all undertakings with more than 50 employees by 2008. This means it will cover three-quarters of the UK labour force. Undoubtedly the Directive will start to have an immediate impact, as management and unions plan for its implementation. In the Directive, consultation is defined as an 'exchange of views and the establishment of dialogue' (Article 2) – implying an ongoing process. Article 4(2) outlines the substantive areas: (a) there is an obligation to provide information on the general business situation of the undertaking; (b) there is an obligation to inform and consult on the likely development of employment and on 'anticipatory measures' that might threaten employment; and (c) there is an enhanced obligation to inform and consult on decisions likely to lead to substantial changes in work organization or in contractual relations. These are minimum mandatory topics, but other topics are permitted to be covered. Consultation must take place at an 'appropriate' time, and so as to enable employee representatives to study the information and prepare for consultation. It shall also be 'at the relevant level of management and representation depending on the subject under discussion' – implying that there should be different levels of representation and consultation within an undertaking. On item (c), the consultation shall be 'with a view to reaching an agreement' (Article 4) – implying an ongoing process of give-and-take. In all cases, management is obliged to provide a reasoned response to representatives' opinions. Representatives are also to be given adequate 'protection and guarantees' to enable them to perform their duties (Article 7). On matters of confidentiality, the employer may withhold information that it is considered would seriously damage the undertaking, and representatives and 'any experts who assist them' may be made subject to an obligation of confidentiality. Sanctions for failure to comply shall be 'effective, proportionate, and dissuasive' (Article 8). Employers and employee representatives may negotiate different arrangements before and after transposition, but these would have to respect the principles of the Directive (Article 5).

The transposition of the Directive into UK law will depend on political circumstances, and the debate will be along a spectrum of what Wedderburn has described as 'soft' and 'strong' rights (Wedderburn, 1997: 34). However, some outcomes are reasonably certain. For example, forms of direct participation will not qualify. Equally, ad hoc and issue-specific arrangements will not qualify, given that the Directive talks about a 'permanent' and 'general' system of consultation (Article 10). Many existing systems of consultation will not qualify, such as where representatives are appointed by management. Trade union collective bargaining will qualify, subject to non-members not being disenfranchised. Moreover, from the wording it seems likely that arrangements will have to be created at multiple levels within enterprises. At the time of writing, other outcomes are more problematic. The following are particularly unclear. How, in the absence of an employer initiative, will a request for a council or committee be instigated? Will there be a process of balloting? Who will be deemed to be representatives, and how will such persons emerge? What will be the exact nature of sanctions? Whatever the legislation, as with all EU-derived law, the transposition will be subject to interpretation by the European Court of Justice, which in the past in areas such as representation, sex discrimination and working time has rendered Directives far-reaching. The implementation of the Directive will seemingly depend on the preferences of employees and capabilities and actions of employers and unions.

On the basis of the foregoing, what can we speculate about this? On the part of employers, their advantage lies in the fact that for some time they have controlled employee relations and in many cases have introduced more sophisticated human resource policies. On the other hand, in addition to the new law, there are other constraints. Employees would seem to want more representative voice at work, and employers now confront more confident unions than they have for many years. Undoubtedly, some employers will seek to avoid new arrangements, arguing either that they already have adequate mechanisms or that their employees do not want arrangements on these lines. This strategy clearly has dangers in that it may be challenged by unions in all or in parts of an enterprise. For other employers, there is an opportunity to establish arrangements, either wholly or partially new, either with or without trade unions.

Union fears must be that employers may use the Directive to exclude or eject them, and that they have neither the leverage nor the capability to mobilize workers to achieve and operate new information and consultation arrangements. However, there is evidence that employees desire more voice at work, many workplaces already have a union presence that can be built on, and unions now have legal supports that they can potentially turn to their advantage. At one end of the spectrum, where unions already have a high level of membership and bargaining coverage, they may eschew new arrangements but use the law to capitalize on what they already have and expand the scope and level of consultation and bargaining. At the other end of the spectrum, where unions have no presence, unions will have little choice for employees but to accept what employers may put into place. Here, unions will have mixed motivations as to whether they wish to see such arrangements succeed. Where arrangements are successful, this may mean permanent union exclusion; where they are less successful, this may mean new opportunities to intervene. It is in situations at the middle of the spectrum, where there is hollow recognition or a partial presence, at some levels or in some parts of an undertaking, that unions will confront challenges and have real opportunities to increase their membership and activities.

Conclusions

To conclude, the UK has a differentiated system of representing workers, where direct voice has been on the increase, indirect voice through joint consultation has held up, and voice through trade unions has shrunk considerably. In terms of indirect mechanisms, in both law and practice, the UK has already moved down the road of multi-channel representation and is likely to move further in this direction in future. British workers clearly want more voice, but with a preference for joint consultative arrangements and based on multi-channel representation. The present situation presents a set of major challenges and opportunities for the industrial relations parties. In the light of the Directive, the opportunity for government is to establish for the first time in the UK a permanent and effective general system of information and consultation at work. Some employers may see this as an opportunity to create weak voice mechanisms; for others, there is an opportunity to establish strong arrangements that may complement one another. The challenge for unions is to be able to build on these arrangements, and to maintain and expand their role within them.

Acknowledgement

We are grateful to Helen Bewley, Alex Bryson and Wayne Diamond for providing help with the statistics. We would like to thank colleagues at King's College, London and the Said Business School, Oxford, who commented on this chapter at seminars.

Chapter 9

A US perspective on the future of trade unions in Britain

Thomas A. Kochan

Reading the chapters in this book from the perspective of a US industrial relations researcher makes me want to repeat one of the classic euphemisms of Yogi Berra's (the New York Yankees' catcher of the 1960s known for his oxymorons): 'it's déjà vu all over again'. The overriding conclusion is that despite their different historical legacies, the situation now looks quite similar with respect to the state of British and US unions, and the factors affecting their growth, decline and future. Indeed, as noted by Gospel and Wood in Chapter 1, British and US unions are not alone. Unions in most countries around the world have been declining for some time. It is important to keep this larger context in perspective in examining the future of British unions.

The chapters in this book provide a solid empirical picture of the current state of union membership, organizing trends, access to union membership among women, young workers and those in new worksites, the role of management, and the factors affecting individual propensities to join a union. However, it is important not to lose sight of the forest by focusing on the trees. Taken together, these studies suggest that, like unions in the USA and other parts of the world, British unions will need to make major changes in the ways they recruit, retain and represent workers if they are to reverse their long-term membership decline.

In what follows I will compare the findings of these studies to similar studies of developments in the US labour movement and industrial relations system, and discuss shifts in union strategies and structures that the evidence to date suggests will be needed if there is to be a revival of unionism in the twenty-first century, in Britain and perhaps elsewhere.

Parallel developments

Magnitude and duration of membership decline

The most obvious commonality, shared among Britain, the USA and most other countries, is not only the magnitude but also the long-term duration of the decline in union membership. In the USA union density began declining from its peak of approximately one-third of the private-sector labour force in the mid-1950s and has continued up to the present time. At approximately 9 per cent today, private-sector union density is at about the same level that it was prior to the passage of the National Labour Relations Act in 1935. When the public sector unionization that emerged in the 1960s and 1970s is factored in, the overall rate of unionization in the USA now stands at just under 14 per cent. As in the UK under Margaret Thatcher's governments, the most precipitous decline in union density in the USA came in the 1980s under the conservative regime of Ronald Reagan. However, the downward trends both predated the arrival and continued after the departure of Mrs Thatcher and Mr Reagan, under seemingly more labour-friendly governments.

Decentralization of industrial relations

Gospel and Wood (see Chapter 1) note that the structure of industrial relations has become more decentralized in Britain. The same is true in the USA, and in many other countries (Katz and Darbishire, 2000). In Britain, decentralization has taken the form of a decline in multi-employer bargaining. The system in the USA was always more decentralized. Only a few industries, such as steel, coal, trucking and construction and apparel (at regional levels) tended to have industry-wide or multi-employer bargaining. With the exception of construction, these have largely either disappeared entirely (as in the steel industry) or now cover a significantly smaller percentage of the labour force in the industry (as in coal mining and trucking). Thus in both Britain and the USA, decentralization has moved the locus of bargaining and industrial relations to the individual firm and in many respects to the individual plant or worksite level. One implication of this decentralizing trend is that not only must bargaining be done more locally; organizing workers also has to be done in smaller and more numerous settings. This further increases the magnitude of the task facing unions today.

Bargaining structures are, however, responsive to variations in the relative power of labour and management. It is possible therefore to see exceptions to the decentralizing trend and movements back towards greater centralization in pockets where unions have been able to maintain or build strength. In the USA, the healthcare sector serves as an example. In the New York City region, bargaining remained centralized between an association of non-profit hospitals and a healthcare union that represents its staff. In Minneapolis–St Paul, the same was true until the employer association broke apart in the mid-1990s. In that case the unions were not strong enough to block the employers' decision to decentralize bargaining. In another healthcare example, the coalition of unions representing the giant healthcare provider and insurer, Kaiser-Permanente, have forged a national partnership and bargaining structure. One feature of the agreement negotiated in this structure was a neutrality clause that has allowed the union to organize approximately 8,000 new members (Kochan *et al.*, 2002: 21).

Thus the dynamics of bargaining structures both reflect the changing balance of power and can have a substantial effect on union decline and growth. The relationship of the structure of bargaining to union density has been noted by others (Swenson, 1989), however, the way in which structure affects membership is often overlooked. How these structural dynamics play out in Britain in the future is likely to have a substantial effect on both the nature of industrial relations and collective bargaining, and the growth or decline of union membership.

Scope of bargaining, and who sets the agenda

Gospel and Wood note that the scope of bargaining has been reduced in many British settings, indicating a reduction in union initiative and bargaining power and a corresponding increase in management control over the agenda for negotiations. In our own writing, we characterized this as one of the signal developments and shifts in collective bargaining and union management relations in the USA in the 1980s (Kochan *et al.*, 1986a). Management brought a renewed focus on gaining flexibility in work rules, taking action to escape unionization wherever possible, and making increased use of replacement workers in strikes. Thus, more than ever before, British and US unions are engaged in defensive struggles to limit the negative impacts of management actions.

The root cause of increased managerial initiatives lies in the intense pressures executives faced in recent years to respond to the interests of investors and their capital market agents. The shift towards an investor-oriented capitalism is the dominant development in management of the last quarter century in both the USA (Useem, 1996) and the UK (Gospel and Pendleton, 2000). To regain momentum, unions will need to once again shift the focus to require managers to attend to workers' interests and be seen as engines of economic and social progress for the workforce and society.

Corporate governance debates

The crisis in corporate governance that exploded onto the scene in the USA with the collapse of Enron, Polaroid, Tyco, WorldCom and others has created an opening for labour to regain the momentum in both collective bargaining and political debate. So far it is not clear, however, that the US labour movement is able to take advantage of the opening. The AFL-CIO has proposed stronger employee voice in the oversight of pensions (representation on pension trust boards) and has taken legal action to upgrade the ranking of employees on the list of creditors of bankrupt companies, but has not pressed for a broader debate or set of reforms aimed at giving employees a stronger voice in corporations. In Britain, the TUC's General Secretary John Monks has been an outspoken and articulate spokesman for the stakeholder view of corporations. Whether approaching the governance of a firm from a stakeholder perspective can be translated into new sources of power for employees remains to be seen. The role of employees and their unions in corporate governance will, I anticipate, be a key battleground for unions in the years ahead in both Britain and the USA, and the outcome is likely to have a substantial bearing on how the workforce perceives labour as a political voice and agent for its interests.

Management ideology and resistance to unions

The one big difference in British and US management actions is that US employers became increasingly open and aggressive in their 'union avoidance' behaviour. While Wood *et al.* (see Chapter 7) show that there is determined opposition to unions in some British management circles (as in all countries), it pales in comparison to the deep anti-union culture that historically and currently pervades US management. By 1980 it became acceptable for US managers to bring their union avoidance ideology out of the closet, and in many organizations it is now a part of their publicly stated personnel policies (Walmart, for example, makes it clear in its employee handbook that it does not believe its employees need any 'third party' representation). Notwithstanding these differences, it is clear that in both Britain and the USA management opposition plays a major part in explaining union membership decline.

Herein lies a major strategic challenge to unions. To date most union rhetoric and effort in both Britain and the USA has focused on chastising management for resisting unions and on attempting to overcome this opposition. Sometimes these efforts are successful, but most of the time they are not. Where they are successful, it is normally after a long battle that is costly in both financial and human terms. An alternative strategy, to which I will return in the final section, would be to take management out of the recruitment process altogether by weaning recruitment from its workplace focus.

Human resource management and its impacts

Both countries witnessed a significant rise in the importance and spread of advanced human resource practices of the kind associated with high involvement management, although the effects of these practices on the desire for unionization, according to the Charlwood study (see Chapter 4), may be more muted in the UK than in the USA. Our research (Kochan *et al.*, 1986b) showed that workplaces that introduced practices designed to involve employees and attend to issues of fairness through such things as non-union grievance or dispute resolution procedures significantly reduced the likelihood of unionization. In the UK this may not be the case, at least in existing establishments. Advanced human resource practices do, however, provide another channel for employee voice on at least some workplace issues of concern to them. So too do works councils, where they are supported or mandated by legislation. Gospel and Willman (see Chapter 8) make this point explicitly by noting that today collective bargaining is no longer the sole or, for the majority of workers, even a significant voice mechanism. Yet there is no inherent reason why unions cannot serve as champions for direct employee participation or for works councils. In Britain, unions have a new opportunity to develop another channel for worker voice through the works councils now mandated by the European Union regulations. German unions have found ways to incorporate works councils into their strategies for representing the workforce, and in doing so have become the dominant force in works council elections and processes (Wever, 1995).

The challenge of new workplaces

Machin (see Chapter 2) documents that new workplaces are significantly less likely to be organized than older workplaces in Britain. This again was a hallmark of the transformation in industrial relations in the USA in the

1980s. Moving from documenting this fact to identifying ways by which new workplaces might be organized is no small task. By their very nature, new workplaces are dominated by employees who are optimistic about the prospects of their company and who share some of the entrepreneurial excitement and spirit, and it is generally hard to convince them that they should distrust their employer or that union membership has much to offer them. This is a big problem for unions that rely on the standard organizing model that builds on worker dissatisfaction and union instrumentality as described by Charlwood. Some positive reason for becoming a member of a union that does not depend on worker distrust of the employer will be needed to make headway in gaining members in new worksites. Moreover, organizing on a worksite-by-worksite basis is very costly, particularly because few unions are aware of new sites until they have already been created and grown to substantial size. The failure rate of new companies is also quite high. Hence investing in organizing sites with uncertain futures is costly. All this suggests that some model of recruitment is needed that is divorced from individual workplaces and retains members even if or when they are forced or choose to move from one workplace to another.

The importance and challenge of youth

Young workers are not only less likely to be union members than older workers; this gap in membership has also increased in recent years. This development is not limited to Britain and the USA. Visser (2002) noted the same thing in the Netherlands, and Gomez *et al.* (2002) document it for Canada and, in unpublished research, find the same patterns among young US workers. The causes are also common. As Gomez *et al.* (2002) show for Canadian youth, and Freeman and Diamond (see Chapter 3) show for their British counterparts, young workers are not less inclined towards unions. Instead they are not exposed to opportunities to join unions, and unions increasingly do not figure in the experiences of young people today. Visser (2002) goes a step further and offers the provocative view that if individuals are not recruited to join a union early in their careers, they are likely to be lost for the remainder of their careers. In this book, Bryson and Gomez (see Chapter 5) suggest that union organizing works best when potential joiners have had positive past experiences (direct or by proxy) of unions. That is, unions would do well to become a more central part of young workers' consciousness by engaging them and their peers in activities that are both of interest to young people and demonstrate the value of membership and representation at an early age. As Freeman and Diamond point out, British unions already engage in an array of such efforts.

Whether or how these translate into deeper knowledge and positive views of unions and into substantial new recruits of young workers, and whether those recruited can be retained as members as they move through their career and family life cycles, remains to be seen. Once again, to do so will require substantial change in union strategies and structures.

Women: recruitment, representation and leadership roles

Men account for a higher percentage of union membership than women; however, women are catching up. Women express at least as strong an interest in organizing as do men. Indeed, in the USA women account for approximately two-thirds of all new union members in the past decade. Yet unions in both countries continue to be largely led by men. The ability of unions to take advantage of the growth potential that women provide will depend on how effective they are in addressing issues of critical concern to women, in ways that women find attractive. This in turn will require transforming unions from their largely male-dominated image and leadership to organizations in which women are visible in the leadership positions that matter most.

Bewley and Fernie (see Chapter 6) show that union recognition in Britain, as in the USA, is positively associated with the presence of a variety of family-friendly practices, especially those that have direct costs associated with them – such as shorter work hours, provision of parental leave, and commitment to review policies for gender equity. Take-up of some of these policies is, however, lower in unionized establishments than in non-union establishments with human resource management policies. Exactly the same patterns have been reported in US workplaces (Bailyn *et al.*, 2001). Thus unions have an opportunity and a challenge to change the culture of the workplace to encourage women and men to use the benefits that they have negotiated.

Limits of the traditional organizing model

Despite the differences between the UK and USA in the ways workers join unions, the models that predict who would like to join a union are quite similar. Essentially, workers need to feel some level of dissatisfaction with their employer and/or job and to view union representation as instrumental to improving their situation. In the British data presented by Charlwood, the instrumentality effect is stronger than the dissatisfaction effect. In the USA, the relative importance of these two forces varies from group to group (or at least from one research study to the next). The lesson, however, is the same: the traditional organizing model of unions in both countries is founded on these two sets of variables.

This may be fatal to unions. I consider that continued reliance on this model is at the heart of the problem and challenge facing unions today. The enactment of the statutory recognition procedure further reinforces this traditional model. The model depends on a majority of workers in a given location or bargaining unit (1) being disgruntled with their employer or work situation; (2) believing that unions can address the causes of their dissatisfaction; and (3) disbelieving their employer's promises to do better on its own. It also requires workers to see their current job as one in which they will be staying for a long enough time to bother with union representation. Those with good external labour-market options or who expect to leave soon will use exit rather than voice as their way of acting on their dissatisfaction. Moreover, once organized, workers retain their membership only so long as they stay employed within this bargaining unit. If they move to another employer or to a job outside the unit, unions have to go through this process all over again. In the end, this model of organizing produces a selection bias in which only the most disgruntled workers and those with the poorest labour-market alternatives are likely to be union members. Some alternative means of recruiting members may be needed.

Chapters 3 and 4 report that the proportions of non-union workers who indicate a preference for unionization are also similar at this juncture – roughly 43 to 47 per cent in both Britain and the USA (see Lipset and Meltz, 1997, for the latest US data). This means that there is a sizeable representation gap in both countries. However, nearly twice as many workers in both countries indicate a preference for forms of consultation and representation that resemble works councils as do for collective bargaining. Thus there is a substantial potential supply of new recruits for unions or other institutions that offer them a voice at work. The problem is that the standard organizing model that relies on feelings of dissatisfaction and instrumentality has not been and is not likely to be capable of reaching most of these potential members.

Role of government

While government policy may affect union growth/decline, its direct and independent effects are limited. At least this is the conclusion Wood *et al.* (see Chapter 7) reach in their analysis of the initial years of Britain's statutory recognition law. They also imply, however, that the potential overall effect of this type of law, if combined with shifts in union strategies and organizing efforts, might yet not be insubstantial. The US private sector experience from the 1930s and the public sector experience from the 1960s and 1970s support this view. In both these periods, the passage of supportive labour legislation encouraged unions to embark on new organizing strategies. In the 1930s, unions adopted an industrial union organizing strategy. In the 1960s, the prevailing view of unions that public sector workers could not be organized because they lacked the right to strike gave way to widespread union efforts to organize public-sector workers, who were gaining the right to bargain without the right to strike. In both cases, unions grew substantially.

In Britain the new statutory procedures have embraced the US basic model of elections, and so far appear to be having a modest direct effect in increasing union-organizing activity and winning new members through elections. It has, however, encouraged more employers voluntarily to recognize unions without going through the formal procedures. This is similar (but of more modest magnitude) to the effects of the National Labour Relations Act in its early years. It clearly had the effect of encouraging US unions to put more resources into organizing; however, the biggest gains in union membership came not through the formal election process but by inducing employers voluntarily (albeit in the shadow of the law) to recognize unions after a show of membership solidarity and in some cases, as in the auto and steel industries, a show of union strength. Thus, labour law is part of a solution to union revival, but standing alone it is not a panacea.

Government's efforts to encourage union–management partnerships (ongoing or continuous efforts to address issues of critical concern to both workers and employers) have met with limited successes. In the USA such efforts have a long history dating back to the US Commission on Productivity and the Quality of Work in the 1970s, efforts of the Carter Administration to foster industry level government–business–labour partnerships, the Department of Labor's Bureau of Labor Management Cooperation in the 1980s, and the Clinton Administration's aborted effort to create an initiative on the Workplace of the Future. The Blair government is now promoting partnerships, as is the Trades Union Congress (TUC). In the USA such efforts all experienced difficulty in sustaining partnerships over time as economic conditions changed and the original union and management champions turned over. Whether the combined support of the TUC and the government will be enough to get parties to adopt and sustain partnerships in Britain remains to be seen.

Broader implications

Like the pieces to a puzzle, each of the chapters in this book provides essential theoretical and empirical material needed to understand the reasons that underlie the long-term decline in unions and their prospects for a turnaround and revival. However, the picture produced by putting them together is more sobering than inspiring. Consider the combined effects of the basic conclusions of these papers:

1 Unions have been declining for nearly a quarter-century through periods of slow and rapid growth, high and low inflation, and Conservative and Labour Governments. Only the pace of the decline has varied over these years, not the direction.

2 Unions are not regenerating themselves by engaging the new entrants to the labour force, the newest workplaces, and the fastest growing industries, occupations or regions.

3 Unions are doing better in recruiting women, and are addressing a number of the key issues women care most about in collective bargaining and in their political lobbying efforts. However, they appear to be less effective in creating a work culture and an environment that encourages women (as well as men) to make use of these benefits. Also, unions are making slow progress in putting women in positions of leadership and power within their individual organizations. Few women have the time to take up part-time union work, their regular jobs at work, and their on-going jobs at home. Moreover, given the political realities of union careers, it is just as hard (or maybe harder) to take time out to start and care for a family and have a successful career in the labour movement as it is in business or government.

4 The standard organizing model continues to dominate the way unions recruit new members, yet this model has limited potential for recruiting and retaining the number and range of new members needed to achieve a union resurgence.

5 While the majority of workers today want a voice at work, the forms of voice and representation workers express the greatest interest in are not necessarily the ones unions have provided in the past. Freeman and Diamond's estimates (see Chapter 3) suggest that perhaps half (taking the union and non-union workforce together) would like to be represented by a union for collective bargaining purposes. However, nearly three-quarters want a direct say in how they do their jobs, and input into the broader array of human resource and corporate practices that affect their long-term economic futures and welfares.

6   The majority of managers prefer and work hard to keep their work-
forces and organizations non-union. Managers therefore play at least
as significant a role in deciding whether or not workers will have
access to union membership as do workers themselves or the unions
that seek to represent them.

7   In some cases where unions are already strong, partnerships can be
used to organize new workers. However, partnerships tend to be
vulnerable to shifting economic conditions and leadership turnover
within unions and employer organizations. So partnerships can be
seen at best as a complement to, not a substitute for, other organizing
and representational strategies for unions that already have achieved
sufficient membership and power to neutralize employer opposition.

8   Government policy might at best provide a level playing field for
workers to join unions, but a fair law or labour-friendly government
will not guarantee a resurgence in union membership in the absence of
union strategies that build on the opportunities created by the law and
a more conducive political environment. More broadly, very few governments today can be seen as 'labour' governments that are tightly
allied with the labour movement, unless the labour movement can
mobilize a broad cross-section of the voting population in support of
its vision and political agenda.

Conclusions

The picture that emerges suggests that continued reliance on current strategies for organizing, representing and servicing workers, or incremental
increases in the resources devoted to these activities, will not be sufficient
to achieve a substantial turnaround and resurgence in union membership
and influence in society. We reached this same conclusion for US unions
(Osterman et al., 2001) and for unions in other parts of the world as well
(Verma et al., 2002). Yet this same body of evidence, if reconfigured somewhat, suggests a range of other options that might produce a resurgence. If
the parallels noted above between Britain and the USA are accurate, the
same possibilities exist in Britain. If workers today want a variety of different forms of participation and representation, then the labour movement
of the future will need to supply and support these different forms. This
implies continuing to promote and support collective bargaining, but also
championing and supporting direct worker participation and voice in
workplace affairs, as well as gaining a voice for workers in corporate
affairs through vehicles such as works councils and/or representation on
corporate boards. It also requires providing a sufficient array of labour

market, education and career services and benefits to retain workers as they move from job to job or in and out of the paid labour force over the course of their working lives. To recruit and retain a representative cross-section of the labour force will require going beyond the standard organizing model by providing an array of services and benefits that give individuals a positive reason for joining a union rather than relying on the existence of a threshold level of distrust or dissatisfaction among a majority of their peers at work to trigger unionization. In some respects, this would signify a return to a form of craft or occupational unionism.

Adopting this approach would give unions a higher probability of reaching the target populations that are critical to their future: women, youths and employees in new workplaces. Even more importantly, by focusing on recruiting individuals independently of who they work for, employers can more readily be taken out of the equation rather than simply neutralized or overcome in traditional union campaigns.

This model of union representation would require new structures that coordinate the transfer of members as they move across jobs that heretofore were the province of, or that cross, traditional union boundaries and jurisdictions. Indeed, a key role for unions will be to facilitate and support workers in making these transitions. It will require unions to harness the potential power of information and the modern modes of communications to both get their message to current and potential members and to mobilize them in support of their common objectives.

Finally, the very definition of what constitutes a union may need to change as unions form coalitions with other advocacy groups that share interests in addressing the needs and interests of workers and their families and communities. It requires new models of union leadership that take advantage of the talents and energies of women, but are sensitive to the multiple pulls on their work, career and family interests and responsibilities.

Whether British unions will adopt some or all of these changes in strategies and structures is an open question. While the effects of doing so may be uncertain, not doing so and continuing on a path of incremental changes or improvements in the standard model is less likely to avert the downward trend in union representation, influence and contribution to the welfare of the British workforce and society.

Bibliography

Advisory Conciliation and Arbitration Service (2001) *Annual Report 2000–2001*. London: Advisory Conciliation and Arbitration Service.

Allan, A. and Monkcom, C. (2001) *Quality of Life in the City: A Report on Work–Life Balance in the City of London*. London: Parents at Work.

Arulampalam, W. and Booth, A.L. (2000) Union status of young men in Britain: a decade of change. *Journal of Applied Econometrics*, 15(3): 289–310.

Bailyn, L., Drago, R. and Kochan, T.A. (2001) *Integrating Work and Family Life: A Holistic Approach*. Cambridge, MA: MIT Sloan School of Management.

Bain, G.S. (1970) *The Growth of White Collar Unionism*. Oxford: Oxford University Press.

Bain, G.S. and Price, A. (1980) *Profiles of Union Growth: A Comparative Statistical Portrait of Eight Countries*. Oxford: Basil Blackwell.

Bakke, E. (1944) Why workers join unions. *Personnel*, 22 July: 2–11.

Barling, J.C., Kelloway, E.K. and Bremermann, E.H. (1991) 'Pre-employment predictors of union attitudes – the role of family socialization and work beliefs. *Journal of Applied Psychology*, 76(5): 725–31.

Baron, R.M. and Kenny, D.A. (1986) The moderator–mediator variable distinction in social psychological research: conceptual, strategic, and statistical considerations. *Journal of Personality and Social Psychology*, 51(6): 1173–82.

Belfield, C. and Heywood, J. (2004) Do HRM practices influence the desire for unionization? Evidence across workers, workplaces and co-workers for Great Britain. *Journal of Labor Research* (forthcoming).

Blanchflower, D. and Bryson, A. (2003) Changes over time in union relative wage effects in the UK and the US revisited. *In:* J.T. Addison and C. Schnabel (eds), *International Handbook of Trade Unions*, Chapter 7. Cheltenham: Edward Elgar.

Booth, A.L. (1985) The free rider problem and a social custom theory of membership. *Quarterly Journal of Economics*, 100(1): 253–61.

Booth, A.L. (1989) What do unions do now? Discussion Paper, Economics, Brunel University: Uxbridge, Brunel University.

Booth, A.L. (1995) *The Economics of the Trade Union*. Cambridge: Cambridge University Press.

Booth, A.L. and Chatterji, M. (1995) Union membership and wage bargaining when membership is not compulsory. *Economic Journal*, 105(4): 345–60.

Boyer, R. (1995) The future of unions: is the Anglo-Saxon model a fatality, or will contrasting national trajectories persist? *British Journal of Industrial Relations*, 33(4): 545–56.

Brammel, D. and Cortiz, C. (1987) Tomorrow's workers and today's unions: a survey of high-school students. *Labor Studies Journal*, 12(1): 28–43.

Bronfrenbrenner, K. (1997) The role of union strategies in NLRB Certification Elections. *Industrial and Labor Relations Review*, 50(2): 195–212.

Brook, K. (2002) Trade union membership: an analysis of data from the autumn 2001 LFS. *Labour Market Trends*, 110(7): 343–54.

Brown, W., Deakin, S., Hudson, C. *et al.* (1999) *The Individualisation of Employment Contracts in Britain*. Department of Trade and Industry, Employment Relations Series. London: Department of Trade and Industry.

Brown, W. and Wadhwani, S. (1990) The economic effects of industrial relations legislation since 1979. *National Institute for Economic Review*, 131, 57–70.

Bruegel, I. and Perrons, D. (1998) Deregulation and women's employment: the diverse experiences of women in Britain. *Feminist Economics*, 4(1): 103–25.

Bryson, A. (1999) Are unions good for industrial relations? *In:* R. Jowell, J. Curtice, A. Park and K. Thomson (eds), *British Social Attitudes: The 16th Report*, pp. 65–95, Aldershot: Ashgate.

Bryson, A. (2001) Employee voice, workplace closure and employment growth. Policy Studies Institute Report No. 876, London: Policy Studies Institute.

Bryson, A. and Gomez, R. (2002a) Marching on together? Reasons for the recent decline in union membership. *In:* C. Bromley, A. Park and K. Thompson (eds), *British Social Attitudes: The 20th Report*, pp. 43–73. Aldershot: Ashgate.

Bryson, A. and Gomez, R. (2002b) You don't know what you're missing: union membership as an experience good. *Mimeo*, Centre for Economic Performance, London School of Economics. London: London School of Economics.

Bryson, A. and Gomez, R. (2002c) You can't always get what you want: frustrated demand for unionisation in Britain. Working Paper No. 1182, Centre for Economic Performance, London School of Economics. Centre for Economic Performance, London School of Economics.

Bryson, A., Cappellari, L. and Lucifora, C. (2002) Why so unhappy? The effect of union membership on job satisfaction. Working Paper No. 1183, Centre for Economic Performance, London School of Economics.

Bullock, Rt Hon Lord (1977) *Report of the Committee of Inquiry on Industrial Democracy (1977)*. Cmnd 6702. London: HMSO.

Carruth, A. and Disney, R. (1988) Where have two million trade union members gone? *Economica*, 55(217): 1–19.

Carter, B. (2000) Adoption of the organizing model in British trade unions: some evidence from MSF. *Work, Employment and Society*, 14(1): 117–36.

Central Arbitration Committee (2002) *Annual Report 2001/2*. London: Central Arbitration Committee.

Certification Office for Trade Unions and Employers' Associations (2002) *Annual Report of the Certification Officer, 2001–2002*. London: Certification Office for Trade Unions and Employers' Associations.

Charlwood, A. (2002) Why do non-union employees want to unionize? Evidence from Britain. *British Journal of Industrial Relations*, 40(3): 463–91.

Claydon, T. (1996) Union derecognition: a re-examination. *In:* I. Beardwell (ed.),

Contemporary Industrial Relations: A Critical Analysis, pp. 151–74. Oxford: Oxford University Press.

Conley, H., Delbridge, R., Heery, E. and Stewart, P. (2001) Part-time workers, full-time members: trade union representation of part-time workers. Paper presented at Gender, Work and Organization Conference, University of Keele. *Mimeo*, Cardiff Business School. Cardiff: Cardiff Business School.

Cregan, C. (1991) Young people and trade union membership – a longitudinal analysis. *Applied Economics*, 23(9): 1511–18.

Cregan, C. and Johnston, S. (1990) An industrial relations approach to the free rider problem: young people and trade union membership in the UK. *British Journal of Industrial Relations*, 28(1): 87–102.

Cully, M., Woodland, S., O'Reilly, A. and Dix, G. (1999) *Britain at Work: As Depicted by the 1998 Workplace Employee Relations Survey*. London: Routledge.

Daniel, W. and Millward, N. (1983) *Workplace Industrial Relations in Britain*. London: Policy Studies Institute.

Dekker, I., Greenberg, L. and Barling, J. (1998) Predicting union attitudes in student part-time workers. *Canadian Journal of Behavioural Science*, 30(1): 49–55.

Department of Trade and Industry (1999a) *Workplace Employee Relations Survey: Cross-Section, 1998 (computer file)*. 4th edn. The Data Archive [distributor], 22 December 1999, SN: p. 3955, Colchester.

Department of Trade and Industry (1999b) Fairness at Work, Cm. 3968, London: Stationery Office.

Department of Trade and Industry (2002) UK Workers Struggle to Balance Work and Quality of Life as Long Hours and Stress Take Hold. Department of Trade and Industry press release, 30 August.

Diamond, W. and Freeman, R. (2000) Liking the workplace you have: the incumbency effect in preferences towards unions. Working Paper 1115, Centre for Economic Performance, London School of Economics. London: London School of Economics.

Diamond, W. and Freeman, R. (2001) *What Workers Want from Workplace Organizations: A Report to the TUC's Promoting Trade Unionism Task Group*. London: TUC.

Diamond, W. and Freeman, R. (2002a) Modelling parental union status transition rates. *Mimeo*, Centre for Economic Performance, London School of Economics. London: London School of Economics.

Diamond, W. and Freeman, R. (2002b) Will unionism prosper in cyber-space?: the promise of the Internet for employee organization. *British Journal of Industrial Relations*, 40(3): 569–96.

Disney, R., Gosling, A. and Machin, S. (1995) British unions in decline: the determinants of the 1980s fall in trade union recognition. *Industrial and Labor Relations Review*, 48(3): 403–19.

Disney, R., Gosling, A. and Machin, S. (1996) What has happened to union recognition in Britain? *Economica*, 63(249): 1–18.

Disney, R., Gosling, A., Machin, S. and McCrae, J. (1998) *The Dynamics of Union Membership in Britain*. Department of Trade and Industry Employment Relations Research, Report No. 3. London: Department of Trade and Industry.

Donovan, Rt Hon Lord (1968) *Report of the Royal Commission on Trade Unions and Employers' Associations 1965–1968*. Cmnd 3623, London: HMSO.

Dundon, T. (2001) Put up and shut up: social mobilization and employee attitudes in non-union firms. *Mimeo*, Department of Management, National University of Ireland. Dublin: National University of Ireland.

Dunn, S. and Metcalf, D. (1996) 'Trade union law since 1979. *In*: I. Beardwell (ed.), *Contemporary Industrial Relations: A Critical Analysis*, pp. 66–98. Oxford: Oxford University Press.

Employment Relations Act (1999) London: HMSO.

EOC (2002) Glass ceiling and sticky floor leave women the poorer sex. Equal Opportunities Commission, press release, 24 January.

Equal Pay Taskforce (2001) *Just Pay: A Report to the Equal Opportunities Commission*. Manchester: EOC.

Ewing, K.D. (1990) Trade union recognition – a framework for discussion. *Industrial Law Journal*, 19(4): 209–27.

Farber, H. (1983) The determination of the union status of workers. *Econometrica*, 51(5): 1417–38.

Farber, H. (2001) Notes on the economics of labour unions. Working Paper 452, Industrial Relations Section, Princeton University. Princeton: Princeton University.

Farber, H. and Krueger, A.B. (1993) Union membership in the United States: the decline continues. *In*: B. Kaufman and M. Kleiner (eds), *Employee Representation: Alternatives and Future Directions*, pp. 163–83. Madison: Industrial Relations Research Association.

Farber, H. and Western, B. (2002) Ronald Reagan and the politics of declining union organization. Working Paper 460, Industrial Relations Section, Princeton University. Princeton: Princeton University.

Feldman, G. (1992) *Army, Industry, and Labor in Germany 1914–1918*. Leamington Spa: Berg.

Fernie, S. and Gray, H. (2002) It's a family affair: the effect of union recognition and human resource management on the provision of equal opportunities in the UK. Discussion Paper 525, Centre for Economic Performance, London School of Economics. London: London School of Economics.

Fernie, S. and Metcalf, D. (1995) Participation, contingent pay, representation and workplace performance. *British Journal of Industrial Relations*, 33(3): 379–415.

Forth, J. and Millward, N. (2002) *The Growth of Direct Communication*. London: CIPD.

Freeman, R. (1995) The future of unions in decentralized collective bargaining systems: US and UK unionism in an age of crisis. *British Journal of Industrial Relations*, 33(4): 519–36.

Freeman, R. and Medoff, J. (1984) *What Do Unions Do?* New York: Basic Books.

Freeman, R. and Pelletier, J. (1990) The impact of industrial relations legislation on British union density. *British Journal of Industrial Relations*, 28(2): 141–64.

Freeman, R. and Rogers, J. (1999) *What Workers Want*, London: ILR Press.

Freeman, R. and Rogers, J. (2002) Open-source unionism: beyond exclusive collective bargaining. Paper presented in the 23rd Middlebury Economics Conference, Changing Role of Unions, 13–14 April. Online. Available Web site: http://www.workingusa.org.

Frick, B. and Lehmann, E. (2001) Corporate governance in Germany: problems and prospects. Paper for ESF-ScSS Network, Cologne. *Mimeo*, Department of Economics and Management, Witten/Herdecke University. Witten, Germany: Witten/Herdecke University.

Gall, G. and McKay, S. (1994) Trade union derecognition in Britain, 1988–94. *British Journal of Industrial Relations*, 32(3): 433–8.

Gall, G. and McKay, S. (1999) Developments in union recognition and derecognition in Britain, 1994–98. *British Journal of Industrial Relations*, 37(4): 601–14.

Gall, G. and McKay, S. (2001) Facing 'fairness at work': union perceptions of employer opposition and response to union recognition. *Industrial Relations Journal*, 32(2): 94–113.

Gall, G. and McKay, S. (2002) Trade union recognition in Britain, 1995–2001: turning a corner? Stirling: Stirling University.

Gershuny, J. (1997) 'Sexual divisions and the distribution of work in the household. *In:* G. Dench (ed.), *Rewriting the Sexual Contract*, pp. 141–52. London: Institute of Community Studies.

GMB. 'Young GMB', online. Available Web site: http://www.gmb.org.uk (accessed January 2002).

Gollan, P.J. (2001) Tunnel vision: non-union employee representation at Eurotunnel. *Employee Relations*, 23(4): 376–400.

Gomez, R., Gunderson, M. and Meltz, N. (2002) Comparing youth and adult desire for unionization in Canada. *British Journal of Industrial Relations*, 40(3): 421–39.

Gospel, H. (1992) *Markets, Firms, and the Management of Labour in Modern Britain*. Cambridge: Cambridge University Press.

Gospel, H. and Lockwood, G. (1999) Disclosure of information for collective bargaining: the CAC approach revisited. *Industrial Law Journal*, 28(3): 233–48.

Gospel, H. and Pendleton, A. (2000) Some effects of financial systems and corporate governance on labour outcomes. Proceedings of the 52nd Annual Meeting of the Industrial Relations Research Association, Madison, WI: Industrial Relations Research Association.

Gospel, H. and Willman, P. (2002) The right to know: disclosure of information for collective bargaining and joint consultation in Germany, France, and Great Britain. Working Paper No. 1178, Centre for Economic Performance, London School of Economics. London: London School of Economics.

Gospel, H., Lockwood, G. and Willman, P. (2002) A British dilemma: disclosure of information for collective bargaining or joint consultation? *Comparative Labor Law and Policy Journal*, 22(2), 101–23.

Gray, H. (2002) Family-friendly working: what a performance! An analysis of the relationship between the availability of family-friendly policies and establishment performance. Discussion Paper, No. 529, Centre for Economic Performance, London School of Economics. London: London School of Economics.

Greer, D. (1992) *Industrial Organization and Public Policy*, 3rd edn. Toronto, Canada: Macmillan Press.

Hartley, J. (1992) Joining a trade union. *In:* J. Hartley and G. Stephenson (eds), *Employment Relations: The Psychology of Influence and Control at Work*, pp. 163–83. Oxford: Blackwell.

Heery, E. and Kelly, J. (1988) Do female representatives make a difference?

Women full-time officers and trade union work. *Work, Employment and Society*, 2(4): 487–505.

Heery, E., Simms, M., Delbridge, R. *et al.* (1999) Organizing unionism comes to the UK. *Employee Relations*, 22(1): 38–57.

Heery, E., Simms, M., Delbridge, R. *et al.* (2000) Union organizing in Britain: a survey of policy and practice. *International Journal of Human Resource Management*, 11(5): 986–1007.

Hepple, B., Coussey, M. and Choudhury, T. (2000) *Equality: A New Framework*. Oxford: Hart Publishing.

Hinton, J. (1994) *Shop Floor Citizens: Engineering Democracy in 1940s Britain*. Aldershot: Edward Elgar.

Hirsch, B., Macphereson, D. and Schumacher, E. (2002) Measuring union and nonunion wage growth: puzzles in search of solutions. Paper presented in the 23rd Middlebury Economics Conference 'Changing Role of Unions', 13–14 April. *Mimeo*, Department of Economics, Trinity University. San Antonio, Texas: Trinity University.

Hogarth, T., Hasluck, C. and Pierre, G. (2001) *Work–Life Balance 2000: Results from the Baseline Study*. Norwich, Department for Education and Employment Research Report 249.

Howell, C. (1992) *Regulating Labor: The State and Industrial Relations Reform in Postwar France*. Princeton: Princeton University Press.

Institute of Management (2001) *A Woman's Place: a Survey of Female Managers' Changing Professional and Personal Roles*. London: Institute of Management.

Jacoby, S. (1985) *Employing Bureaucracy: Managers, Unions, and the Transformation of Work in American Industry, 1900–1945*. New York: Columbia University Press.

Jacoby, S. (1997) *Modern Manners: Welfare Capitalism since the New Deal*. Princeton: Princeton University Press.

Jagpal, S. (1999) *Marketing Strategy and Uncertainty*. New York: Oxford University Press.

Jowell, R., Curtice, J., Park, A. and Thomson, K. (1999) *British Social Attitudes: The 16th Report*. Aldershot: Ashgate.

Katz, H.C. and Darbishire, O. (2000) *Converging Divergences*. Ithaca, NY: Cornell University ILR Press.

Kelloway, E.K. and Newton, T. (1996) Pre-employment, predictors of union attitudes: the effects of parental union and work experiences. *Canadian Journal of Behavioural Science*, 28(2): 113–20.

Kelloway, E.K. and Watts, L. (1994) Pre-employment predictors of union attitudes: replication and extension. *Journal of Applied Psychology*, 79(4): 631–4.

Kelloway, E.K., Barling, J. and Agar, S. (1996) Pre-employment, predictors of children's union attitudes: the moderating role of identification with parents. *Journal of Social Psychology*, 136(3): 413–15.

Kelly, J. (1998) *Rethinking Industrial Relations*. London: Routledge.

Kerr, A. and Waddington, J. (1997) *Unions for Young Workers?* A UNISON report on a survey of young workers. London: UNISON.

Kirton, G. and Healy, G. (1999) Transforming union women: the role of women trade union officials in union renewal. *Industrial Relations Journal*, 30(1): 31–45.

Klemperer, P.D. (1995) Competition when consumers have switching costs: an overview with applications to industrial organization, macroeconomics, and international trade. *Review of Economic Studies*, 62(4): 515–39.

Kochan, T.A. (1979) How American workers view labor unions. *Monthly Labor Review*, 104(4): 23–31.

Kochan, T.A. (1980) *Collective Bargaining and Industrial Relations*. Homewood, IL: Richard D. Irwin.

Kochan, T.A., Katz, H.C. and McKersie, R.B. (1986a) *The Transformation of American Industrial Relations*. New York: Basic Books.

Kochan, T.A., McKersie, R.B. and Chalykoff, J. (1986b) Corporate strategy, workplace innovation and union members. *Industrial and Labour Relations Review*, 39(4): 487–501.

Kochan, T.A., Eaton, S.C. and McKersie, R.B. (2002) The Kaiser Permanente Labor Management Partnership: The First Five Years. *Mimeo*, MIT Sloan School of Management. Cambridge, MA: MIT School of Management.

Kodz, J., Harper, H. and Dench, S. (2002) *Work–life Balance: Beyond the Rhetoric*. Brighton: Institute for Employment Studies Report 384.

Kotler, P. (2000) *Marketing Management: International Edition*. London: Prentice Hall.

Lambin, J.J. (1997) *Strategic Marketing Management*. London: McGraw-Hill.

Lancaster, K. (1966) A new approach to consumer theory. *Journal of Political Economy*, 74(2): 132–57.

Lewis, S. (1997) Family-friendly employment policies: a route to changing organizational culture or playing about at the margins? *Gender, Work and Organization*, 4(1): 13–23.

Lipset, S.M. and Meltz, N. (1997) Canadian and American attitudes towards work and institutions. *Perspectives on Work*, 1(3): 14–19.

Logan, J. (2002) Consultants, lawyers and the 'union free' movement in the United States since the 1970s. *Industrial Relations Journal*, 33(3): 197–214.

McCarthy, W. (1967) *The Role of Shop Stewards in Industrial Relations*. Research Paper Number 1, Donovan Royal Commission.

McCarthy, W. (2000) Representative consultations with specified employees – or the future of rung two. *In:* H. Collins, P. Davies and R. Rideout (eds), *Legal Regulation of the Employment Relation*, pp. 529–56. London: Kluwer.

Machin, S. (1995) Plant closures and unionization in British establishments. *British Journal of Industrial Relations*, 33(1): 55–68.

Machin, S. (2000) Union decline in Britain. *British Journal of Industrial Relations*, 38(4): 631–45.

Machin, S. (2002) Factors of convergence and divergence in union membership. Discussion Paper 554, Centre for Economic Performance, London School of Economics. London: London School of Economics.

Machin, S. and Blanden, J. (2002) Cross-generation correlations of union status for young people in Britain. Discussion Paper 553, Centre for Economic Performance, London School of Economics. London: London School of Economics.

Manpower Services Commission (1978) *People and Their Work*. London: Manpower Services Commission.

Metcalf, D. (1990) Union presence and labour productivity in British manufacturing industry. *British Journal of Industrial Relations*, 28(2): 249–66.

Metcalf, D. (1991) British unions: dissolution or resurgence? *Oxford Review of Economic Policy*, 7(1): 18–32.

Metcalf, D. (1999) New Labour's industrial relations programme. *Perspectives on Work*, 3(1), 12–17.

Metcalf, D. (2001) British unions: dissolution or resurgence revisited. *In:* R. Dickens, J. Wadsworth and P. Gregg (eds), *The State of Working Britain*, pp. 25–33. London: Centre for Economic Performance.

Millward, N. and Stevens, M. (1986) *British Workplace Industrial Relations 1980–1984: The DE/ESRC/PSI/ACAS Surveys*. Aldershot: Gower.

Millward, N., Stevens, M., Smart, D. and Hawes, W.R. (1992) *Workplace Industrial Relations in Transition: The ED/ESRC/PSI/ACAS Surveys*. Aldershot: Dartmouth.

Millward, N., Bryson, A. and Forth, J. (2000) *All Change at Work? British Employment Relations 1980–1998, as Portrayed by the Workplace Industrial Relations Survey Series*. London: Routledge.

Milner, S. (1995) The coverage of collective pay setting institutions: 1895–1990. *British Journal of Industrial Relations*, 33(1): 69–91.

Mitbestimmung Kommission (1998) *Mitbestimmung und neue Unternehmenskulturen – Bilanz und Perspektiven*. Gütersloh: Bertelsmann Stiftung.

Monks, J. (2001) The union renaissance. Lecture at Leeds University Business School. Online. Available Web site: http://www.tuc.org.uk/leedslecture.

MORI, http://www.mori.com/specarea/trade.htm (accessed 26 January 2000).

Morrell, J., Boyland, M., Munns, G. and Astbury, L. (2001) *Gender Equality in Pay Practices*. Equal Opportunities Commission Discussion Series, Manchester: EOC.

Morris, J. (2002) *Changing Times: The TUC Guide to Work–Life Balance*. TUC. Online. Available Web site: http://www.tuc.org.uk/changingtimes/casestudies.htm (accessed June 2002).

Naylor, R.A. (1989) Strikes, free riders and social customs. *Quarterly Journal of Economics*, 104(4): 771–86.

Nelson, P. (1970) Information and consumer behaviour. *Journal of Political Economy*, 78(3): 311–29.

Office of National Statistics (2001) *Employment Gazette*. London: HMSO.

Olsen, M. (1965) *The Logic of Collective Action: Public Goods and the Theory of Groups*. Cambridge, MA: Harvard University Press.

Osterman, P., Kochan, T.A., Locke, R. and Piore, M. (2001) *Working in America*. Cambridge, MA: MIT Press.

Pencavel, J. (2001) The surprising retreat of union Britain. *Mimeo*, National Bureau of Economic Research. Cambridge, MA: National Bureau of Economic Research. Forthcoming in D. Card and R. Freeman (eds), *Seeking a Premier League Economy*. Chicago, IL: University of Chicago Press for NBER.

Porter, M. (1976) *Interbrand Choice, Strategy and Bilateral Market Power*. Cambridge, MA: Harvard University Press.

Premack, S.L. and Hunter, J.E. (1988) Individual unionization decisions. *Psychological Bulletin*, 103(2): 223–34.

Rees, A. (1966) Information networks in labour markets. *American Economic Review*, 56(2): 559–66.

Reinstein, D. and Snyder, C. (2000) The influence of expert reviews on consumer demand for experience goods: a case study of movie critics. Working Paper, University of California, Berkeley.

Riddell, C. (1993) Unionization in Canada and the United States: a tale of two countries. *In:* D. Card and R. Freeman (eds), *Small Differences That Matter: Labor Markets and Income Maintenance in Canada and the United States*, pp. 109–49. Chicago: University of Chicago Press.

Rooney, M. (1998) Decision-making for the Future Report. Young Members' Strategy, Equality Development Unit, AEEU.

Simpson, R. (1979) Judicial control of ACAS. *Industrial Law Journal*, 8(2): 69–84.

Skinner, D. (1999) The reality of equal opportunities: the expectations and experiences of part-time staff and their managers. *Personnel Review*, 28(6): 425–38.

Smith, P. and Morton, G. (1993) Union exclusion and the decollectivization of industrial relations in contemporary Britain. *British Journal of Industrial Relations*, 31(1): 97–114.

Stewart, M. (1983) Relative earnings and individual union membership in the United Kingdom. *Economica*, 50(198): 111–25.

Stigler, G.J. (1961) The economics of information. *Journal of Political Economy*, 69(3): 213–25.

Swenson, P. (1989) *Fair Shares: Unions, Pay and Politics in Sweden and West Germany*. Ithaca, NY: Cornell University Press.

Thelen, K. (1991) *Union of Parts: Labor Politics in Postwar Germany*. Ithaca: Cornell University Press.

Towers, B. (1997) *The Representation Gap: Change and Reform in the British and American Workplace*. Oxford: Oxford University Press.

Trades Union Congress (1995) *Your Voice at Work: TUC Proposals for Rights to Representation at Work*. London: TUC.

Trades Union Congress (1996) *Testament of Youth: A Manifesto for Young Workers*. London: TUC, Campaigns and Communications Department.

Trades Union Congress (1999) *Winning the Organized Workplace: A Manual for Tutors*. London: TUC.

Trades Union Congress (2002) *Trade Union Trends: Focus on Recognition*, London: TUC.

Troy, L. and Sheflin, N. (1985) *Union Sourcebook: Membership, Structure, Finance, Directory*, 1st edn. West Orange, NJ: IRDIS.

Turner, L. (1991) *Democracy at Work: Changing World Markets and the Future of Unions*. Ithaca, NJ: Cornell University Press.

UNIFI. *Organising Young Workers*. Online. Available Web site: http://www.unifi.org.uk/research/youngworkers.htm (accessed February 2002).

UNISON (2002) *Unison Campaigns: Work–life Balance*. Online. Available Web site: http://www.unison.org.uk/worklifebalance/index.asp (accessed August 2002).

UNISON *Young Members' Officers*. Online. Available Web site: http://www.unison.org.uk (accessed January 2002).

USDAW (1996) Union of Shop Distributive and Allied Workers, Young People, Executive Council Statement, *Unions21 Building Tomorrow's Unions*. Online. Available Web site: http://www.unions21.org.uk/newgen (accessed February 2002).

Useem, M. (1996) *Investor Capitalism*. New York: Basic Books.

Verma, A., Kochan, T. and Wood, S. (2002) Union decline and prospects for revival: Editors' introduction. *British Journal of Industrial Relations*, 40(3): 373–84.

Visser, J. (2002) Why fewer workers join unions in Europe: a social custom explanation of membership trends. *British Journal of Industrial Relations*, 40(3): 403–30.

Wagar, T.H. and Rahman, A. (1997) Determinants of union joining and voting intention: evidence from Canadian high school students. *Journal of Collective Negotiations in the Public Sector*, 26(2): 161–8.

Walters, S. (2002) Female part-time workers' attitudes to trade unions in Britain. *British Journal of Industrial Relations*, 40(1): 49–68.

Wedderburn, W. (1997) Consultation and collective bargaining in Europe: success or ideology? *Industrial Law Journal*, 26(1): 1–34.

Wever, K. (1995) *Negotiating Competitiveness*. Boston: Harvard Business School Press.

Whitley Committee (1918) *Ministry of Reconstruction, Interim Report of the Committee on Relations between Employers and Employed* (Cd. 8606, 1917–1918) and *Final Report* (Cd. 9153).

Wills, J. (2001) Community unionism and trade union renewal in the UK: moving beyond the fragments. *Transactions of the Institute of British Geographers*, 26(4): 465–83.

Wood, S. (2000) Learning through ACAS: the case of union recognition. *In:* B. Towers and W. Brown (eds), *Employment Relations in the UK: Britain's Advisory Conciliation and Arbitration Service 1974–2000*, pp. 123–52. Oxford: Basil Blackwell.

Wood, S., Moore, S. and Willman, P. (2002) 'Third time lucky for statutory union recognition in the UK? *Industrial Relations Journal*, 33(3): 215–33.

Index